Elvis

™

Elvis Presley
aus dem CinemaScope-Film
THMUS HINTER GITTE
Foto MGM

A CELEBRATION

IMAGES OF ELVIS PRESLEY® FROM THE ELVIS PRESLEY ARCHIVE AT GRACELAND®

MIKE EVANS

LONDON, NEW YORK, MUNICH,
MELBOURNE, DELHI

Produced for DK Publishing, Inc. by
The Ivy Press Limited

Creative Director: Peter Bridgewater
Publisher: Sophie Collins
Editorial Director: Steve Luck
Design: Clare Barber
Editor: Stephanie Horner

Dorling Kindersley Limited
Managing Art Editor: Heather McCarry
Editors: Gary Werner, Margaret Parrish

First published in the USA and Great Britain
in 2004 by Dorling Kindersley Limited,
80 Strand, London WC2R 0RL

A Penguin Company

02 03 04 05 10 9 8 7 6 5 4 3 2 1

A Cataloging-in-Publication record for this book
is available from the Library of Congress
(US) ISBN 0-7566-0769-8

A CIP catalog record for this book
is available from the British Library
(UK) ISBN 1-4053-0703-X

Reproduced by Hong Kong Graphics

Printed in China

Contents

[1935-1977]

"Elvis is the greatest cultural force in the 20th century. He introduced the beat to everything, music, language, clothes, it's a whole new social revolution."

– *Leonard Bernstein*

OK, so that was going too far. The man who composed the music for *West Side Story* should have known better. Elvis simply didn't "introduce the beat to everything," but he was the first to acknowledge the roots of his music in blues, gospel, country, and all the other rhythmically based popular music that America had created through the first half of the 20th century.

Likewise, the jive-talk language and sharp clothes that were adopted by Elvis and other early rock'n'rollers—and soon taken up by the newly identified generation of "teenagers"— weren't invented overnight, but had their basis in the bebop slang and zoot-suit fashions of big city jazz musicians in the 1940s.

Having said that, Bernstein was right about Elvis being an incalculable cultural force. It's hard to appreciate the impact Elvis had on what we call popular culture, that melting pot of music, art, attitudes, and manners that found its most vital catalyst and dynamo for change in the America of the last century. And, like Louis Armstrong, Jackson Pollock, Scott Fitzgerald, cowboy movies, and boogie woogie, Elvis and his music were uniquely American; it just wouldn't have happened, couldn't have happened, anywhere else.

In that media-driven century that has so recently come to a close, the century of the photograph, motion pictures, and television as well as records and radio, image was all important. The visual record of people and events that burned onto the mass consciousness was more potent than newsprint, more memorable even than the voices of radio pioneers who gave us history as it happened over the airwaves. When his music exploded on an unsuspecting world in the early weeks of 1956, the first impression most people got of Elvis Presley, other than the almost hypnotic atmosphere of "Heartbreak Hotel," were the black-and-white photographs of the "Hillbilly Cat" in action. And in many ways the still camera, creating innumerable images frozen for all time, was the medium that defined Elvis as icon throughout the rest of his life.

From the image that for millions was the first glimpse of Elvis, mouth open, legs apart—it was clear that here was something different. Was he playing the guitar, or making love to it? Those pants looked like they were going to split at any moment! Was he singing, or shouting, was this a performance or some act of defiant celebration? It was both—as the picture found its way round the world, it was clear that things were never going to be the same again.

The early television appearances, beamed coast to coast across a stunned-into-silence America, certainly upset a lot of adult folk, and got the kids on their toes, but these were mere flickering box-in-the-corner images compared to the real thing. Curiously, the combination of the records themselves and an increasing flood of photographs was far more potent propaganda for the rock'n'roll revolution.

RCA Records soon caught on to this. From the start they sensed that this kid looked different. The first time he hit their studios in New York City, there was a photoshoot that revealed the strange beauty of the guy. From Arkansas to Australia, bedroom walls were soon covered with that look. Wallpaper manufacturers, along with big band crooners, righteous preachers, teachers, and parents, held up their hands in horror.

Compared to TV, still in its infancy, the movies were a different matter. Here was a chance for the mass of people, in and outside the US, to see him move for the first time. But his first movie, *Love Me Tender*, was in truth something of an anticlimax as far as seeing the real Elvis was concerned. He played his part convincingly, and brought tears to the eyes of fans when he died at the end, but it was a never-ending chronicle of photographs that recorded the phenomenon that was barnstorming across America in the wildest series of live performances ever seen in the history of show business.

On stage, backstage, on trains, in hotel rooms, signing autographs, eating in diners, meeting the press, sitting exhausted with just his thoughts; we see more of the true Elvis in moments captured by photographers, photo-journalists, and fans than in all his Hollywood output played end to end. Possibly the most memorable visual set-piece in any of his movies, the title song sequence in *Jailhouse Rock*, was only truly rendered an icon in the still images that were subsequently reproduced forever after.

Even during the mid-Sixties, the "movie years," when Elvis spent most time in the privacy of recording and film studios, photographers reported his every move: his private life became public property by virtue of his fame.

Launched via television, Elvis' celebrated comeback to live performance in the late Sixties heralded a new image, and one that was to be the closest to an unofficial Elvis Presley brand identity. Purists may not like it, but the much-caricatured stereotype of white jumpsuit, sunglasses and big sideburns is the most popular symbol of Elvis in common currency. But the real image is sustained by a couple of highly charged film documentaries following Elvis in live concert performances, and in a mountain of photography.

The great Duke Ellington once said music is like a flower: you can't appreciate its beauty by dissecting it. The same can be said of Elvis' contribution to contemporary culture. He was singer, musician, entertainer, actor, but much more than all these put together. The value of everything he did, particularly the records that provided a soundtrack to a period of unprecedented change, is enhanced when seen in the context of the society and lives he touched so fundamentally—and it's in the photographic record that this becomes most apparent. The epic saga of Elvis' life, from small town Mississippi to the neon-lit Las Vegas of hoofers, high rollers, and Hollywood stars, was made real for ever in a million photographs.

The pictures reproduced in the pages that follow are just some of them ...

Prologue

CHILD & TEENAGER

[1935–1955]

1941 TUPELO In striped pants and suspenders, six-year-old Elvis stands in front of the modest rented house the Presleys had moved into at 510½ Maple Street, Tupelo Mississippi, toward the end of 1940.

1941 c1937 c1941 c1950

Tupelo, Mississippi, was deep in sharecropper country back in the 1930s. The land was impoverished, and most of the people were too—Vernon and Gladys Presley were no exception.

The first picture many of us see of the young Elvis, born January 8, 1935, shows him between his parents, aged just two, all of them staring at the photographer like folks did then, when they didn't get their picture taken often.

Throughout his childhood Elvis would hear music from the dozens of radio stations that beamed country, gospel, and blues to the local communities. Sometimes, on their Philco Radio Phonograph, the family would tune in to syndicated stations, either big-name shows networked coast-to-coast or programs with a regional coverage. Most famous of these in the South were Nashville's Grand Ole Opry and the Shreveport-based Louisiana Hayride.

Despite giving the impression of being a shy youngster, Elvis opened up when it came to performing music, whether entertaining friends with guitar sessions or appearing at a talent show; all of which would be recalled years later, with varying degrees of accuracy, by those privileged to be there.

1950 1954 1955

Elvis was 13 years old when his parents decided to move to the big city. Memphis, 90 miles northwest of Tupelo, sprawls across the southwest corner of Tennessee where the stateline touches Mississippi in the south and Arkansas across the river to the west. With its black blues and white country music, and gospel songs that were common to both communities, Memphis was rich with music, and the teenage Elvis was all ears.

He was all eyes too, and soon noticed the way the music-makers dressed, the Western swing players in their wild floral shirts like hipcat cowboys, the bluesmen sharp as knives in zoot suits straight from Lansky's clothes store, on the corner of Second Street and Beale.

The neon-night honky tonk heaven that was Beale Street was long a landmark in the city as a catalyst in the evolution of blues, and it soon became a magnet for the adolescent kid who still stared at that camera, be-jeaned legs apart, holding a toy gun, sitting on the sidewalk with an early girlfriend, or looking ultra-cool in some flash new duds between two highschool buddies.

And very soon, it seemed like the cameras would never go away.

↑ c1937 **ELVIS AND PARENTS** Gladys Love Smith, born April 25, 1912, had married Vernon Elvis Presley (four years her junior, born April 10, 1916) on June 17, 1933. Eighteen months later, on January 8, 1935, in the small two-room house on Old Saltillo Road, East Tupelo, that Vernon had built with help from his father and brother, she gave birth to twin boys: Jesse Garon and Elvis Aaron. Jesse Garon was stillborn at 4.00 AM. The second of the twins, Elvis Aaron, was born 35 minutes later.

→ 1941 **ELVIS AND PARENTS** The picture with Vernon and Gladys outside their house on Maple Street, East Tupelo, was taken around the time Elvis started grade school in the fall of 1941 at the East Tupelo Consolidated School on Lake Street.

↑ 1940 ELVIS AT FIVE It was a turbulent time for the Presleys' fortunes. Vernon was released from a short jail sentence after a minor offence and the rest of the year saw the family struggling financially while he got back on his feet. By the time the young Elvis entered grade school in 1941, his father was more or less regularly in work, though in an itinerant capacity. It wasn't until they moved from Tupelo to Memphis, Tennessee in 1948 that life seemed relatively settled.

→ c1941 CHILDHOOD Elvis' mother was, if anything, overprotective of her young son. "I couldn't go down to the creek with the other kids. Sometimes . . . I used to run off. Mama would whip me, and I thought she didn't love me."

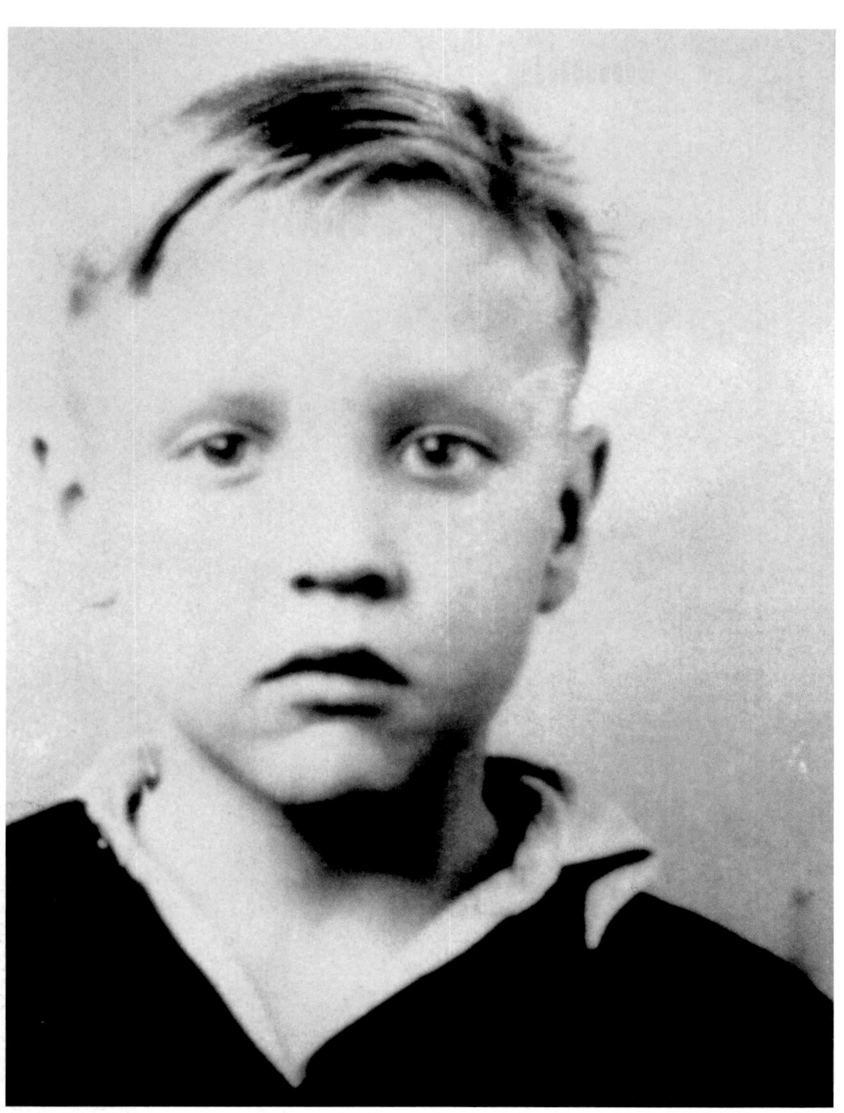

c1945 **TUPELO** The fact that the young Elvis was increasingly fascinated by music was first evident when he made his first public performance, age ten, on the Children's Day at the Mississippi–Alabama Fair and Dairy Show Fairgrounds in downtown Tupelo. It was October 3, 1945, and Elvis took part in a children's talent contest. He remembered clearly that he had had to stand on a chair to reach the microphone, and that his rendition of the ballad "Old Shep" went down well.

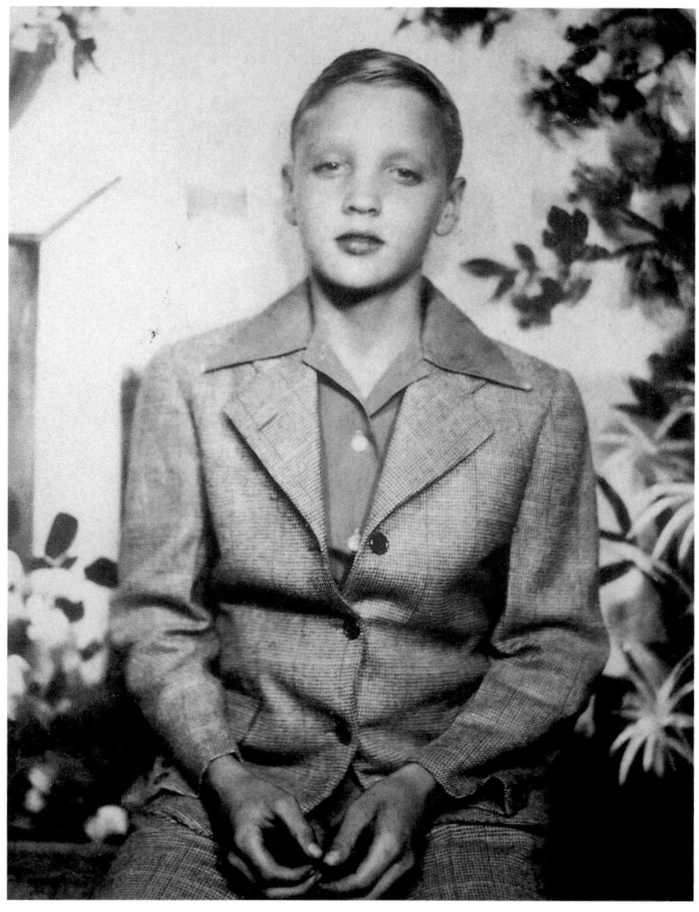

1946 **GUITAR MAN** Soon after his appearance at the Fair talent contest, just as significantly, Elvis was to get his first guitar. He recalled later on that the reason he sang unaccompanied at the Fair was because he didn't have a guitar at that point, and his mother subsequently bought him one for his eleventh birthday the following January. He was soon absorbing the music and picking up hints by listening to the performers on the Grand Ole Opry radio show, and the local radio "amateur hour" WELO Jamboree.

1947 **SCHOOL PORTRAIT** On the back of the portrait was written: "Elvis Presley 1947–1948 Tupelo, Miss. Tupelo School." Elvis first began taking a guitar to school when he was in seventh grade, and already voicing an interest in gospel music.

1947 **MILAM JUNIOR HIGH** The sixth grade class at the end of the school year; Elvis appears far right, second row from top. He started at Milam in the fall of 1946, after the Presleys had moved from East Tupelo to the center of town.

1953 CLASS OF '53 The L. C. Humes High School Class upon graduation in June 1953. Elvis is in the center of the second row up from the bottom. He had entered the school after the family moved to Memphis in November 1948. On April 9, he had performed at the school's annual Minstrel Show. He later recalled, "When I came on stage I heard people kind of rumbling and whispering and so forth 'cause nobody knew I even sang. It was amazing how popular I became after that."

1950

c1950 MEMPHIS SIDEWALK Elvis sits on a Memphis sidewalk with one of his first regular girlfriends, Betty Anne McMahan, who lived in the same apartment house, the much sought-after public housing project Lauderdale Courts. The Presleys had moved to 185 Winchester, Apartment 328 in the Courts in September 1949. The family had initially migrated to Memphis in November 1948, first settling in Washington Street, then moving to Poplar Avenue near the Courts. In an interview years later Elvis recalled how they had moved with all their belongings on top of their '37 Plymouth: "We were broke, man, broke, and we left Tupelo overnight . . . we just headed for Memphis. Things had to be better."

c1950 ROTC CADET Most American high schools in the 1950s had a branch of the Reserve Officers Training Corps attached. Elvis joined in 1950. Years later, Elvis was to donate new uniforms to his old school's ROTC drill team.

1950 EARLY TEENS Posing with a toy gun outside Lauderdale Courts, Elvis is dressed in turned-up jeans and a sports-style jacket and starting to look like a real teenager. Before the 1950s the concept of "teenagers" didn't exist.

c1951 **THE COURTS** Another shot taken outside Lauderdale Courts: this time Elvis sports a flowered shirt. He was already developing a dress-consciousness that would become more and more pronounced as he grew into his late teens.

c1953–54 **THE IMAGE** By his late teens Elvis was starting to look like the rock'n'roll stereotype that he himself created almost single-handedly. Within a year (*see overleaf*) the sideburns and quiff appeared, and his hair was slicked back.

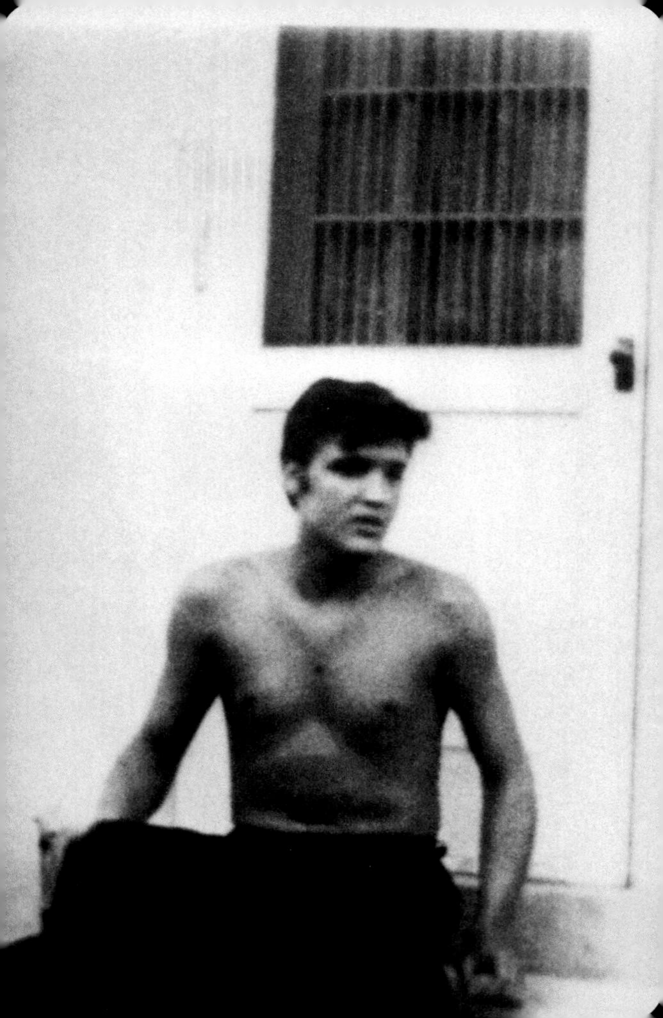

1951 **SIXTEEN** With aviator-style fur collar and hair greased, Elvis was developing a look: a hybrid of styles picked up from movie magazines, country singers, and the rhythm and blues singers who worked the clubs on Beale Street.

c1953 **TEENAGER** When the news media in the early Fifties coined the word "teenager" to describe the growing army of young people with new spending power, Elvis' appearance at the time typified what they had in mind.

1953

➔ **c1953 ROCKER** Elvis as a young rocker. The picture was taken around the time Elvis left high school in 1953. It was used a year or so later as a very early publicity shot when he started releasing records on the Sun label, and playing professionally with Scotty Moore and Bill Black in clubs and dancehalls around the Memphis area.

953
FAIR
AMUSEMEN

1953 PARDNERS Two cool cowpokes: Elvis and his cousin Gene Smith, dressed for the West at the Mid South Fair in Memphis, September 1953. The two spent a lot of leisure time together in their late teens, and also worked together briefly at the Precision Tool Company in Memphis.

1954 BUDDIES One year on, and life is changing fast. By now a budding rock'n'roll singer, and dressed for the part, Elvis poses with Buzzy Forbess (*left*) and Farley Guy, outside Lauderdale Courts, where all three teenagers were neighbors. With a fourth Court resident, Paul Dougher, they had been almost inseparable for the past three or four years. The picture is believed to have been taken after Elvis returned from one of his earliest appearances on the Louisiana Hayride.

1953 PHOTO BOOTHS As with ny teenager in the early 1950s there vere the inevitable pictures from photo ooths. In such pictures we see that this kid had a kind of . . . look. His hair was reased back and quiffed now, his shirt collar usually upturned, jackets casually smart. It was 1953, and 2,000 miles west in Burbank, California, Marlon Brando was shooting *The Wild One*. The world was changing fast, and Elvis was going to be part of the change in a big, big way.

1953

1955 HIGH SCHOOL PROM Hey good lookin'. With girlfriend Dixie Locke, about to go to the South Side High School Prom, May 6. Also in the picture is Elvis' cousin Gene Smith and his girlfriend Bessie Wolverton. Dixie was a regular date of Elvis' from early in 1954. Their relationship finally came to an end not long after the High School Prom, as Elvis' life became more and more consumed with his musical career, and his circle of friends broadened to include local music and media folk.

1955 HIGH SCHOOL PROM Whoa' there, man, keep that camera steady! The amateur snapper cut off the top and bottom of Elvis as he prepared for the Prom, but we can still dig that cool tuxedo, neat necktie, and one of those crazy shoes.

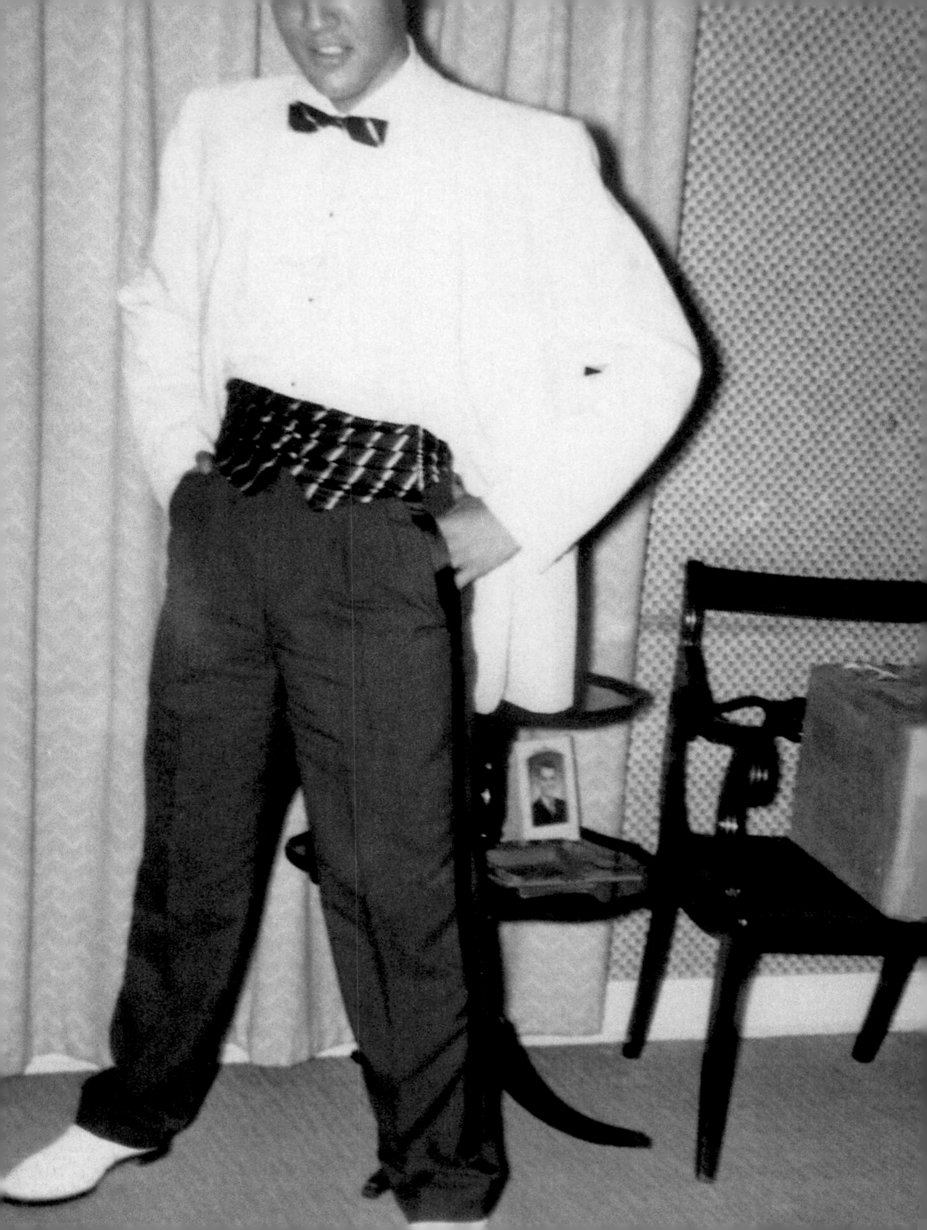

Elvis™

Elvis, Scotty & Bill

THE SUN YEARS

[1954–1955]

← **1955 TAMPA, FLORIDA**
A publicity photograph, taken backstage at a package show that Elvis was appearing on at the Fort Homer Hesterly Armory in Tampa, Florida on July 31, 1955.

January 1955 *October 1955* *August 1955* *December 1956*

1954–1956

Memphis was hot, real hot, in the summer of 1953, and when Elvis walked into Sam Phillips' Memphis Recording Service, he was 18. He seemed so nervous that Phillips found it hard to believe that he had ever sung in public. The studio at 706 Union Avenue doubled as the home of Sun Records, which was almost 100% a blues label at that time. The studio was also a "walk in" facility, and the young Elvis did just that, to make an $8 acetate dub of his own singing voice. He made a second acetate the following January, but it was June before Phillips called him back for a try out on various songs that might prove commercial, with none proving quite right.

Early in July, Phillips got a local guitarist, Scotty Moore, and bass player Bill Black, to play on a trial session with Elvis. Both played in a band called the Starlite Wranglers. Against Phillips' idea of what to expect (he told Moore that Elvis was a ballad singer) the most sensational take, in a session that up till then had the three just busking some ideas, was "That's All Right," by blues singer Arthur "Big Boy" Crudup. In that moment, rock'n'roll was truly born.

Summer 1955 *July 1955* *1955*

In the summer of 1954 Elvis eventually teamed up with Scotty and Bill (and subsequently D. J. Fontana on drums) and started—debuting from the Bon Air club in Memphis on July 17—to barnstorm across the South like a tornado.

Via the pioneering records masterminded by Sam Phillips and the hugely popular Louisiana Hayride radio show, something wild was being let loose, that nobody could control. It wasn't just about the music. For white kids from Phoenix, Arizona to Clarksdale, Mississippi, it was a true liberation; for their parents, Elvis was something inexplicable, even downright dangerous.

The timing couldn't have been more perfect. Young people across the Western world, and particularly in the United States, had surplus money to spend for the first time, and a liberty and identity as never before. The media even gave them a new name, and for the politicians and pundits it stood for a new social class: teenagers. Elvis, at 19, was one of them.

Elvis, Scotty, and Bill, as they were labeled on the Sun 45s, conquered all in an 18-month campaign of a new kind of cool that took no prisoners.

1954

1954 SUN STUDIO Sam Phillips founded his Sun Studio in 1950, specializing in black rhythm and blues players. He had a "record yourself" facility on which Elvis recorded his first acetate—"My Happiness" and "That's When Your Heartaches Begin." Sam also recorded local country-style musicians, and among them were Bill Black and Scotty Moore, whom he teamed up with Elvis. *Below*, Elvis, with Bill and Scotty. Sam Phillips is in the control booth.

1954 SUN SINGLES Seven-inch 45 rpm singles by Elvis on the Sun label—of which he made only five, released between July 1954 and August 1955—with their distinctive yellow labels and sleeves, now sell for phenomenal prices. Even rarer are the 78 rpm shellac discs also released at the time.

1954 ELVIS, SCOTTY, AND BILL An early publicity shot with Scotty and Bill sporting some wild cowboy shirts. They were still the Starlite Wranglers—a country swing outfit, hence the shirts—when Elvis teamed up with them at the Bon Air Club. Indeed, the "western" association stuck with Elvis: in this first explosion of popularity he was billed sensationally as the "Hillbilly Cat."

1955 ELVIS SIGNS New Year's Day, and Elvis signs a management deal with Memphis radio DJ Bob Neal, seen on the right with Sam Phillips (*left*). Neal nurtured Elvis through his early days on the road, only to be eclipsed by the more strident—and commercially inspired—Tom Parker.

RCA
VICTOR

1955 RCA STUDIOS From the first series of publicity shots made by RCA after signing Elvis in November for an unprecedented $40,000. Elvis was about to record in the label's studios in Nashville and New York, with the addition of session players (while retaining Scotty Moore, Bill Black, and D. J. Fontana), plus vocal group The Jordanaires.

1956 MILLION-DOLLAR QUARTET Still with Sun Records in Memphis were (*from left to right*) Jerry Lee Lewis, Carl Perkins, and Johnny Cash. All three participated in a sensational "ad lib" session with Elvis, which was never intended for release, and later became known as the "Million-Dollar Quartet." Elvis jammed with Perkins and Lewis, while Johnny Cash never actually appeared in the subsequent tapings, which circulated for years as bootlegs before being released on CD.

1956

1955

1955 TAMPA A backstage publicity shot taken in Tampa, Florida, in July 1955 for a showcase of stars from the Grand Ole Opry, headlined by comedian Andy Griffith. Posters proclaimed that Elvis, Scotty, and Bill were added "By Popular Demand."

1955 BACKSTAGE Elvis poses backstage with local radio DJ "Texas Bill" Strength at the 8th annual Country Music Jamboree promoted by Bob Neal, at the Overton Park Shell amphitheater in Memphis. It attracted 4,000 people.

⊖ ⊕ 1955 MEMPHIS Elvis backstage at the Overton Park concert (*opposite*), and (*above*) on stage at Ellis Auditorium, Memphis, in a show on February 6, 1955, which was compered by the local WHBQ disc jockey Dewey Phillips, the first DJ to play an Elvis record on the air, "That's All Right" in 1954. Elvis is playing the Martin D-28 guitar that he bought in July 1955; it had a custom-made tooled leather cover to protect the back of the guitar from being scratched by Elvis' belt buckle.

1955

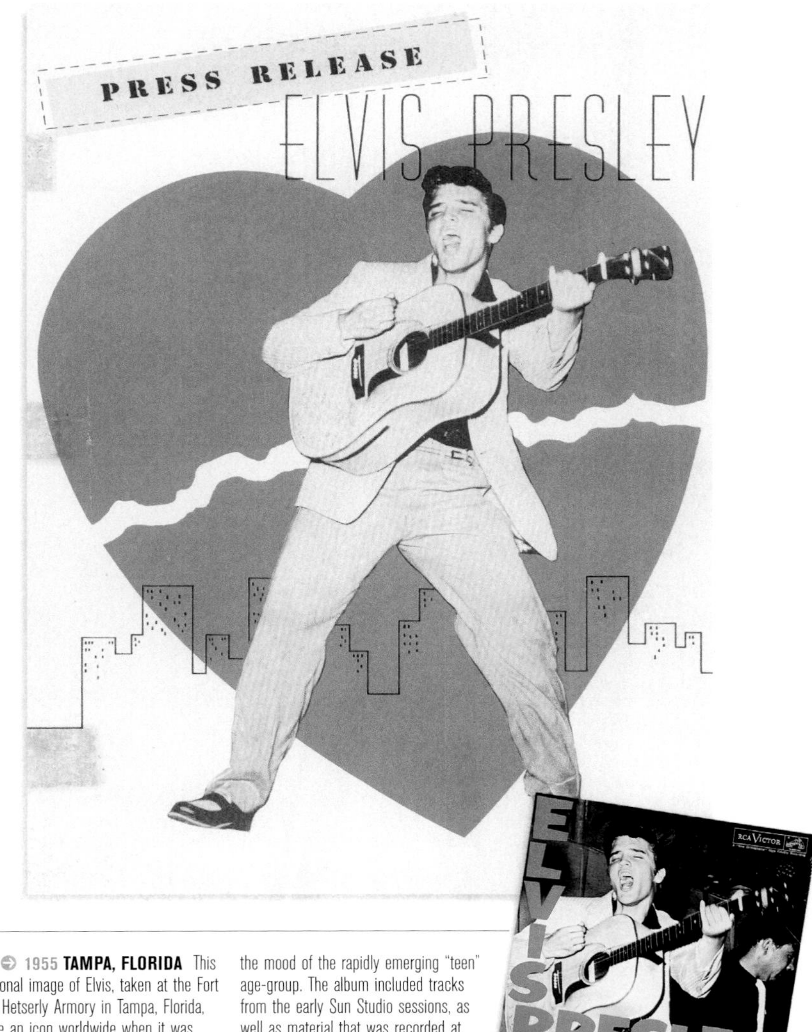

1955 **TAMPA, FLORIDA** This sensational image of Elvis, taken at the Fort Homer Hetserly Armory in Tampa, Florida, became an icon worldwide when it was used on the cover of his debut album. The picture seemed to accurately portray the mood of the rapidly emerging "teen" age-group. The album included tracks from the early Sun Studio sessions, as well as material that was recorded at RCA Records' studios in both Nashville and New York.

1956 LOUISIANA HAYRIDE The Louisiana Hayride was a radio show that beamed music across the rural South, and it became a crucial showcase for Elvis. The main competitor to the Grand Ole Opry, the Hayride was carried by 190 local stations in 13 states, and, when in November 1954 Elvis signed a one-year contract for 52 Saturday night appearances, it was a big step forward. The pictures above were taken during Elvis' last performance on the Hayride.

1955 **THE HAYRIDE** Elvis' regular radio stints on the Hayride were particularly important as they led to his being featured on most of the Hayride live package shows that toured the South. The Hayride deal was fixed while he was still with his original manager Bob Neal, and it was via the Hayride that he met Colonel Tom Parker.

1955 ANDY GRIFFITH SHOW Listen to "Blue Moon of Kentucky" with that slapped bass from Bill Black driving things crazy: this was cowboy music with a swivel. Shot during the Tampa, Florida, debut on the Andy Griffith show, July 31, 1955.

Andy Griffith Show Slated At Peabody

Andy Griffith, who made his reputation on recordings of such numbers as "What It Was — Was Football" and "Make Yourself Comfortable" is coming to Daytona Beach next weekend.

His show, which will also include several country and Western entertainers, is booked for two

ANDY GRIFFITH

ELVIS PRESLEY

performances, at 7:30 and 9:30 p. m. Saturday at Peabody Auditorium.

Elvis Presley, young singer from the Louisiana Hayride Show, will be one of the personalities in the show. Presley, a singer who combines country music with bop, has made a name for himself with such records as "That's All Right Mama," "Blue Moon of Kentucky," "I Don't Care If The Sun Don't Shine" and "Good Rockin' Tonight." He'll be accompanied by Scotty Moore, on the guitar, and Bill Black, bass.

A group of Grand Ole Opry artists will include Ferlin Huskey, Simon Crum, and Marty Robbins. Tommy Collins, of Hollywood, and Glenn Reeves are also scheduled to perform.

As a special attraction on the program there'll be Jimmie Rodgers Snow, son of the famous Hank Snow, and his Tennessee Playboys.

Griffith, star of the show, made his name in television on the show, "No Time For Sergeants," and will have a starring role in the production when it opens on Broadway in September.

COMING

Thursday and Friday
July 28 and 29—8:15
NEW
BASEBALL STADIUM

IN PERSON
THE ANDY GRIFFITH SHOW

NOW SEE HIM IN PERSON

PLUS STARS OF
GRAND OLE OPRY
★ FERLIN HUSKEY
with His Hush Puppies
and SIMON CRUM
★ MARTY ROBBINS
with JIMMY FARMER
SPECIAL ADDED ATTRACTIONS
★ TOMMY COLLINS
★ GLENN REEVES
JIMMY
★ RODGERS SNOW
and His Tennessee Playboys

EXTRA — EXTRA
By Popular Demand
★ ELVIS PRESLEY
with SCOTTY & BILL
Don't You Dare Miss It

Tickets on sale at both Dixie Music Stores and all McDuff ... Gen. adm. advance—only $1.00.

The Cash Box, Music — Page 79 — July 2, 1955

HANK SNOW ATTRACTIONS TOURS BIG SUCCESS

WESTERN UNION

HANK SNOW ATTRACTIONS PRESENTS
(Unit One)
In Person
The
HANK SNOW SHOW
With An All-Star Cast
Starring
HANK SNOW
"The Singing Ranger"
RCA Victor
The Rainbow Ranch Boys
•
...ISS MARTHA CARSON
and the
...OUNTRY GENTLEMEN
RCA Victor
•
...MOTHER MAYBELLE
and the
CARTER SISTERS
(Anita & Becky)
RCA Victor
•
...E DAVIS SISTERS
(Skeeter & Georgia)
RCA Victor
•
...E RODGERS SNOW
RCA Victor
•
Unit Manager
TOM DISKIN

...nks, Dee Jays, for voting "I DON'T HURT ANYMORE" by HANK SNOW . . . "THE MOST PROGRAMMED COUNTRY RECORD OF THE YEAR."
Sincerely,
Hank

HANK SNOW ATTRACTIONS PRESENTS
(Unit Two)
In Person
The
ANDY GRIFFITH SHOW
Starring
ANDY GRIFFITH
Capitol
•
FERLIN HUSKEY
Capitol
•
SIMON CRUM
Capitol
•
TOMMY COLLINS
Capitol
•
MARTY ROBBINS
Columbia
•
ELVIS PRESLEY
Sun
•
Unit Manager
COL. TOM PARKER

Special Guest on Florida Tour
GLENN REEVES
Singin' his latest TNT Record
"Wasted Time, Wasted Tears"
b/w
"I Ain't Got Room To Rock"

UNIT ONE :-: TOUR PUBLICITY: MAE AXTON ON TOUR IN JULY :-: UNIT TWO

HANK SNOW ATTRACTIONS

COL. TOM PARKER, GEN. MGR.

P. O. BOX 417, MADISON, TENNESSEE — Phone NASHVILLE 2-6770

"It's What's in THE CASH BOX That Counts"

1954–55 THE PRESS Right from the start, Elvis was aware of the power of the press. In addition to reviews of performances there was the advertising that promoters put into papers to publicize their upcoming attractions. Elvis was way down the bottom on many of these bills at first, but not for long. Later it was national publicity via the music trade press, then—as Elvis became newsworthy generally—the regular media. By the end of 1956, Elvis Presley was headline news worldwide.

1955

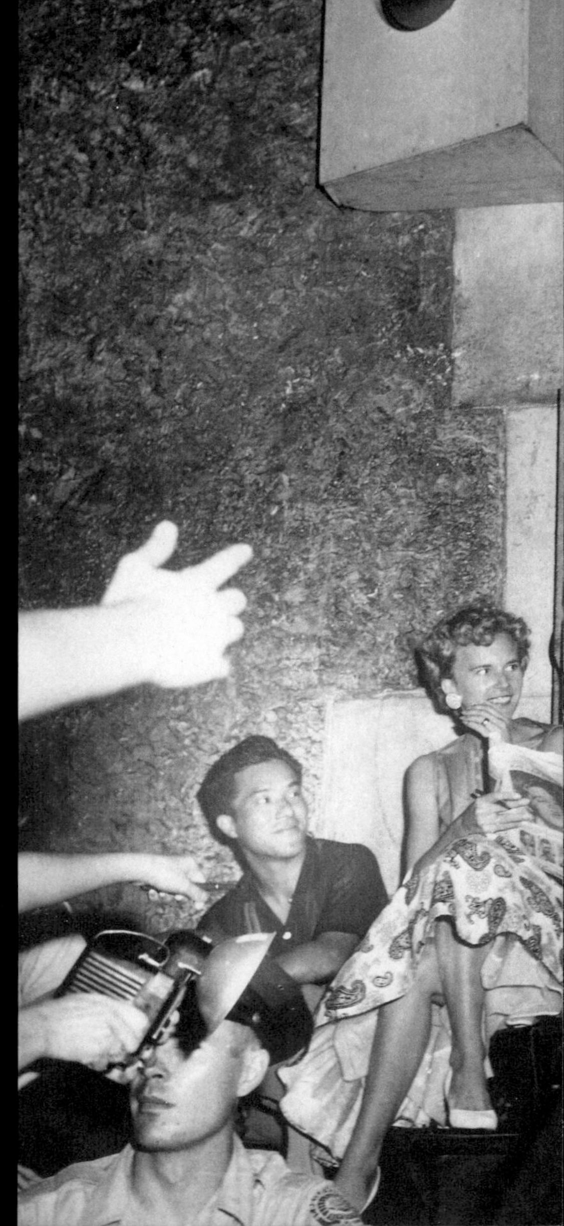

➔ **1955 CONTACT** The level of Elvis' contact with his audience was unprecedented, and no matter how remote he would inevitably become due to superstardom, his stage shows always managed to retain that bond.

➔➔ **1955 PRESLEY FANS** These sweet southern girls (*following pages*), like all mid-teens, were experiencing something new in their lives. This wasn't something Mom would understand when she remembered her own flowering youth; this was different from anything that had gone before.

➔ **1955 BACKSTAGE** During those riotous gigs of 1955, Elvis' fan base mushroomed. First of all the backstage encounters, signing autographs and chatting, were friendly affairs. But as the hysteria increased, the fans were mobbing him rather than meeting him. More and more Elvis found himself escorted, by local police, security men—and later his own personnel—from hotel to bandroom to stage, and vice versa, with a diminishing contact that he clearly regretted.

1955 TAMPA The venue of Fort Homer Hesterly Armory in Tampa, Florida where Elvis played on July 31, might sound unusual but no venues were really typical at this time. Dance halls, sports stadia, theaters, cinemas, rodeo arenas, municipal auditoriums—as his popularity grew, the only thing the places he played had in common was that they got bigger. A local promoter contemplating booking a show with Elvis on the bill had to work out how to cope with the capacity crowds he was attracting.

1955 **CLEVELAND** Backstage with fans during a trip to Cleveland, Ohio, in October 1955. On Thursday, an afternoon gig at Brooklyn High School in the city—also starring Bill Haley, Pat Boone, and the Four Lads—is filmed for a proposed minidocumentary. It never appeared. Later that evening, a near-riotous appearance by Elvis ensued when, after breaking his guitar strings, he smashed the instrument on the stage. The subsequent outburst of crowd hysteria was only just controlled by police.

1955 BILL HALEY A backstage shot (October 20, 1955) at the Brooklyn High School Auditorium, Cleveland, Ohio, with the first king of rock'n'roll, Bill Haley. Haley and his "Comets" came from the same country-swing tradition as Elvis. Haley also looked to black rhythm and blues for much of his material. But at 10 years older than Elvis, despite worldwide smashes like *"Rock Around the Clock"* and *"Shake Rattle and Roll,"* once Elvis raised the sex-appeal stakes there was no contest.

1955

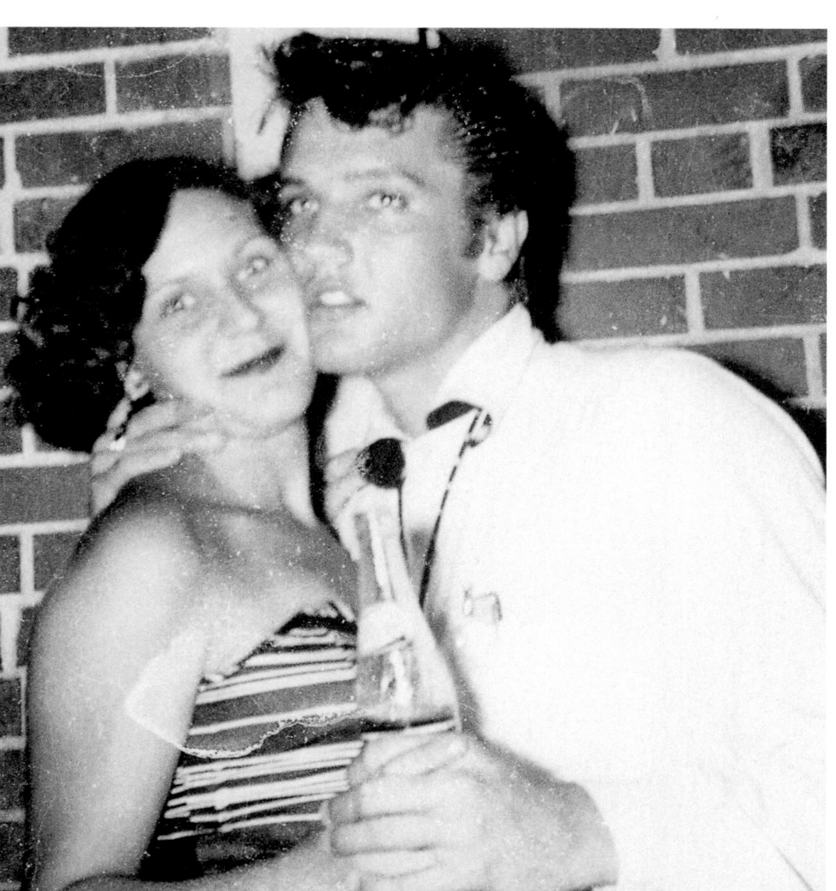

◀ 1955 **MAE BOREN AXTON** The lady on the right is Mae Boren Axton, who worked as publicist on the Florida leg of Elvis' 1955 dates. She went on to cowrite "Heartbreak Hotel" with Tommy Durden, the launchpad for Elvis Presley worldwide.

▲ 1955 **JACKSONVILLE, FLORIDA** This photograph was taken at the gig on May 13 in Jacksonville Ball Park. The gig was a milestone in Elvis' career, the occasion when rioting fans chased him into his dressing room, tearing off his clothes.

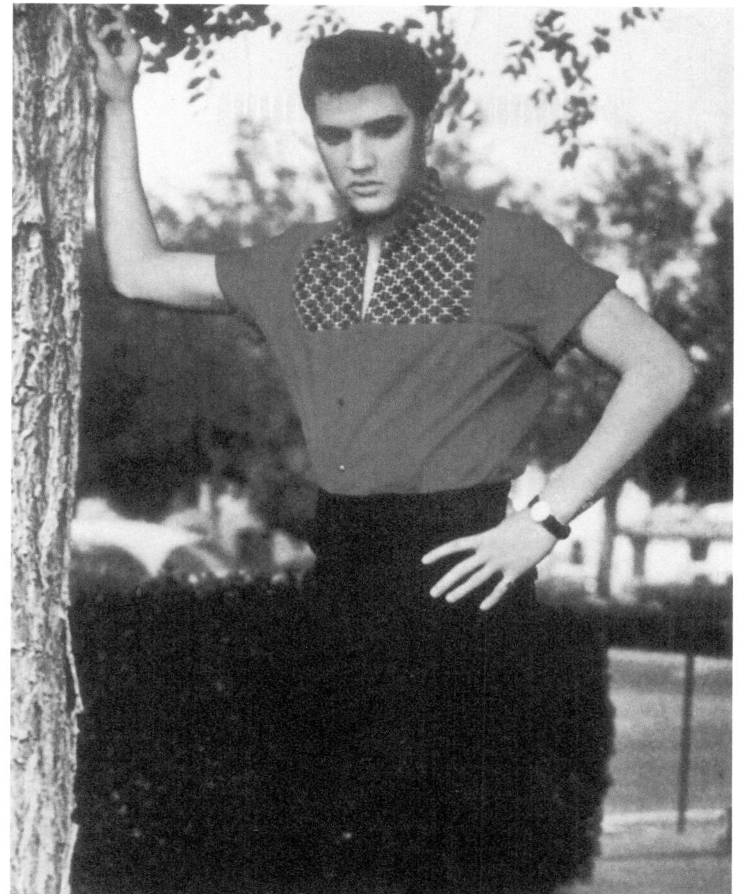

⬅ 1955 **MEMPHIS** William Speer, a Memphis-based photographer, captured a smouldering Elvis in a series of portraits that guaranteed his status as a new kind of sex symbol. The photographs were akin to the pinup pictures of Hollywood movie stars.

⬆ 1955 **MEMPHIS** There weren't that many color shots of Elvis back in 1955, and this one by an unknown photographer was used as publicity material by Colonel Tom Parker, who became the singer's manager in the latter half of that year. Parker had promoted some of the Louisiana Hayride and other package shows on which the Presley trio had appeared. His skill at negotiating in Elvis' favor made him a yardstick by which showbiz managers were subsequently measured.

Elvis™

Shake, Rattle & Roll

SUPERSTARDOM

[1956–1957]

← **1956 LAS VEGAS** By the middle of 1956 Elvis was truly a superstar, fêted by fans and celebrities alike. Among the many famous faces who visited him backstage during his first-ever Las Vegas season was Liberace. Elvis reciprocated (*left*) when the pianist entertainer played the Riviera Hotel in Las Vegas in November 1956.

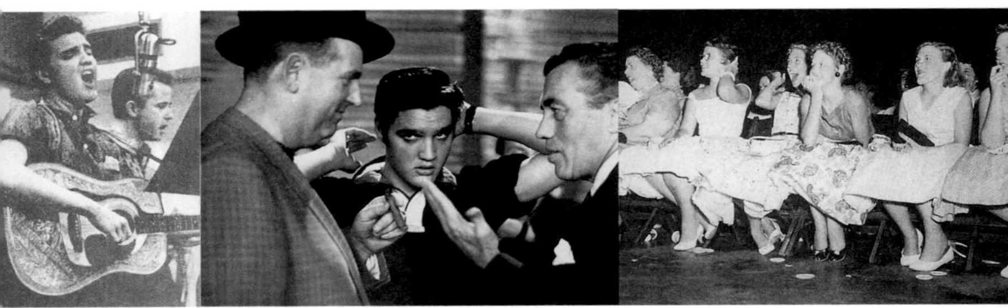

April 1956 *October 1956* *May 1956*

1956

Released in January in 1956, "Heartbreak Hotel" was much more than just another pop record. Rock'n'roll was still in its infancy, and its main characteristic, be it by Bill Haley, Little Richard, or the "Hillbilly Cat" from Memphis, was as dance music to bop the blues away. Yet the disc that triggered the seismic musical and social changes wasn't some up-tempo jive side at all. Quite the opposite, it was dark, sinister in its brooding melancholy, the new-to-the-ear "echo chamber" sound taking a whole generation down to the end of Lonely Street. But it did smack of the blues, with the simple but insistent guitar break and Floyd Cramer's evocative piano being more "down home" than any previous single by a white artist—indeed, many on first hearing it on the radio imagined it was a black singer, making Elvis' teen-appeal even more controversial, especially in the still-segregated South.

But that was only the start of it. Through the following 11 months of that year he had no less than 10 singles, nine EPs, and two albums released by RCA. The statistics were staggering; after "Heartbreak Hotel" went to number one in the US (and in many other territories worldwide) his debut LP was RCA

July 1956 *c1956* *September 1956*

Records' first to sell over a million copies. As well as both sides of "Hound Dog"/"Don't Be Cruel" topping the charts, plus "I Want You, I Need You, I Love You," and "Love Me Tender" hitting the number three and number one spots respectively, 4-track Extended Players also regularly made the US singles charts. In August 1956, RCA released seven singles on the same day, six of which were culled from Elvis' debut album of a few months earlier.

Elvis' ascendance through 1956 was due in no small part to Colonel Tom Parker, who had taken over complete management responsibilities in October 1955, after what could only be described as an uneven relationship with Elvis' previous representative Bob Neal, a local DJ and promoter, who himself had replaced the even more informal management role played by Scotty Moore.

Elvis Presley rocketed to fame so quickly that by the end of the summer he was making his first movie, *Love Me Tender*, in which his ambition to be a "serious" actor was frustrated by the studio's insistence on including musical items that had no bearing on the plot. But it was a huge hit, and confirmed, by the end of the year, Elvis' position as the undisputed King of Rock'n'Roll.

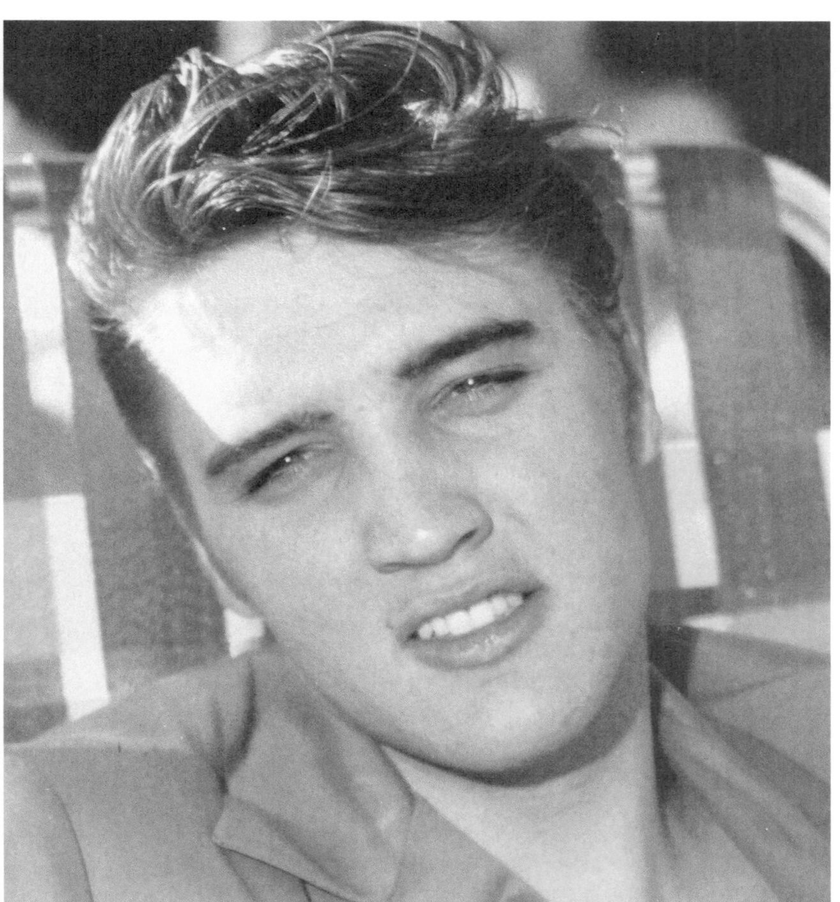

1956 HEARTTHROB It was the era of a new kind of teenagers' hero, represented primarily by smouldering screen actors like Marlon Brando and James Dean, who were able to identify directly with the new youthful audiences. But it was Elvis, with his stunning looks and captivating music, who was the first to bring this kind of image to the role of pop singer. It heralded the new phenomenon of early rock'n'roll as popular music aimed almost exclusively at teenagers.

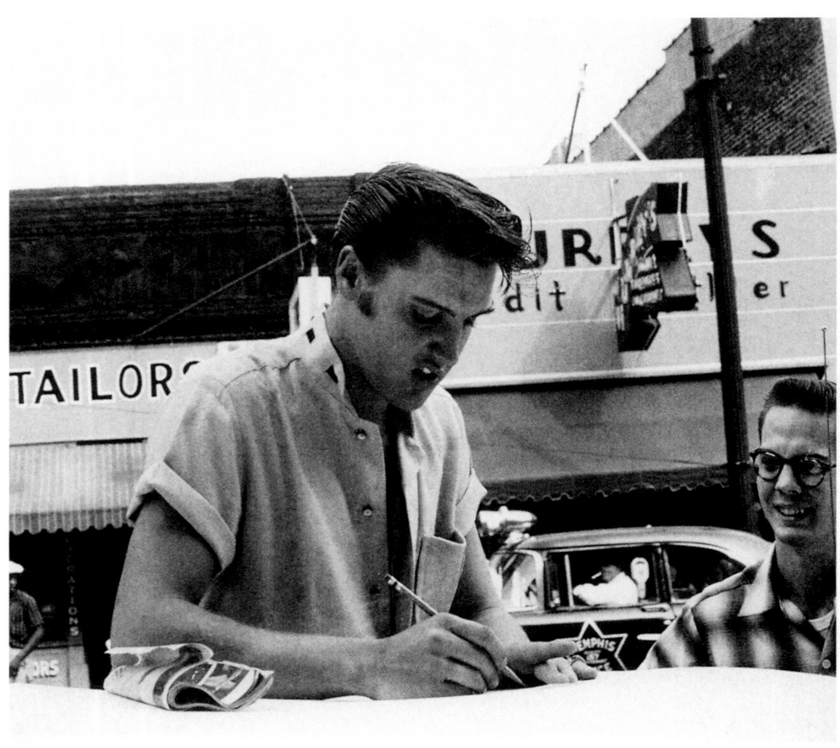

1956 **LOCAL HERO** Elvis signs an autograph in downtown Memphis in the summer of '56. Even at the height of the first wave of Elvis fan-mania in the mid-Fifties, he tried to move around his home town as freely as circumstance would allow. He would ride out to favorite restaurants and hamburger joints, and even go to the movies. Later, when things got just a little too hectic, he sent out for his food and would rent an entire movie theater for after-hours showings with his friends.

1956

1956 AUDUBON DRIVE In March 1956 Elvis purchased a new house for himself and his parents in a comfortable suburb of Memphis, at 1034 Audubon Drive. This shot was taken in July. A seemingly extravagant gesture for someone who had only recently achieved fame, the purchase created a convention for young rock'n'roll stars, who almost invariably signaled their success by buying a house for their folks. In less than a year the Presleys, meanwhile, had moved to Graceland.

1956

1956

← **1956 AUDUBON DRIVE** The face that appeared in a million bedrooms. Elvis reclines against his own bed at Audubon Drive, while all over the country, and increasingly the world, his image on photographs and posters covered fans' walls, was reproduced on bedside lamps, vanity sets, bedspreads, even pajamas.

1956

IN PERSON - ON THE STAGE - THREE TIMES DAILY
ELVIS PRESLEY - TV & RECORDING STAR AND HIS STAGE SHOW
ON THE SCREEN
"THE SQUARE JUNGLE"
ELVIS PRESLEY AND HIS STAGE SHOW IN PERSON
ON THE SCREEN - TONY CURTIS IN "THE SQUARE JUNGLE"
ON THE STAGE
IN PERSON
ELVIS PRESLEY
STAGE SHOW
IN PERSON
ELVIS PRESLEY

1956 ON THE ROAD Spurred on by 11 guest appearances on network TV shows through 1956, the live stage shows got even wilder. The work schedule for Elvis, plus the musicians, the Jordanaires and the road crew, was frantic. In the first two months of the year Elvis performed over 30 live dates, some involving double or triple appearances at a venue on the same day, in addition to four TV shows in the "Dorsey Brothers' Stage Show" and five days in the recording studio.

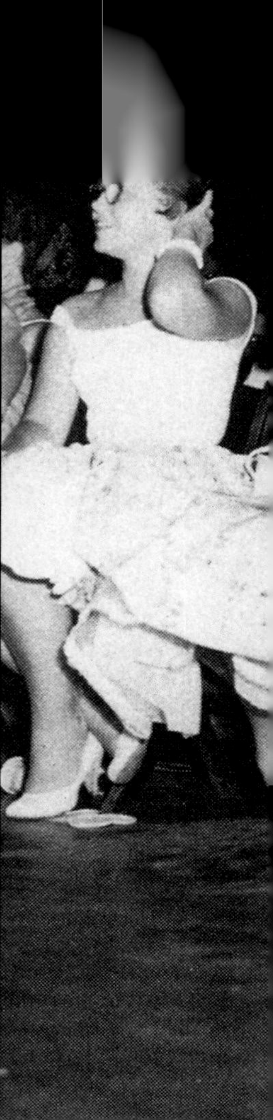

1956 ELVIS MANIA Theaters
the United States of America had
een anything like it. The bobby
had jived in the aisles for jazz stars
nny Goodman and Harry James in
Band era, the fans swooned as
Frank Sinatra crooned, and audiences literally wept for the "Cry Guy" Johnnie Ray, but the reaction to Elvis was altogether different again. Like Elvis' performances, the impact he had on the audience could only be described as physical.

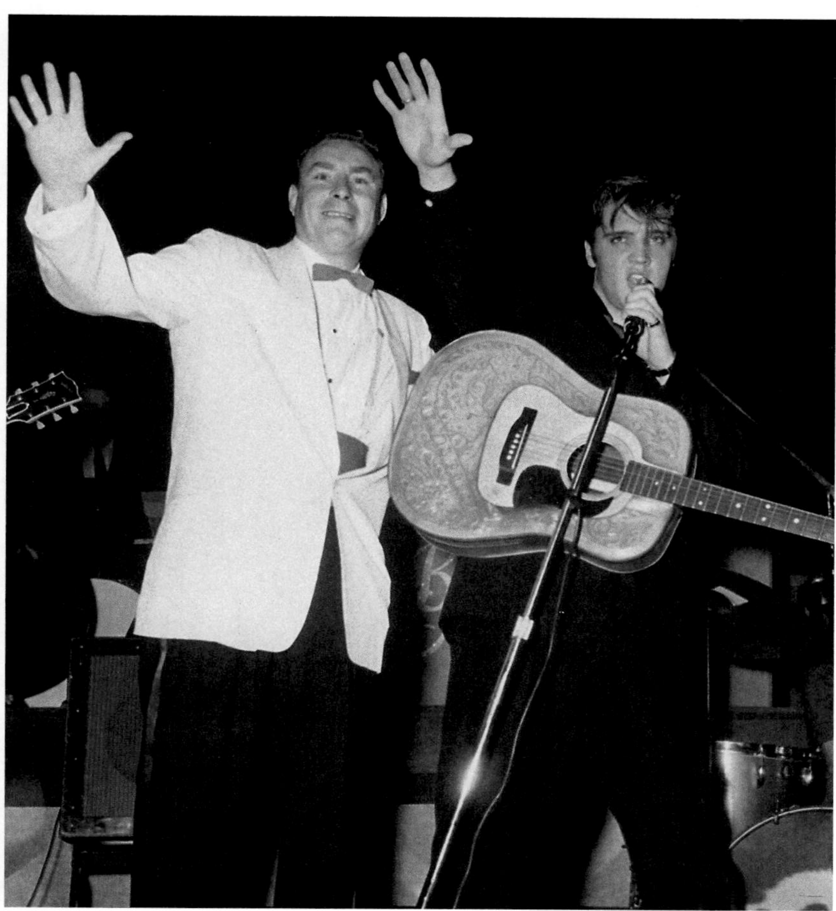

← **1956 DALLAS, TEXAS** A concert at the Cotton Bowl in October 1956 grosses nearly $30,000. Elvis' drummer, D. J. Fontana, later described the sight of thousands of flashbulbs in the darkened arena—"It looked like war out there."

↑ → **1956 ON STAGE** Elvis' whole persona—the way he swung his body (*here and overleaf*)—along with the hairstyle, the scowl, and every detail of his image—became a template for thousands of white male rock'n'roll artists who followed him.

1956

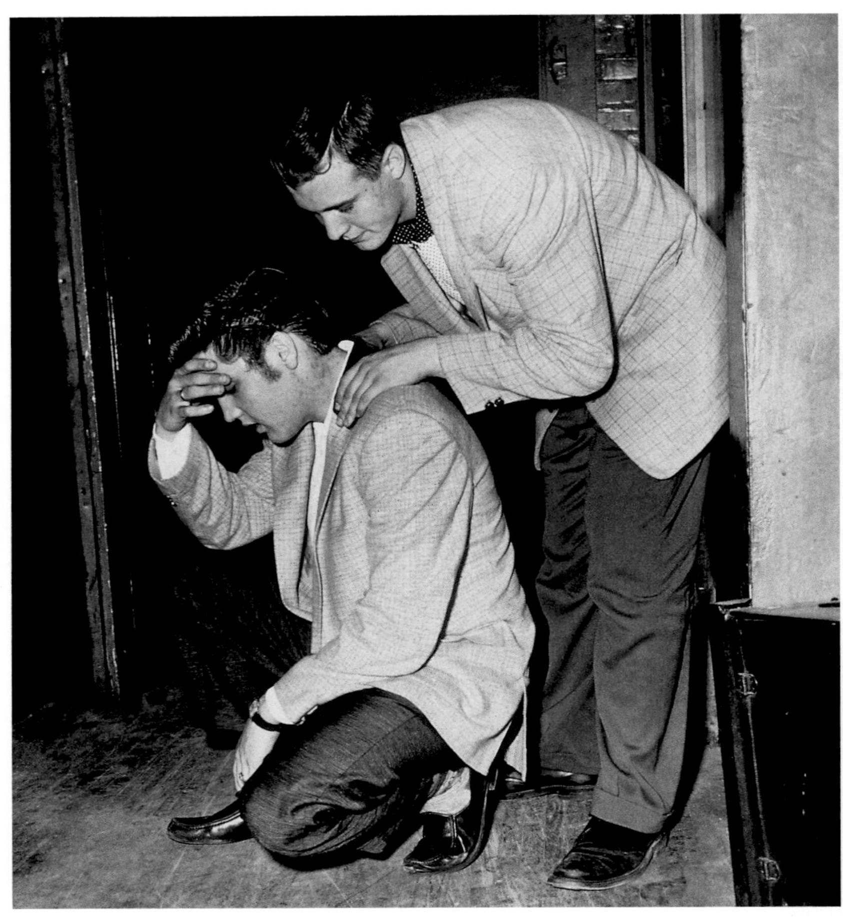

1956

⬆ 1956 **ST. PAUL, MINNESOTA** The stage shows and their frequency could be, physically, extremely exhausting. Elvis is seen here backstage at an afternoon show at the Auditorium in the Minnesota state capital of St. Paul, on May 13.

➡ 1956 **BACKSTAGE, LAS VEGAS** Fans besiege Elvis when he agrees to sign autographs during his two-week engagement at the Venus Room of the New Frontier Hotel in Las Vegas. Soon this kind of intimacy became virtually impossible.

ELVIS PRESLEY
RCA Victor Artist
ELVIS
Autographs
VENUS ROOM
PRESLEY

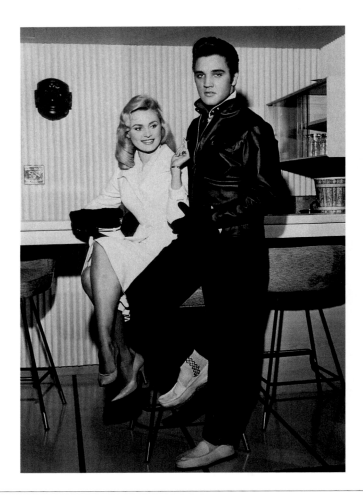

1957 LAS VEGAS One of a series of pictures of Elvis with Hannerl Melcher, a Las Vegas showgirl and Miss Austria 1957, who spent Christmas of that year with him at Graceland. Some of the photographs show them sitting astride a motorcycle.

1956 MEMPHIS This photo, taken in Memphis, shows Elvis with yet another admiring female fan. Although during this period Elvis enjoyed a lot of female company, he was yet to settle into a long-term relationship.

EP

1956

1956 RCA, NASHVILLE A Nashville recording session on April 14, 1956, which produced Elvis' second single for RCA, *"I Want You, I Need You, I Love You."* He is with Gordon Stoker from the Jordanaires, who were soon to work with him regularly.

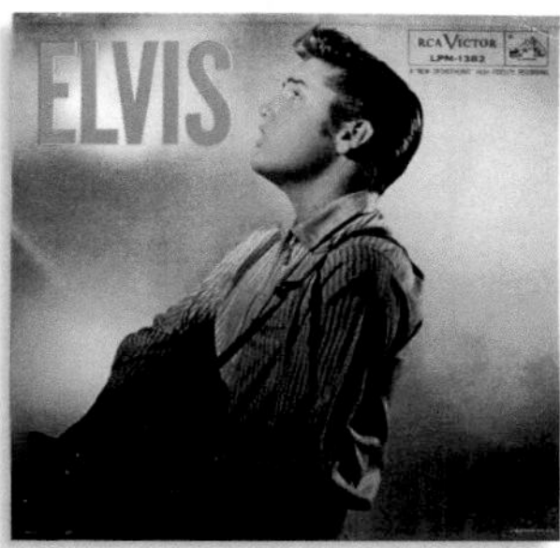

1956 RECORD BLITZ By the end of 1956, Elvis had released two albums. The second featured a mixture of ballads and hard-hitting rockers. RCA was still able to mine the back catalog it had inherited from Sun Records for material, hence on the October-released EP *"Any Way You Want Me"* (*left*), apart from the title track the other three songs had all originally been singles on Sun.

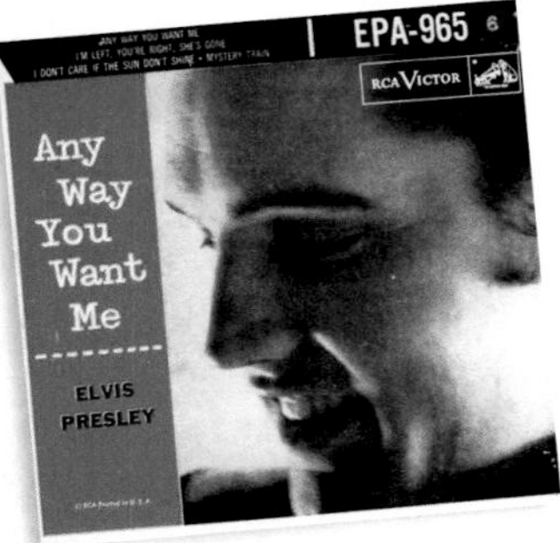

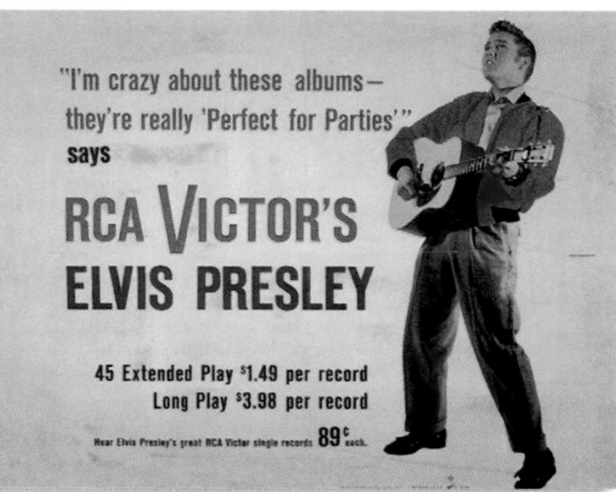

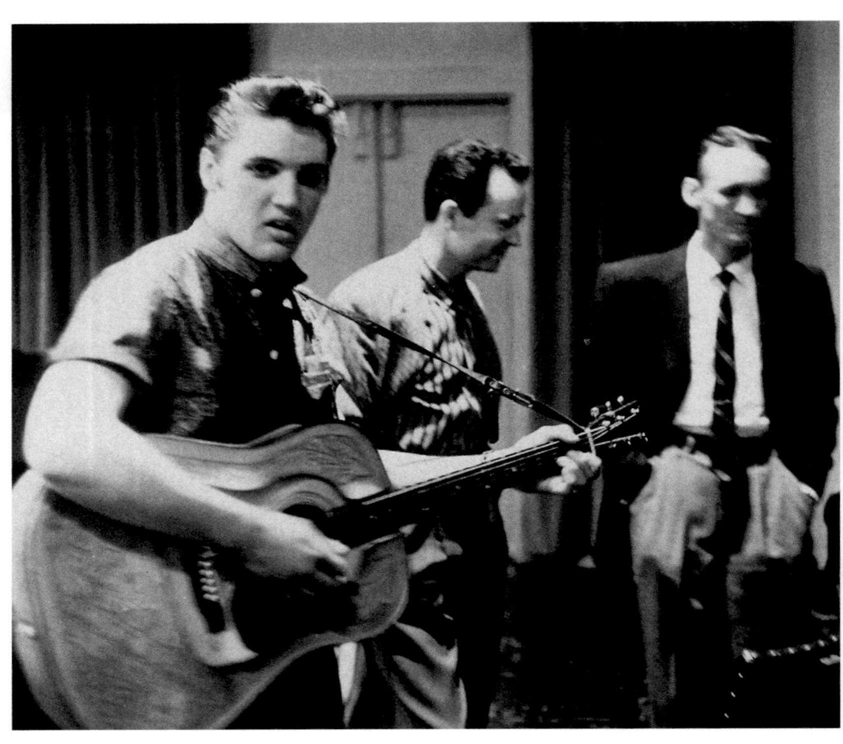

1956

1956 RCA, NASHVILLE More photographs from the "I Want, I Need You, I Love You" session. *Above*, Elvis with vocalists Gordon Stoker and Brock Speer in the background. On this session Stoker and the brothers Ben and Brock Speer did the backing vocals. Opposite, Elvis is flanked by Ben Speer and (on his right) the legendary Nashville guitarist Chet Atkins. Atkins was an early regular on the Grand Ole Opry. A talent scout for RCA records from 1952, he rose to the position of vice president.

1956

1956 MERCHANDISE Many merchandised products bearing Elvis' name and image started to appear in 1956. Items from clothes to cosmetics, toys (like the plastic guitar *above*) to neckties, and buttons (*right*)—all aimed at teenagers—fueled a multimillion-dollar industry. In fact in the long term, the sale of Elvis material has far outstripped any other—including products related to the Beatles—being marketed in virtually every country in the world for more than 40 years.

In Person
ELVIS PRESLEY

1956 NEW FRONTIER HOTEL On May 23, 1956, Elvis made a debut in a Las Vegas hotel showroom. He played two weeks in the New Frontier Hotel as an "extra added attraction" to Freddy Martin's Big Band and comedian Shecky Greene.

1956 TRADING CARDS Some of the pictures taken next to the New Frontier pool appeared on a set of fan trading cards. Trading cards had long been a craze for sports fans, and the Elvis series launched in 1956 pioneered their use of rock'n'roll stars.

1956 ELVIS CONTRACT The Colonel had highly personalized documents made for Elvis' live appearances. Part of the deal involved Elvis being prominently displayed in promotional material, such as the table flyers *(center)* at the New Frontier.

1956

➔ **1956 NEW FRONTIER HOTEL** The Las Vegas dates represented a new frontier for Elvis in more ways than just name. It was his first move into the seemingly more sophisticated, and certainly financially better-off, world of middle-class, middle-aged cabaret audiences, as opposed to the teen-dominated crowds that packed his tour concerts. And right from the start, he loved it. Although nervous about the reaction he was getting on the first few dates, Elvis went on record as taking to Las Vegas in a big way. He felt relaxed there, as pictures taken around the hotel pool suggest.

Best Wishes
Elvis Presley

1956 AUTOGRAPHS Some of the pictures taken next to the New Frontier pool were to appear on fan photographs, with a facsimile of Elvis' autograph. In an era when most photography was in black-and-white, these color pictures were quite spectacular.

1956 NATALIE WOOD A small-time Hollywood-based actor, Nick Adams became a close friend of Elvis after Elvis' first work in the movie capital on the feature *Love Me Tender*. Adams was to later introduce Elvis to the young star actress Natalie Wood, who was basking in her success in the hit movie *Rebel Without a Cause*. During Halloween night in 1956, Natalie Wood arrived in Memphis for a three-day visit. These pictures show the two young stars at the WHBQ radio station.

1956 BACKSTAGE, MEMPHIS On September 29, 1956, Elvis and Nick Adams visited the Mid-South Fair. Elvis signed some autographs, and they watched the show "Stars Over Dixie." Elvis appeared briefly on stage with headliner Dennis Day.

1956

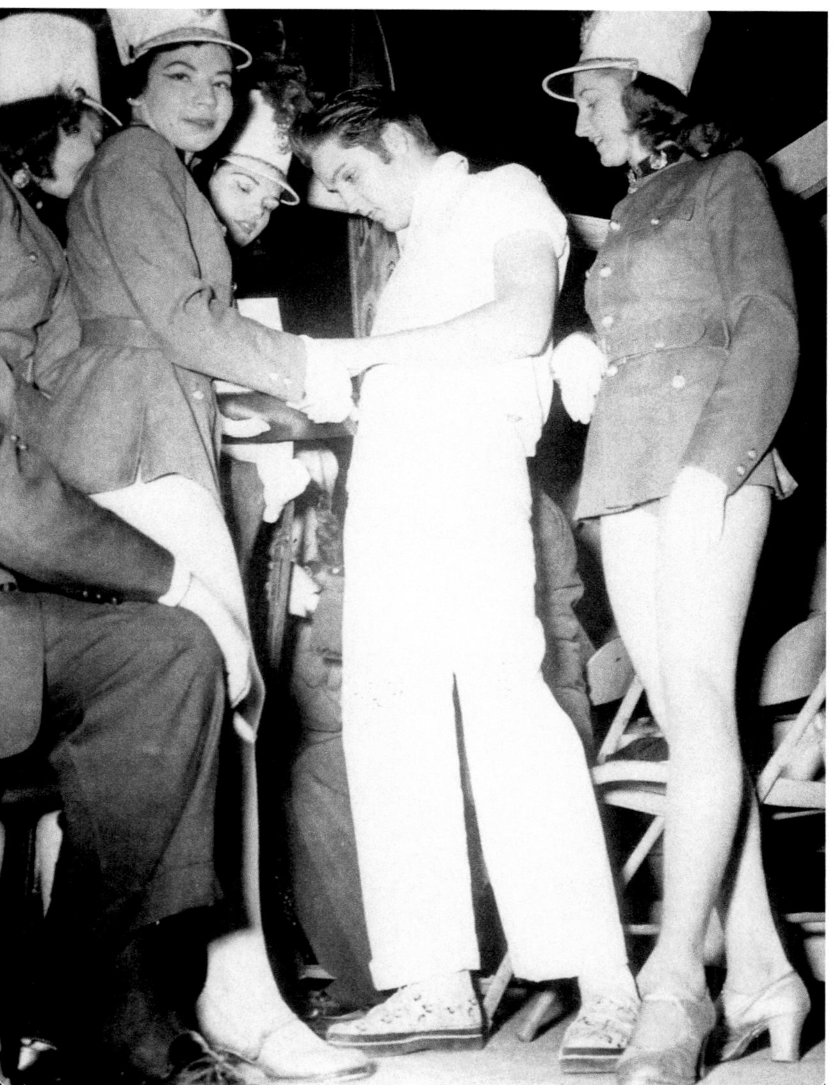

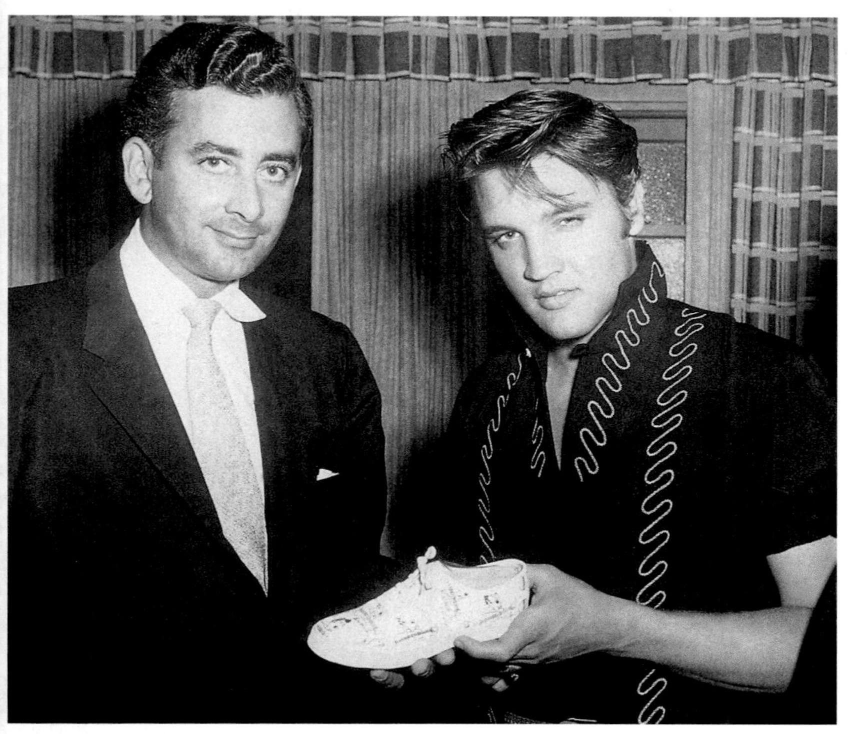

1956 HOLLYWOOD A very early example of product merchandise, Hank Saperstein presents Elvis with a sport shoe that features his name. The Colonel had signed a lucrative deal with Saperstein in July 1956 in which they (he and Elvis) would receive $35,000 dollars against 45% of licensing fees and royalties, and which gave the merchandiser exclusive rights to exploit the image of Elvis Presley in just about everything—from bracelets to bedroom slippers.

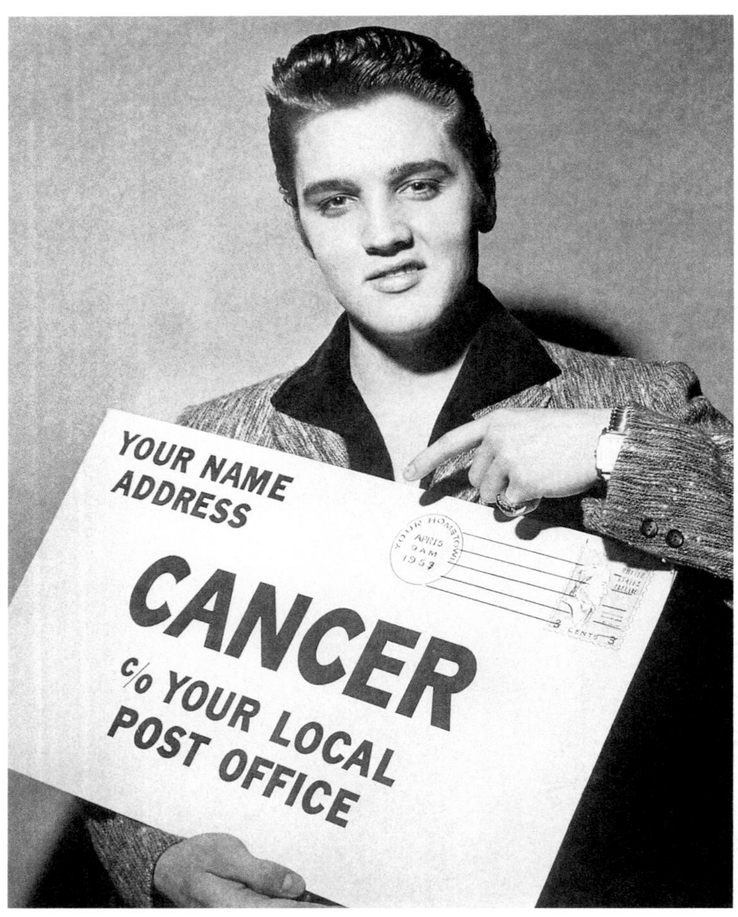

1956 **CHARITY** Toward the end of 1956 Elvis became more concerned with charitable causes. One nationwide charity venture was the annual March of Dimes, and in November Elvis made a promotional announcement to urge people to contribute to the 1957 March. Among others, Elvis identified himself with a Memphis charity for the blind, the Goodwill Revue (a fund-raising event organized by the WDIA radio station), and a US Marines drive for toy donations for underprivileged children.

1956

JOIN
MARCH
OF
DIMES

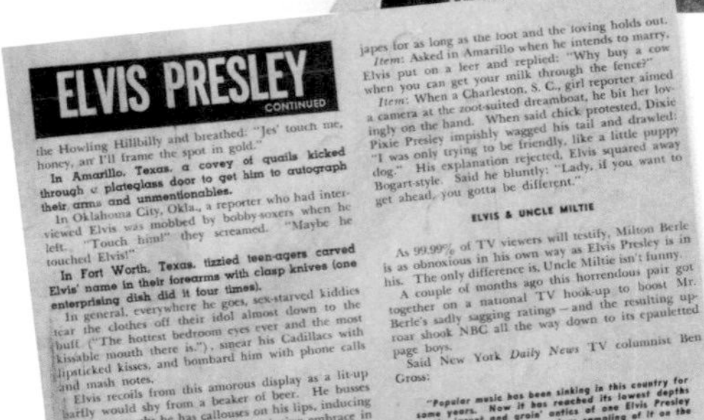

ELVIS PRESLEY

CONTINUED

the Howling Hillbilly and breathed: "Jes' touch me, honey, an' I'll frame the spot in gold."

In Amarillo, Texas, a covey of quails kicked through a plateglass door to get him to autograph their arms and unmentionables.

In Oklahoma City, Okla., a reporter who had interviewed Elvis was mobbed by bobby-soxers when he left. "Touch him!" they screamed. "Maybe he touched Elvis!"

In Fort Worth, Texas, tizzied teen-agers carved Elvis' name in their forearms with clasp knives (one enterprising dish did it four times).

In general, everywhere he goes, sex-starved kiddies tear the clothes off their idol almost down to the buff ("The hottest bedroom eyes ever and the most kissable mouth there is."), smear his Cadillacs with lipsticked kisses, and bombard him with phone calls and mash notes.

Elvis recoils from this amorous display as a lit-up barfly would shy from a beaker of beer. He busses so many mouths he has callouses on his lips, inducing one doll to remark, after a disappointing embrace in Washington, D. C.: "I don't know what's happened, but he was kissing a lot better in Winston-Salem." And in at least two encounters with reporters, he has indicated that he intends to encourage these Jukes-like japes for as long as the loot and the loving holds out.

Item: Asked in Amarillo when he intends to marry, Elvis put on a leer and replied: "Why buy a cow when you can get your milk through the fence?"

Item: When a Charleston, S. C., girl reporter aimed a camera at the zoot-suited dreamboat, he bit her lovingly on the hand. When said chick protested, Dixie Pixie Presley impishly wagged his tail and drawled: "I was only trying to be friendly, like a little puppy dog." His explanation rejected, Elvis squared away Bogart-style. Said he bluntly: "Lady, if you want to get ahead, you gotta be different."

38

ELVIS & UNCLE MILTIE

As 99.99% of TV viewers will testify, Milton Berle is as obnoxious in his own way as Elvis Presley is in his. The only difference is, Uncle Miltie isn't funny.

A couple of months ago this horrendous pair got together on a national TV hook-up to boost Mr. Berle's sadly sagging ratings—and the resulting uproar shook NBC all the way down to its epauletted page boys.

Said New York *Daily News* TV columnist Ben Gross:

"Popular music has been sinking in this country for some years. Now it has reached its lowest depths in the 'grunt and groin' antics of one Elvis Presley. The TV audience had a noxious sampling of it on the Milton Berle show.

"Elvis was appalling musically. Also, he gave an exhibition that was suggestive and vulgar, tinged with

1956 LOVE ME TENDER Elvis on the set of his first film, *Love Me Tender.* He is wearing the Sunday best in which he serenades everyone in the film. At first, he had not intended to sing in this drama, but the producers eventually succeeded in including four songs.

1956 PRESS CUTTING An early example of "serious" journalism covering the Elvis phenomenon, a highly critical piece from a mid-1956 edition of the much-respected *Life* magazine. It knocked just about every aspect of Elvis' music, stage act, and mannerisms.

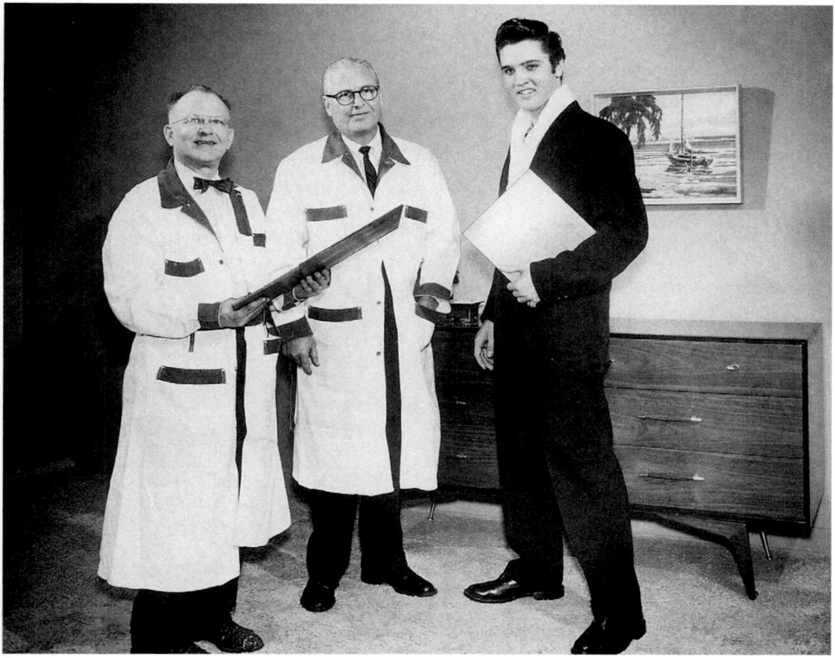

1956 BUREAU
These pictures show Elvis in a proposed product endorsement. He poses by a fashionable piece of furniture, a bureau in the "contemporary" style of the day, in a promotional shoot for Hungerford Furniture. The sales people at the furniture company subsequently decided that Elvis' appeal was far more likely to be toward teenagers rather than their parents who probably bought the furniture for the home. For this reason the ad was eventually scrapped.

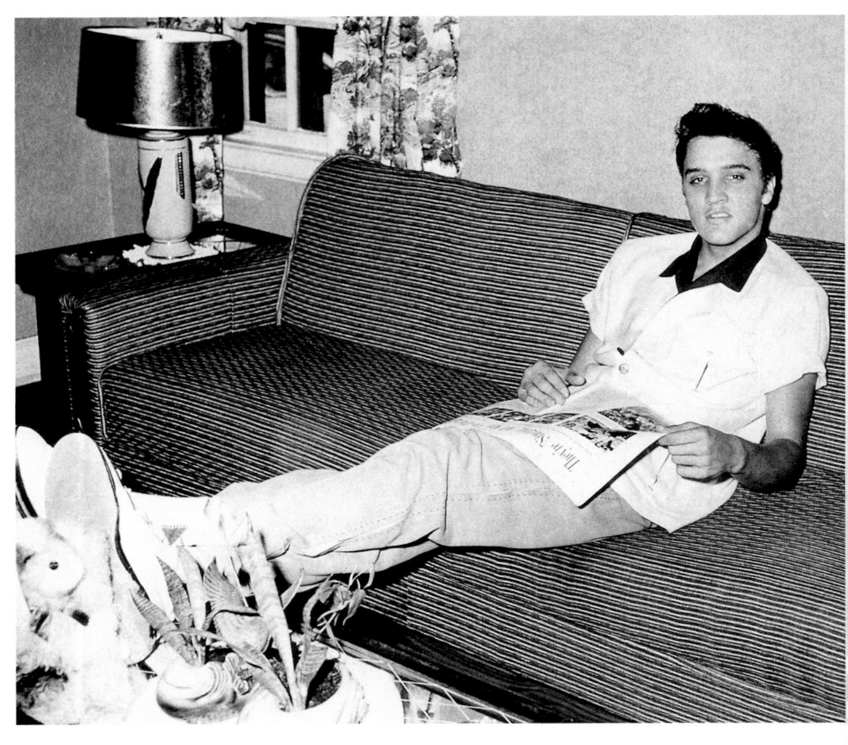

1956 **RELAXING** Elvis "relaxes" at home for a photo-shoot, and *(opposite)* examines a pop music fan magazine called *Dig*. One of the big commercial by-products of the rock'n'roll revolution was an explosion of magazines aimed at teenagers. The spending power of young people was greater than ever before, and along with fashion, music, and movies catering for the juvenile sector came reading matter covering and promoting those areas. Fan magazines led the field in this respect.

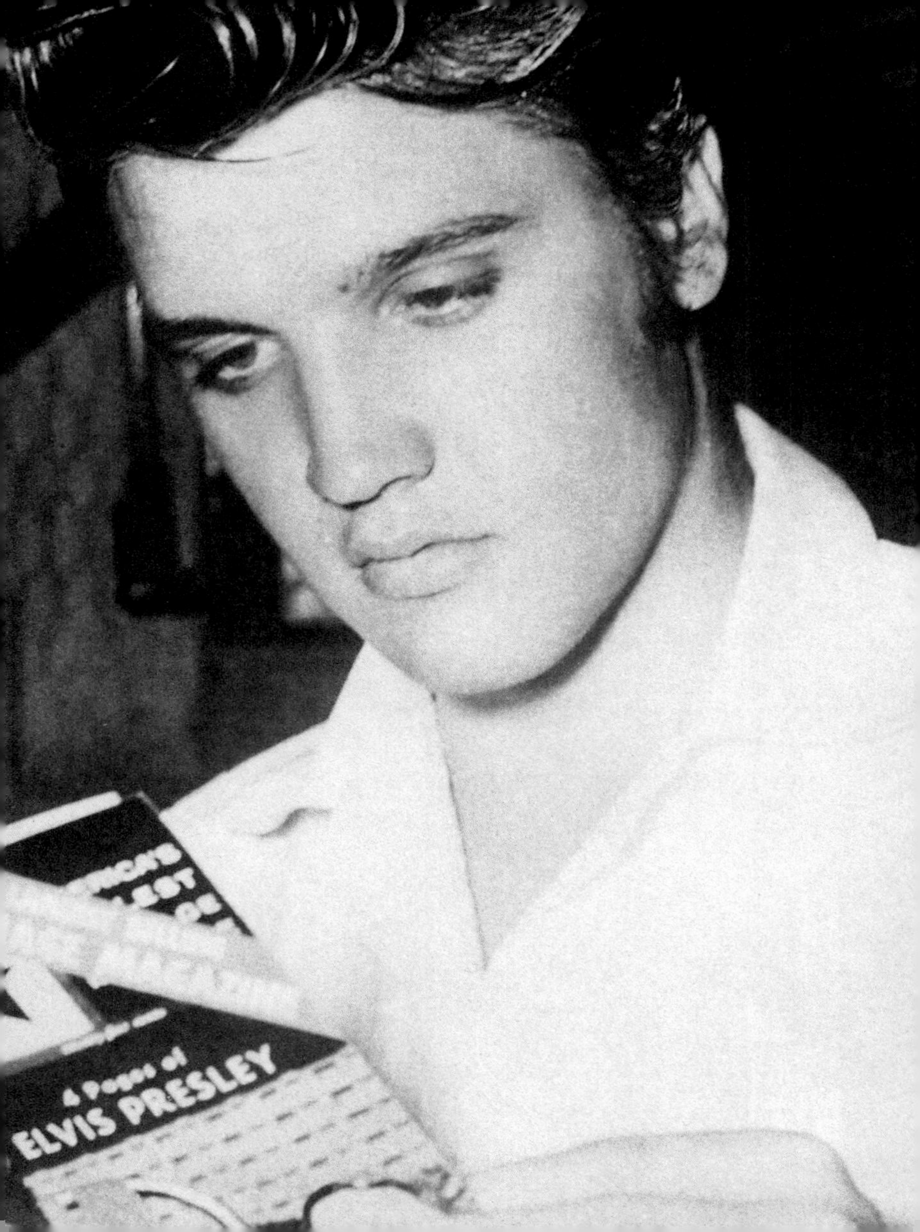
4 Pages of
ELVIS PRESLEY

1956 **MEMPHIS** Despite the fact that it was becoming increasingly difficult for Elvis to move around in public without attracting attention, he still made a habit of driving around the Memphis area in one of his many cars. He clearly had an amiable relationship with the local police; the officer above is a captain, Fred Woodward, who knew Elvis and had personally escorted him as security. Despite the "teenage rebel" image surrounding early rock'n'roll, Elvis always had a respect for officers of the law.

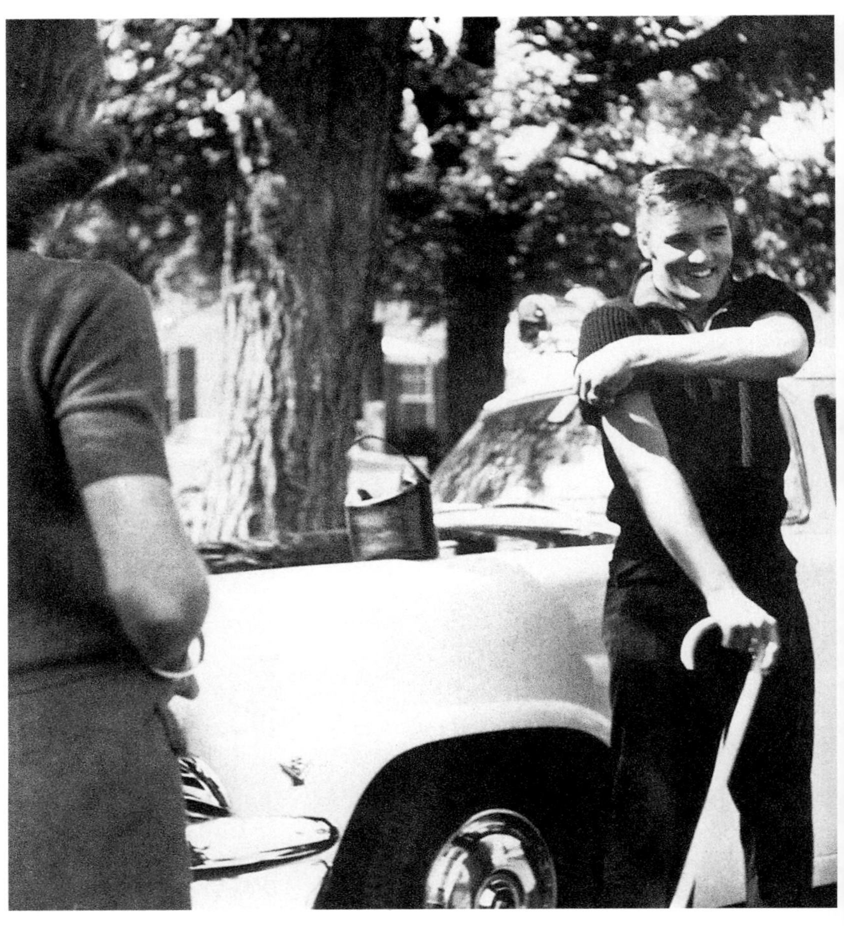

1956 **MEMPHIS** Here, Elvis had just been talking to the police captain (*see previous page*) in a Memphis street, and right away the passing fans saw an opportunity not to be missed, to meet and greet their idol.

1956 **MEMPHIS** Another cop—is it an autograph or a ticket? Elvis' flashy cars were highly conspicuous on the Memphis streets, even though it was during that period of the mid-Fifties when the streets were full of spectacular automobiles.

Royal
MODERN METHOD STORE
205
MA
LOEWS

1956

1956 MEMPHIS
The *de rigueur* status symbol, especially with the young, in mid-Fifties America was the most ostentatious car possible, and that usually meant the biggest, and that usually meant a Cadillac. Elvis very quickly became famous for his spectacular collection of Cadillacs.

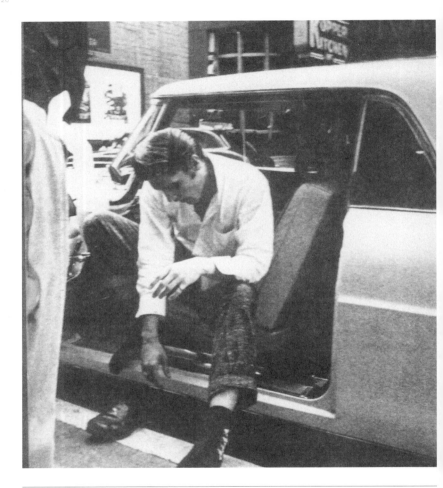

1956 FLORIDA At the beginning of August 1956, Elvis played a series of dates in Florida. He had driven from Memphis to Miami in a brand new lavender Continental Premier *(above)*. By the end of the week, the Premier was already defaced with fan graffiti. Elvis famously commented on the increasing nuisance of his fans scratching their names on his cars: "Sure they tear off my clothes, they scratch their initials on my cars, they phone my hotel all night . . . when they stop, I'll start to worry."

➊ **1956 MEMPHIS** Here, Elvis is
ttending to one of his cars. He had a
apidly growing fleet of automobiles,
articularly favoring Cadillacs; Elvis was
amous for giving these away. As the

modest carport at Audubon Drive became too small. When the family moved to Graceland in 1957, a larger facility was arranged. Visitors to Graceland today can see his car fleet in the automobile museum

➋ **1956 MEMPHIS** Elvis had a great interest in big, fast motorcycles, particularly Harley-Davidsons. Here he is shown sporting a cap that took its inspiration from the Marlon Brando character in *The Wild One*,

1956 MOTORCYCLES Elvis was getting a lot of negative press, and this "juvenile delinquent" image of bikes didn't help; but, as RCA assured the Colonel, it all helped in selling records. Motorcycles were a symbol of youthful rebellion and bikers in general came in for some unsavory press during the 1960s with the association with California's notorious Hell's Angels. Elvis (*left*) sits on a Harley outside the house at Audubon Drive, and (*above*) poses with the biker's obligatory leather jacket.

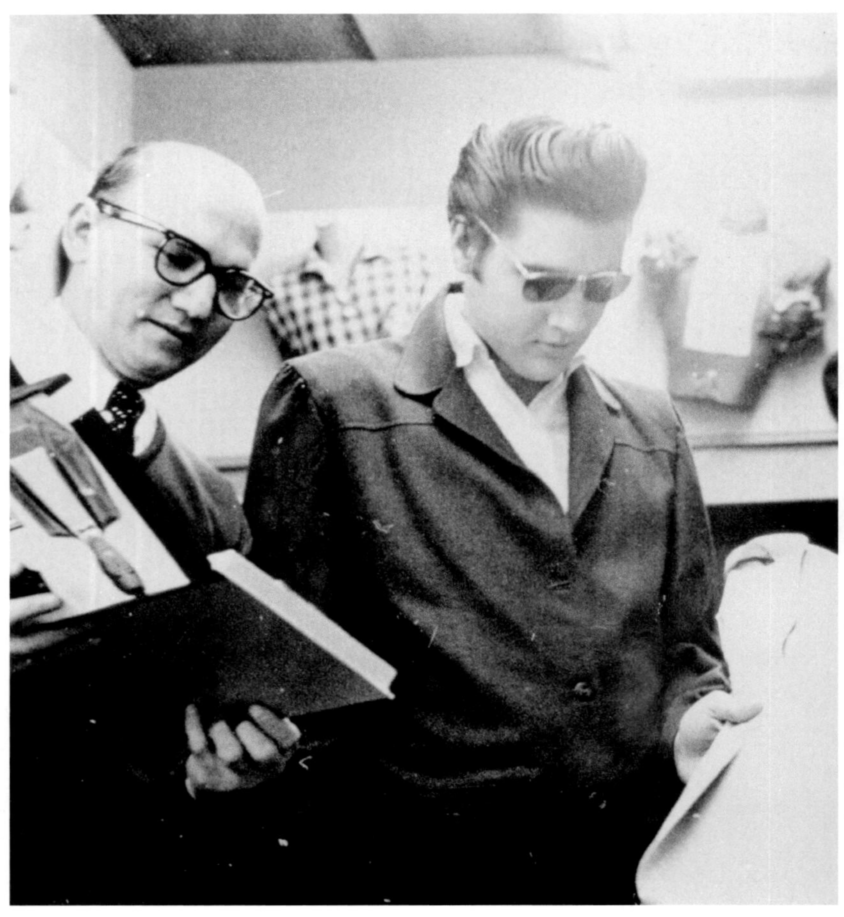

1956 BILOXI, MISSISSIPPI In summer 1956 Elvis dated June Juanico from Biloxi, Mississippi. A rumor began to circulate that the couple were to be engaged. In order to set the record straight Elvis was forced to appear on a local radio station in New Orleans to assure the public that this wasn't the case. As a favor to Eddie Bellman, a friend of June's mother, Elvis made an appearance at Dave Rosenblum's Biloxi clothing store (*above*) in which Bellman owned the shoe department.

1956

➊ **1956 ED SULLIVAN SHOW** At he time, the Ed Sullivan show was the nost prestigious variety program on TV. Elvis is pictured here during rehearsals or his first appearance on the show on Charles Laughton because Sullivan had been involved in a car accident. Elvis performed *"Don't Be Cruel," "Love Me Tender," "Ready Teddy,"* and *"Hound Dog."* Broadcast live, the show attracted an

➋ **1956 ED SULLIVAN SHOW** Before his second appearance on the show, Elvis spoke of his influence on teenagers: "My Bible tells me that what he sows he will also reap, and if I'm sowing evil and

➔ 1956 ED SULLIVAN SHOW Elvis on his second appearance on the Ed Sullivan show on October 28, in full throttle with the Jordanaires.

← 1956 BUTTON BADGE This novelty button utilized the then-new technique in which alternate images were visible when it was moved slightly, to show Elvis gyrating!

↑ 1956 ED SULLIVAN SHOW Ed Sullivan only booked Elvis onto his program after his rivals had upped their ratings when Elvis appeared on their shows. Here on his return date in October 1956, Elvis chats to Ed Sullivan with the Colonel.

1956

1956 **LOVE ME TENDER** A drama set in the aftermath of the Civil War, Elvis' debut movie was titled *Love Me Tender*, after one of the songs featured in the film. The song, which was actually a reworking of an old Civil War ballad "Aura Lee," made it to the top of the singles chart. The movie opened nationally in the United States–and thereafter worldwide–on November 21, 1956, amid great ballyhoo, and reached Number 2 in *Variety* magazine's weekly list of top films.

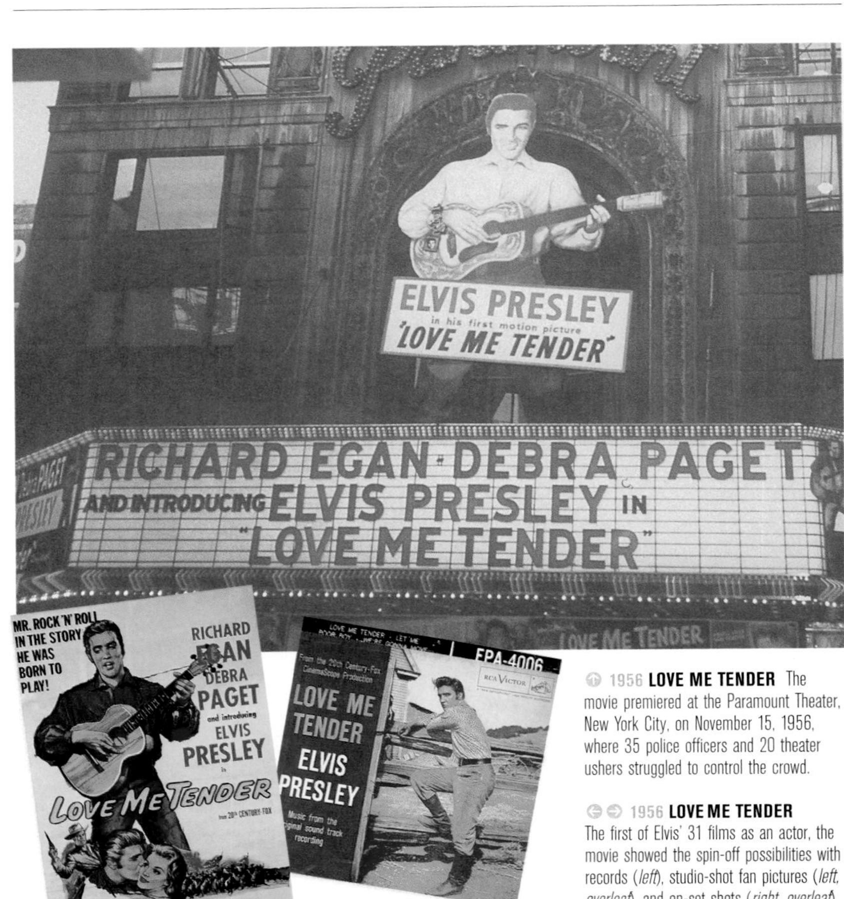

1956 **LOVE ME TENDER** The movie premiered at the Paramount Theater, New York City, on November 15, 1956, where 35 police officers and 20 theater ushers struggled to control the crowd.

1956 **LOVE ME TENDER** The first of Elvis' 31 films as an actor, the movie showed the spin-off possibilities with records (*left*), studio-shot fan pictures (*left, overleaf*), and on-set shots (*right, overleaf*) that were still hot publicity fodder.

Sincerely
Elvis Presley
Elvis Presley

1956 LOVE ME TENDER
On the outdoor set with the Colonel and Elvis' cousin Gene Smith. This was the only Elvis film for which he did not receive top billing, that honor going to leading man Richard Egan.

1956 LOVE ME TENDER
Elvis poses with costar Mildred Dunnock *(left)*. A solid Hollywood character actress, Dunnock specialized in motherly roles, and other major films she appeared in included *Viva Zapata*, *The Jazz Singer*, and, the same year as *Love Me Tender*, *Baby Doll*. On the outdoor set *(right)* with female lead Debra Paget and Elvis is the Colonel's wife Marie.

↑ → → **1956 PORTRAITS** In *Love Me Tender* Elvis was cast in the part of Clint Reno. The film, which was made in black-and-white in the then-new Cinemascope wide-screen process, ended with Clint Reno dying, and uttering the concluding words "Everything's gonna be all right." The scene brought his mother, Gladys, to tears when she first viewed it. Later in his prolific movie career Elvis went on to make two more dramatic Westerns with little or no music involved, *Flaming Star* and *Charro!*

1956 PORTRAITS *Love Me Tender* was the first opportunity people outside the United States had of seeing the famous Elvis hips and legs in action. So the film proved an important stage in the promotion of Elvis' image worldwide. And with it came the posed portraits (here and previous pages) promulgated by the film studio, which were a promotional element of every big Hollywood movie, in which the star often appeared in costume but obviously in a photo studio.

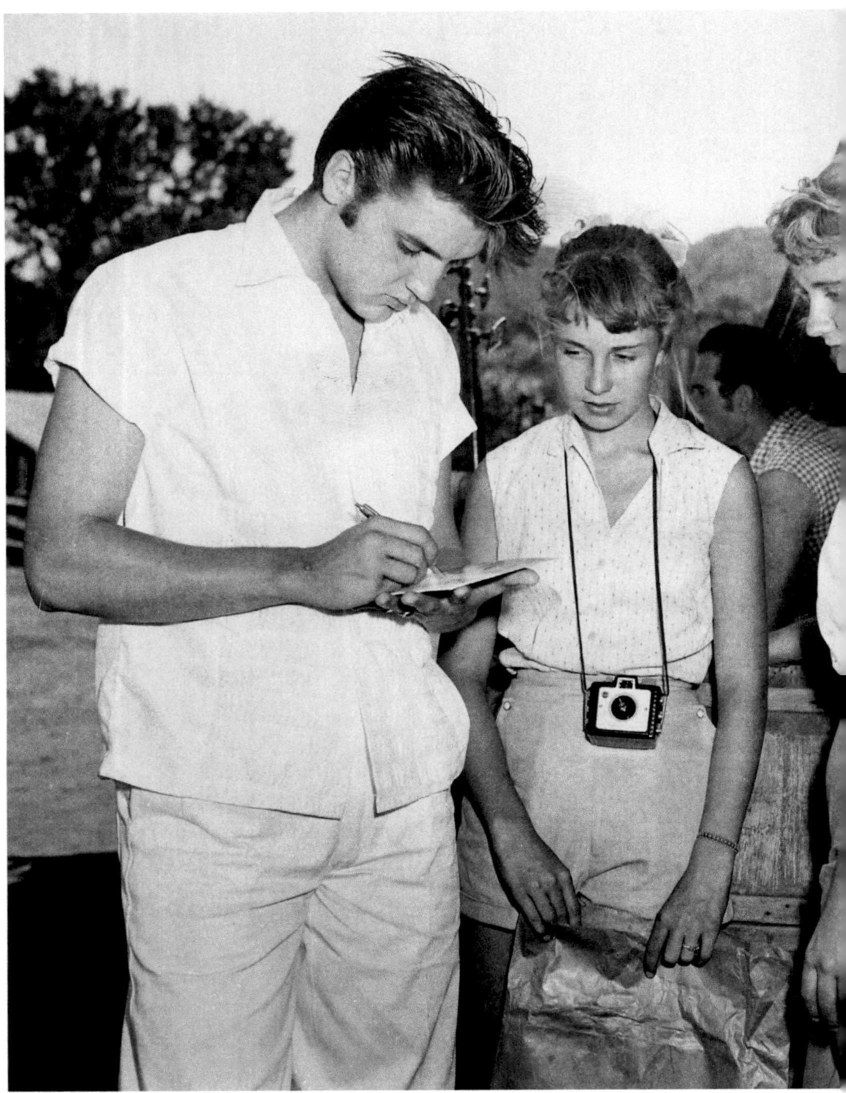

1956

1956 LOVE ME TENDER
Elvis signs autographs for fans who were allowed on to the set. Filming started on August 22, 1956, with the exterior shots being done in the San Fernando Valley near Los Angeles and the interiors at the Twentieth Century-Fox studios in Hollywood. The souvenir plaques (*above*), although referring to the movie's title, actually used pictures taken in the poolside shoot outside the New Frontier Hotel in Las Vegas.

1956 MERCHANDISE The graphic images of Elvis were usually based, though often not well drawn, on familiar photographs. Those on the change purse and wallet above were clearly taken from the shots used on his debut album, while the line drawing is a version of one of the "poolside" poses at the New Frontier Hotel in Las Vegas.

1956 AUTOGRAPHS A young fan (*opposite*), allowed onto the *Love Me Tender* set between takes. Everywhere Elvis went, whether a Memphis street (*above*), a New York hotel lounge, or a California beach, it was open season for the autograph hunter.

Tupelo Ain't Nothin' but a Town Agog

Hometowners Give Elvis Long, Tall Rally

By JOHN SEIGENTHALER
Staff Correspondent

TUPELO, Miss. — A surging screaming crowd of thousands of frenzied teenagers yesterday welcomed a jerking, jumping, guitar-thumping Elvis Presley back to the town where he was born.

"It's the greatest thing that ever happened to me," Presley said. "I've really looked forward to it."

The young prince of rock 'n' roll, who is a guitar playing Pied Piper for millions of youngsters across the nation, turned two grandstand show appearances at the Mississippi-Alabama state fair into a near riot with his singing and accompanying twitches and gyrations.

A cordon of 40 Mississippi state police officers and Tupelo city police surrounded the stage to keep back the hysterical bobby-sox set who had come from all over the South and Midwest to welcome their idol back to his birthplace.

At the second performance, the police were backed up by 20 national guardsmen called out to help control the riot.

In a voice at times barely audible above the screams of the fans, the new singing sensation with the long hair and sideburns

(Continued on Page 18, Column 5)

UPELO, Miss. — Screaming teenagers mob rock 'n' roller Elvis Presley at a frenzied state rformance here in the singer's home town. —Staff photo by Eldred Reaney

Tupelo Daily Journal

Gates Open For Fair's 49th Show

Grand Ole Opry Appears Tonight

The Welcome Mat Is Out For Presley Homecoming

Elvis Traffic Brings Ban On Main Parking

'Presley Ruse' Excites Union Crowd At Fair

That Man's Their Boy--Elvis, That Is

—Staff photo by Eldred Reaney

TUPELO, Miss—"He likes to eat hearty," Mrs. Vernon Presley tells reporters at a press conference for her son, Elvis. Presley's father, right, added that Elvis "hasn't got too big for his britches yet."

1956 HOMECOMING On September 26, 1956, Elvis returned to his hometown of Tupelo, Mississippi, to make a sensational open-air appearance at the annual Mississippi-Alabama State Fair and Dairy Show. Memorable images of the concert were captured in an item filmed for Fox Movietone News. This was back in the days when movie houses showed newsreels between feature films. The local newspapers' treatment of the "local boy made good" say it all. He was given a real hero's return.

1956

1956 TUPELO The fans' outstretched arms signify the absolute adoration that Elvis commanded at his live appearances in the Fifties. The Tupelo homecoming was a triumph, for the town as well as for Elvis, and his performance with Scotty, Bill, D. J., and the Jordanaires was acclaimed by close Elvis watchers as one of the most sensational he had ever given.

All Shook Up

THE KING OF ROCK'N'ROLL

[1957–1958]

1957 LOS ANGELES Elvis, arms outstretched and flanked by the Jordanaires and Scotty Moore, at a concert at the Pan Pacific Auditorium, Los Angeles, in September 1957.

September 1957 *March 1957* *September 1957*

1957-1958

Colonel Tom Parker was determined to consolidate Elvis' hold on the public imagination after the media onslaught that had dominated 1956. He succeeded in this through a number of shrewd moves that involved the dovetailing of Elvis' activity in the fields of recording, live appearances, and movies. The once-billed "Memphis Flash" was now truly the King of Rock'n'Roll, and wasn't going to abdicate the crown as his detractors had predicted.

While *Love Me Tender* was still packing in the audiences, Elvis began work on his second movie in January 1957, *Loving You*. This time the movie was shot in color, and unlike his debut picture it had a solid musical basis to the plot.

Meanwhile he continued touring America, which was in the grip of a fan mania that far outstripped any afforded to previous idols like Frank Sinatra or Johnny Ray, and made his only appearances outside the US when he played dates in Canada. The concerts got wilder and wilder. He was now a superstar in nearly every country in the world. There was even a black market demand for his discs in the Soviet Union, where his records were officially banned.

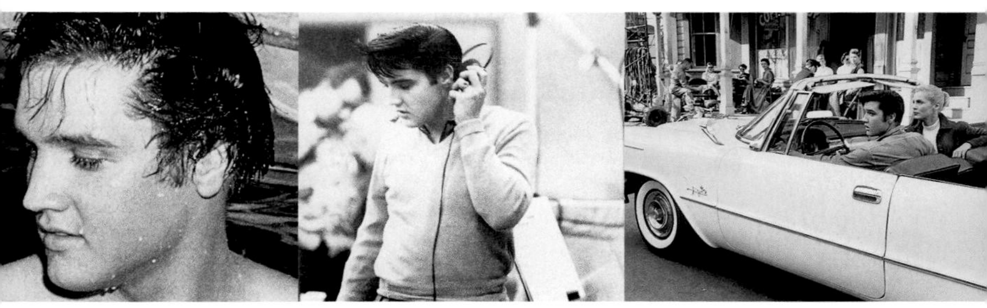

February 1957 *February 1957* *February 1957*

It was the discs which were still the backbone of his success. Rock classic followed rock classic, with singles like "All Shook Up," "Teddy Bear," "Loving You," "Jailhouse Rock," and "King Creole" following each other into the charts in swift succession. The last was the title track to Elvis' fourth movie, completed early in 1958, his third picture being one that provided one of the great rock'n'roll visual icons of all time, the title number sequence in *Jailhouse Rock.*

Another image of Elvis that became a true icon from this period was when he wore the celebrated gold lamé suit. It was created for him by Nudie Cohen of Hollywood, famous for designing flamboyant outfits for country music stars, and although it proved impractical, it was as much a part of Elvis' visual persona at the time as were the ubiquitous white jumpsuits in the Seventies.

In the spring of 1957 he bought the Graceland mansion, on Highway 51 in the southern suburbs of Memphis, for himself, his parents, and his grandmother to live in. At the end of the year, he also received his draft notice, which saw him inducted into the United States Army on March 24, 1958.

1957 CANADA Elvis backstage during the brief Canadian concert visit he made in the spring. Despite many offers of engagements worldwide, Elvis never performed outside the US mainland apart from dates in Hawaii and Canada.

1957 JAM SESSION Elvis takes part in an impromptu "jam session" in the poolroom at Graceland. Sessions like this often took place on the road, when Elvis found that more time was spent waiting around backstage than actually working.

1957 BACKSTAGE, TUPELO In September Elvis returned to the Fairgrounds in Tupelo, where he had appeared the year before. He took an active interest in the social concerns of his birth town; this was a benefit concert to raise funds for an Elvis Presley Youth Recreation Center. Elvis performed to a crowd of 12,000, and is pictured here backstage—wearing the jacket of his celebrated gold lamé suit—with members of the Jordanaires, his backing group, and the now inevitable security men.

1957 GOLD SUIT Alongside promotions of Elvis' image such as the record store display above, in Bayonne, New Jersey, another publicity item was his $2,500 gold lamé suit, which was to appear on the sleeve of the 1959 album *50,000,000 Elvis Fans Can't Be Wrong*. However, Elvis wore the suit only a few times on live dates. Although popular with audiences, Elvis soon discovered that the trousers in particular were hot and uncomfortable. Subsequently, Elvis was seen in just the jacket with black pants (*see following pages*).

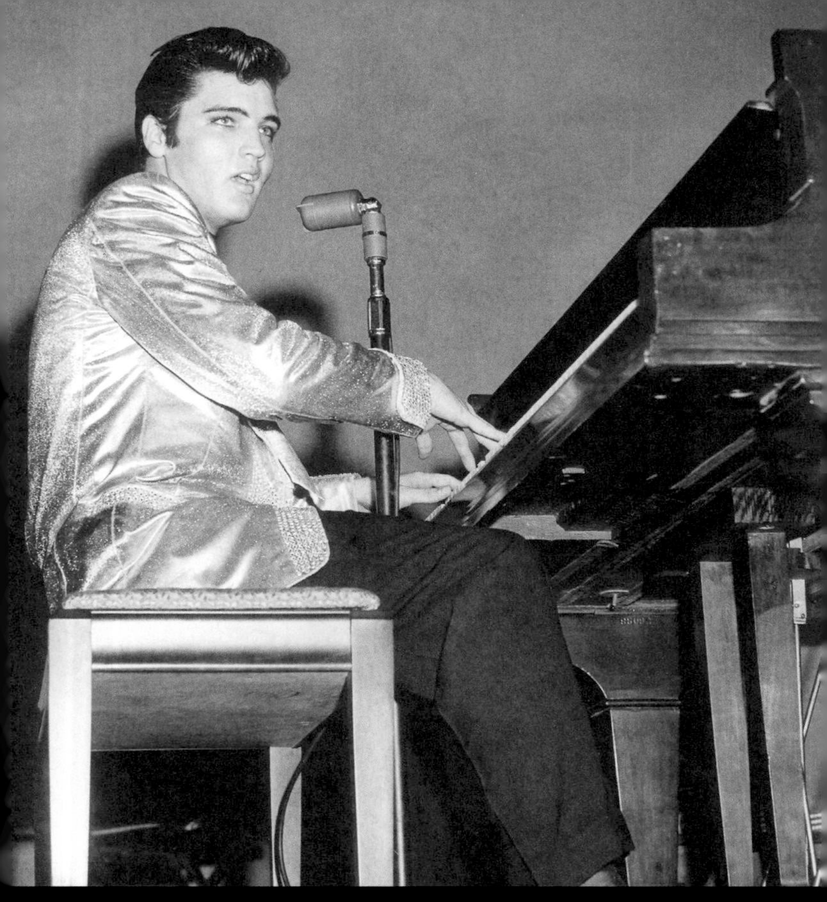

1957 TUPELO The open-air
...irgrounds arena provided a sensational
...tting for Elvis' increasingly dynamic
...age act. His up-tempo numbers were
...mpered by the occasional slower ballad,
...th Elvis playing his own accompaniment

1957 TUPELO Security became an ever-increasing problem at live appearances. Not only did the police have to provide protection for Elvis but they also had to keep order and try to avoid injuries among near-riotous crowds of fans as well.

1957

1957 **PRESS CONFERENCE** Elvis at one of the frequent press conferences that were held while he was on tour. These confrontations with the media helped keep Elvis' name in the news, and enabled him to answer the more hysterical criticisms, such as those accusing his "lewd" stage act of being a bad influence on the nation's youth. As the Colonel often commented, "any publicity is good publicity," but he did like Elvis to have the opportunity to put the record straight.

1957 **OTTAWA** In the spring of 1957, Elvis visited Canada. This picture was taken March 3, backstage at the Ottawa Auditorium. He had appeared in Toronto the day before and was to perform in Vancouver later in the year.

1957

➔ **1957 AUDUBON DRIVE** It's March and Elvis, having just returned from Hollywood where he has been filming his second feature movie *Loving You*, poses for a photograph by one of his Cadillacs in the carport at Audubon Drive. His collection of cars is getting bigger, but it's not only the carport that is becoming insufficient for his and the family's needs. The Presleys needed more privacy as Elvis' more demonstrative fan following started to become a problem, and as soon as he got back from the West Coast he began shopping around for a new, and more secluded, home.

← **1957 ON TOUR** Candid pictures showed the rigors of touring. Elvis was to famously describe how fame hit him: "Everything happened so blame fast I don't know where I was yesterday and I don't know where I'll be tomorrow."

↑ **1957 HOUND DOG** Following his July 1956 appearance on the Steve Allen TV show, on which he sang "Hound Dog" to a real live canine, Elvis adopted the idea in a variety of publicity opportunities, and the Colonel made toy dogs a merchandise item.

↑ **1957 RECORDS** *Top,* some of Elvis' biggest hits. *Elvis' Christmas Album* came out in October 1957 and hit number one in the *Billboard* album charts. In March 1958 *Elvis' Golden Records* reached number three. And the singles kept coming.

1957 **HOUND DOGS** The single "Hound Dog," with its flipside "Don't Be Cruel" was, in the summer of 1956, one of Elvis' biggest-ever hits. It was the perfect example of Elvis taking a rhythm and blues number and making it his own. Rather than by aping the original, or–as in the case of many other white pop singers–by watering down its dynamism, his version was often even tougher. From then on the hound dogs appeared at public relations events such as press conferences (*above*).

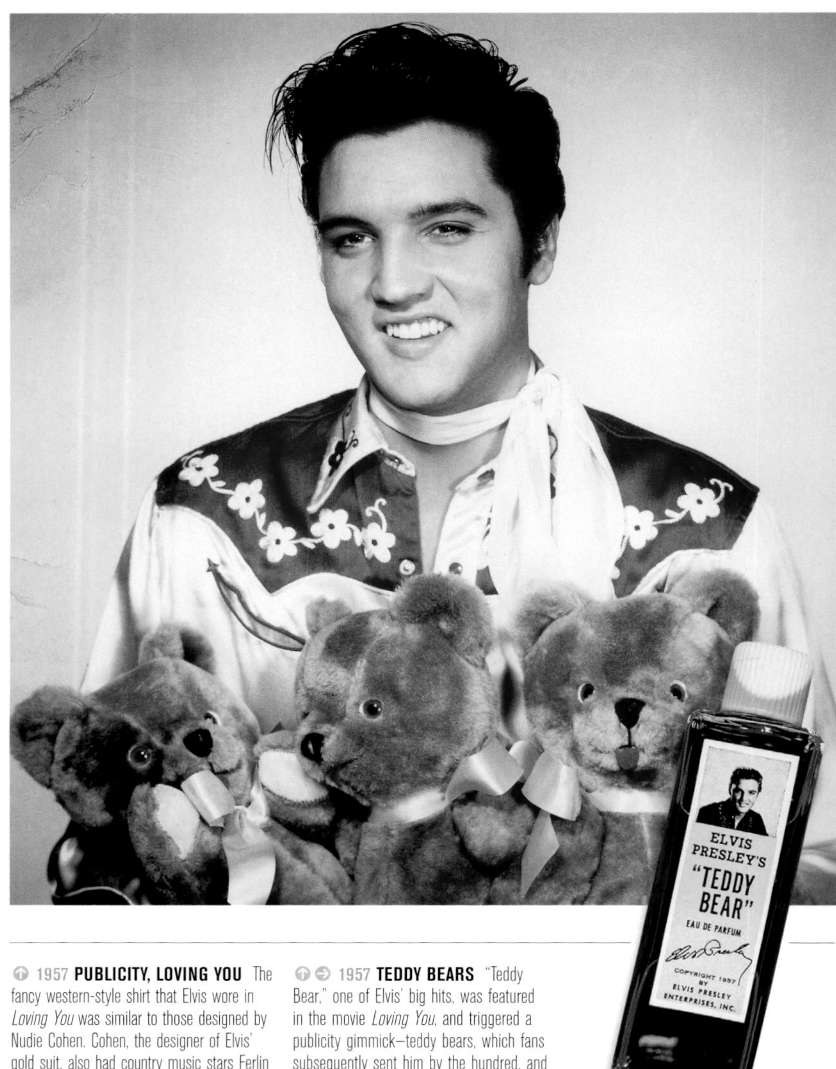

ELVIS
PRESLEY'S
"TEDDY
BEAR"
EAU DE PARFUM
COPYRIGHT 1957
BY
ELVIS PRESLEY
ENTERPRISES, INC.

1957 **PUBLICITY, LOVING YOU** The fancy western-style shirt that Elvis wore in *Loving You* was similar to those designed by Nudie Cohen. Cohen, the designer of Elvis' gold suit, also had country music stars Ferlin Huskey and Hank Snow among his clients.

1957 **TEDDY BEARS** "Teddy Bear," one of Elvis' big hits, was featured in the movie *Loving You*, and triggered a publicity gimmick–teddy bears, which fans subsequently sent him by the hundred, and which appeared on merchandise.

1957

1957 **LOVING YOU** On the set of his second feature film, *Loving You*, Elvis investigates the workings of a movie camera *(above)* while awaiting the next take. The movie was mostly shot on the Paramount studio lot.

1957

COMING! HAL WALLIS PRODUCTION "LOVING YOU"
in Beautiful VISTAVISION
STARRING
ELVIS PRESLEY
LIZABETH SCOTT
WENDELL COREY
HEAR — HEAR
RCA VICTOR'S ELVIS PRESLEY
Sing Title Song! "LOVING YOU" and Other Great Song Hits!
A Paramount Picture
DIRECTED BY HAL
PARAMOUNT PRESENTS
ELVIS PRESLEY
LIZABETH SCOTT
WENDELL COREY
VISTAVISION
LOVING YOU
A HAL WALLIS PRODUCTION
TECHNICOLOR

1957 LOVING YOU Elvis' second movie role was far more in character. He plays a country singer, Deke Rivers, whose path to fame is strewn with fist fights and amorous clinches. This photograph, shot during the movie's production, shows Elvis and costar Lizabeth Scott in a Chrysler Imperial that was used in the film. The sultry blonde had made her name mainly in B-movies through the 1940s and early 1950s and this was one of her last movies.

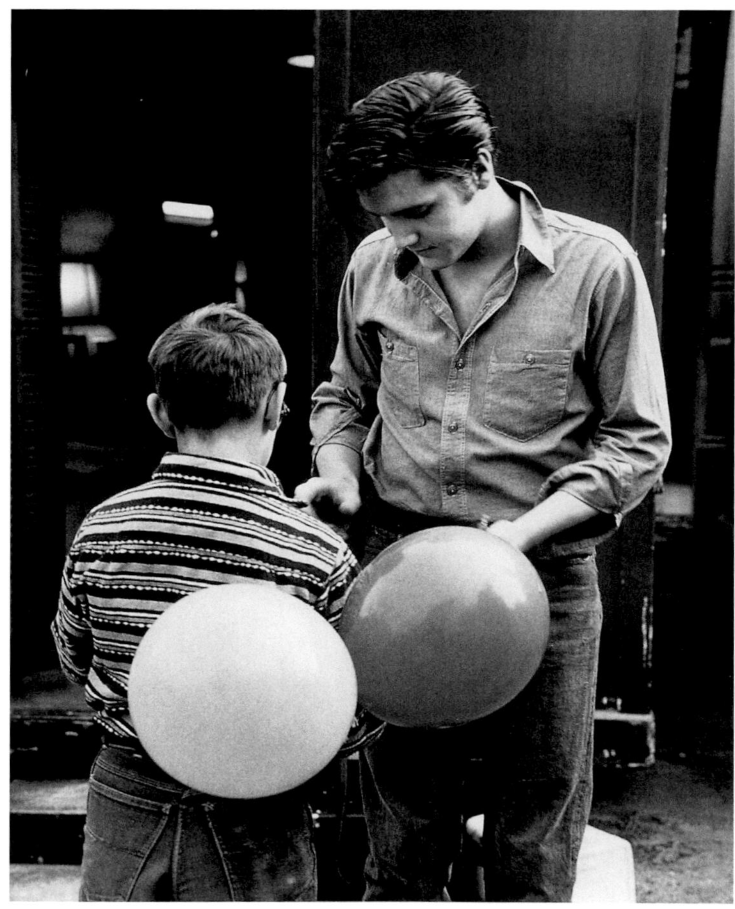

1957

⬆ 1957 **LOVING YOU** A casual shot of Elvis wandering around the *Loving You* set. The jeans he is wearing were from the studio wardrobe department, part of the on-screen costume of the character Elvis played in the movie, Deke Rivers.

➡ 1957 **PARAMOUNT STUDIOS** While cycling around the Paramount studio lot Elvis encounters the inevitable group of fans, and signs the obligatory autograph. Gladys and Vernon Presley visited the shoot, appearing as extras in one scene.

1957 GRACELAND Two fans greet Elvis as he cruises up the driveway at Graceland. He's driving the 1956 Cadillac Eldorado convertible he bought in July 1957 and had customized with purple paintwork, purple-and-white interior, and monogrammed "EP" floor mats. The purchasing power of his young female fan base was exploited in many ways, including an Elvis Presley lipstick.

1957

1957 GRACELAND Elvis stands proud inside his newly acquired home, Graceland (*right*), on Highway 51 in the south Memphis suburb of Whitehaven. He purchased the house for himself and his parents in March 1957 for just over $100,000. The gates (*below*) were custom designed with musical notes and a guitar motif. The news story on the front page of the *Memphis Press-Scimitar* illustrates how much local interest there was in the life of the city's most famous resident.

Memphis Press-Scimitar

Elvis Looks Over Graceland

Mansion Fit for a (Rock 'n' Roll) King

Presley Is Eager To Redecorate

He Has Plenty of His Own Ideas To Try Out on His New Home

1957

1957 GRACELAND Elvis outside Graceland mansion. Although he would later buy a number of houses on the West Coast, and a ranch in the country, Graceland remained Elvis' base for the rest of his life. It was here that friends and family gathered at Christmas, where Elvis had sing-along-sessions at the piano with fellow musicians, and where he recorded an entire album in the Jungle Room. Graceland became the focal point of pilgrimage for millions of fans when it was opened to the public

1957 JAILHOUSE ROCK A shot from the poolside scene in Elvis' third movie, *Jailhouse Rock*. In real life, one of the first things Elvis did after settling with his family into Graceland was to have installed a kidney-shaped swimming pool. This was very much a status symbol at the time, popular with Hollywood stars. Contrary to popular myth, Elvis never actually had a guitar-shaped pool. Elvis' main indulgence of this kind seems to have been the musical motifs on the Graceland gates.

1957

1957 AUTOGRAPHS Rumor had it–again, a popular myth that later grew up around the Beatles as well–that there was an army of scribes in Elvis' publicity and fan club offices, solely employed to sign autographs on his behalf. While he was touring continually, both in the 1950s and 1970s, he must have signed hundreds of thousands of autographs–without any assistance–though it is acknowledged that he did have others authorized to sign for him in some circumstances.

1957

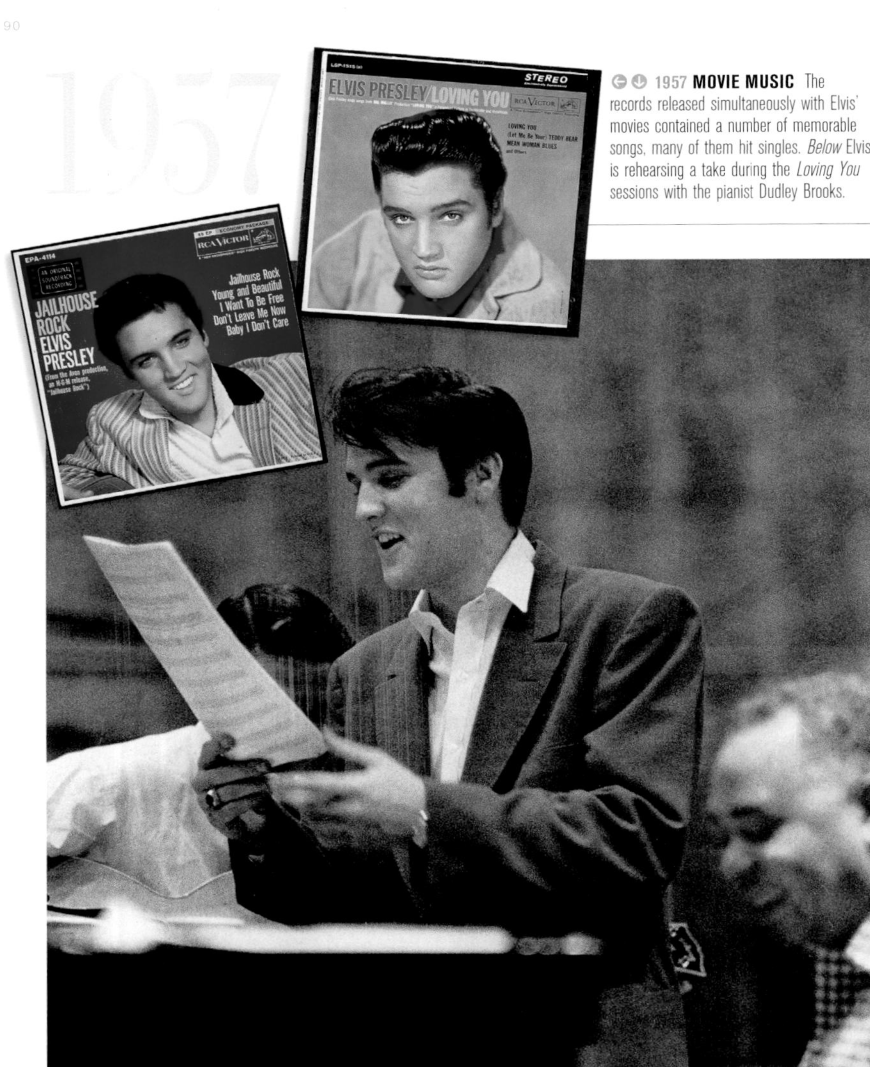

1957 **MOVIE MUSIC** The records released simultaneously with Elvis' movies contained a number of memorable songs, many of them hit singles. *Below* Elvis is rehearsing a take during the *Loving You* sessions with the pianist Dudley Brooks.

1957 PARAMOUNT Another shot from the *Loving You* recording sessions in Hollywood, which were at the Paramount sound stage and the Radio Recorders studios–where this shot of Elvis at the mike was taken on St. Valentine's Day, 1957.

1957

1957 LOVING YOU SESSION Elvis with drummer D. J. Fontana during one of the recording sessions. Also playing were pianist Dudley Brooks (*left*) and guitarist Tiny Timbrell (*background*), as well as Elvis' regular musicians.

1958 KING CREOLE SESSION The *King Creole* sessions were held in January and February at the Paramount sound stage and Radio Recorders. Here, an animated Elvis is dubbing his vocals on a largely Dixieland-styled set of songs.

216-7/26

16-2/22

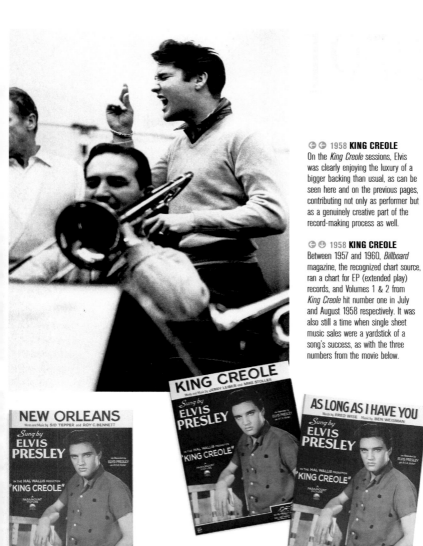

1958 KING CREOLE
On the *King Creole* sessions, Elvis was clearly enjoying the luxury of a bigger backing than usual, as can be seen here and on the previous pages, contributing not only as performer but as a genuinely creative part of the record-making process as well.

1958 KING CREOLE
Between 1957 and 1960, *Billboard* magazine, the recognized chart source, ran a chart for EP (extended play) records, and Volumes 1 & 2 from *King Creole* hit number one in July and August 1958 respectively. It was also still a time when single sheet music sales were a yardstick of a song's success, as with the three numbers from the movie below.

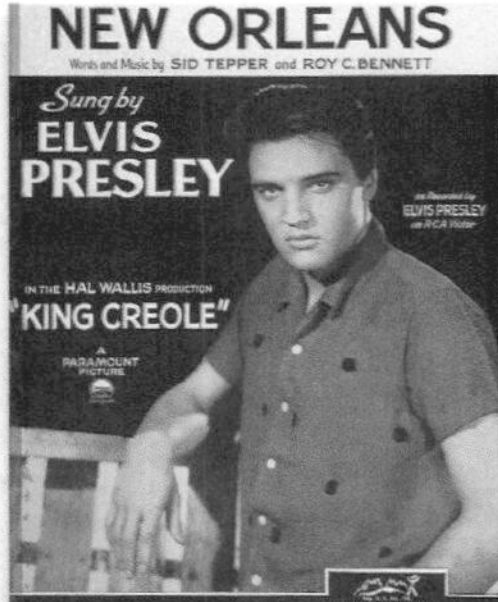

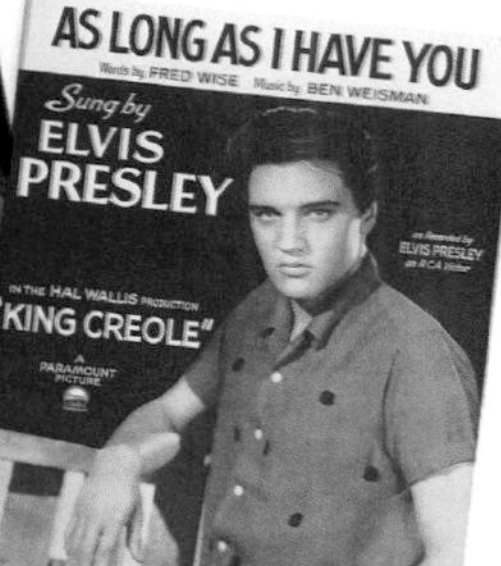

1957

1957 JAILHOUSE ROCK With just six songs performed by Elvis, his third movie could hardly be called a musical, and the dramatic storyline and black-and-white photography underlined this. Indeed, it was billed as "his first big dramatic singing role!" in the movie's publicity. He plays Vince Everett, a singer who gets into trouble with the law, and featured at least three Presley classics in "Treat Me Nice," "(You're So Square) Baby I Don't Care," and the sensational title song which was penned by the now-legendary rock'n'roll tunesmiths Jerry Leiber and Mike Stoller.

1957 JAILHOUSE ROCK Still the hits continued, now via the movies. *Jailhouse Rock* featured a number one single with the title song, in September 1957, plus a number one EP at the end of the year, in time for the Christmas market.

1957 JAILHOUSE ROCK The role Elvis played in *Jailhouse Rock* included fight scenes. Former boxer Johnny Indrisano acted as technical adviser. He had advised similarly in the 1956 movie *Somebody Up There Likes Me*, starring Paul Newman.

⬆ ➡ 1957 **JAILHOUSE ROCK** The publicity pictures that accompanied Elvis' movies were also used to promote the records that were released at the same time. The pictures then appeared on merchandise and pinup pictures worldwide.

1957 RELAXING Elvis takes
ime out during the filming of *Jailhouse
Rock*, made at MGM's Culver City studios
n May and June. The movie had its
premier in Memphis on October 17, and
opened across America on November 8.

1957

1957

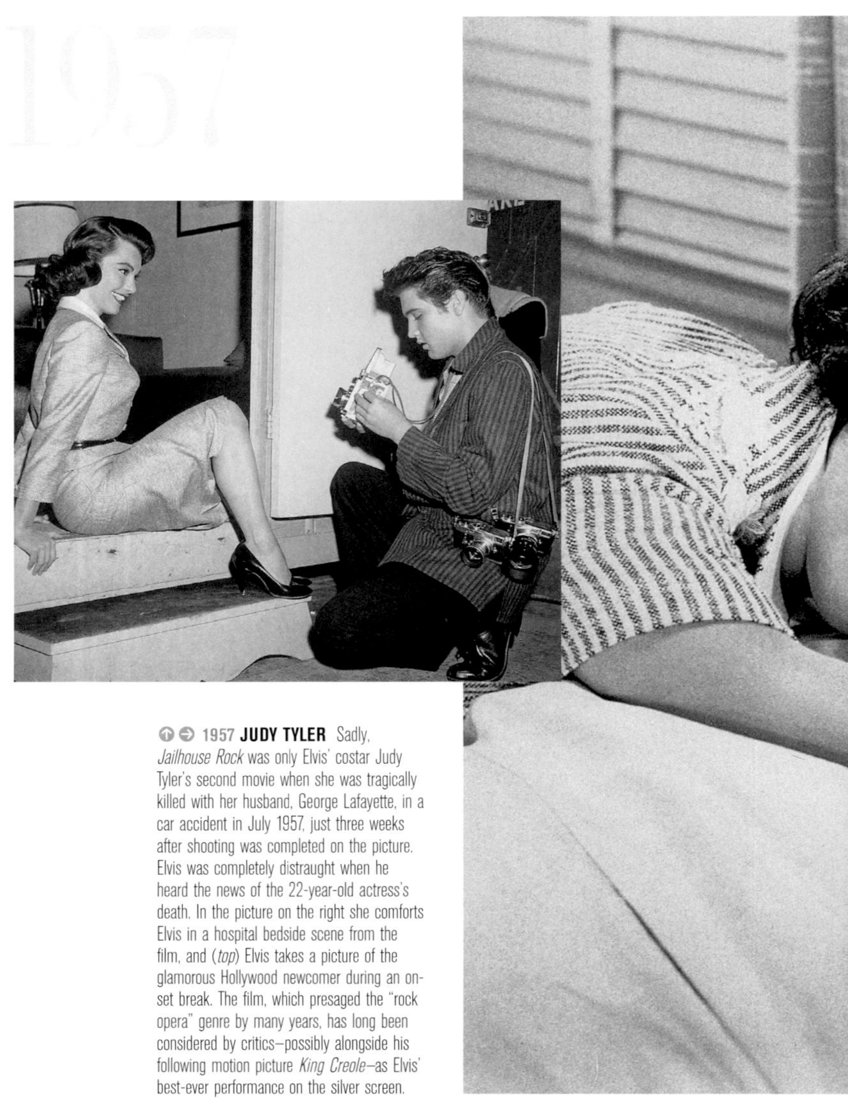

1957 JUDY TYLER Sadly, *Jailhouse Rock* was only Elvis' costar Judy Tyler's second movie when she was tragically killed with her husband, George Lafayette, in a car accident in July 1957, just three weeks after shooting was completed on the picture. Elvis was completely distraught when he heard the news of the 22-year-old actress's death. In the picture on the right she comforts Elvis in a hospital bedside scene from the film, and (*top*) Elvis takes a picture of the glamorous Hollywood newcomer during an on-set break. The film, which presaged the "rock opera" genre by many years, has long been considered by critics—possibly alongside his following motion picture *King Creole*—as Elvis' best-ever performance on the silver screen.

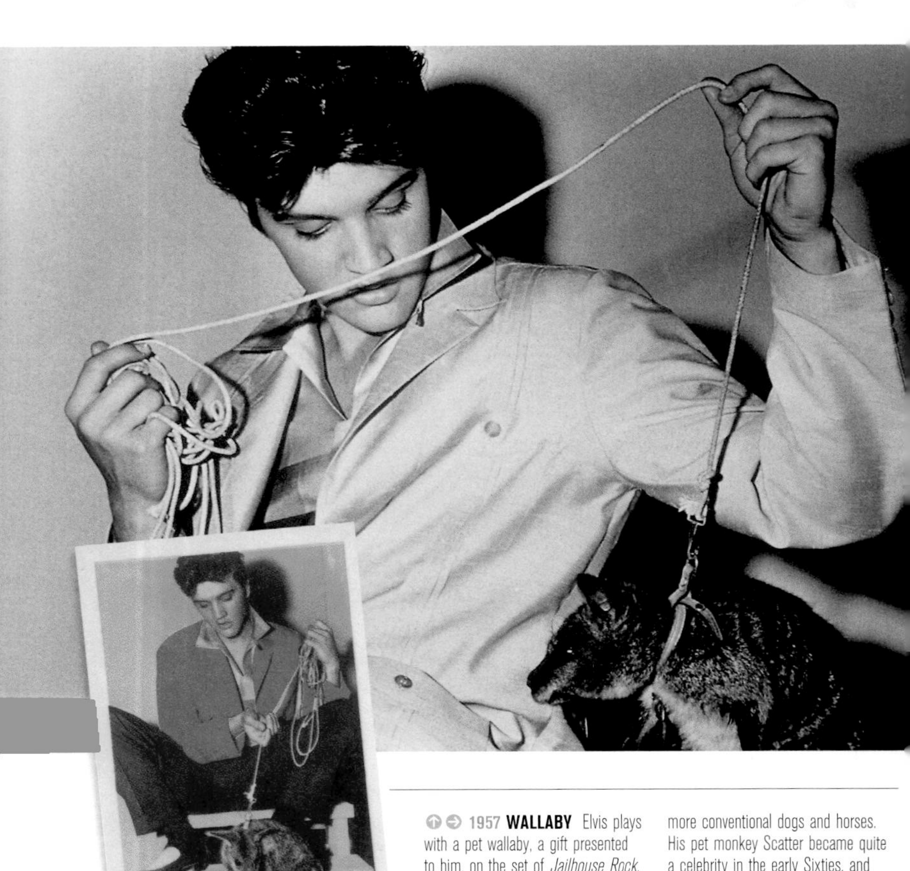

1957 WALLABY Elvis plays with a pet wallaby, a gift presented to him, on the set of *Jailhouse Rock*. Elvis acquired numbers of animals over the years, including parrots and other exotic creatures alongside the more conventional dogs and horses. His pet monkey Scatter became quite a celebrity in the early Sixties, and Elvis later became increasingly involved with horses and riding toward the end of the decade.

1957

1957 FANS Right through his career, Elvis was conscious of keeping in personal contact with his fans as far as possible. He knew that without them he would be nothing; they bought the records and the merchandise, and filled the concert venues.

1957 BOARD GAME The Elvis Presley merchandizing possibilities got more and more imaginative. This board game was an example of his name lending itself to marketing a product that had no direct link with his music, movies, or any facets of his success, except the image itself.

↑ 1957 **FANS** Elvis loved to goof around with fans. This "photo booth" style shot was taken around the time he was making *Loving You*, and is simply inscribed "Sadie, Elvis, and Linda."

← 1957 **"I LIKE ELVIS"** The "Elvis for President" publicity stunt had button badges that echoed the campaign slogan for the President, Dwight D. Eisenhower, ("I Like Ike") with "I Like Elvis." There was even an "Oy Gevalt Elvis" one for Yiddish speakers!

1957 MEMPHIS SHOW In June, TV entertainer Danny Thomas organized a Shower of Stars benefit for a Memphis children's hospital. Elvis made a brief stage appearance, posing here with comedian Lou Costello and Hollywood actress Jane Russell.

1957 TUPELO SHOW Elvis and his entourage backstage at the Tupelo Fairgrounds charity show in September 1957. The blonde girl is Anita Wood, a beauty contest winner from Memphis who was a regular date of Elvis'.

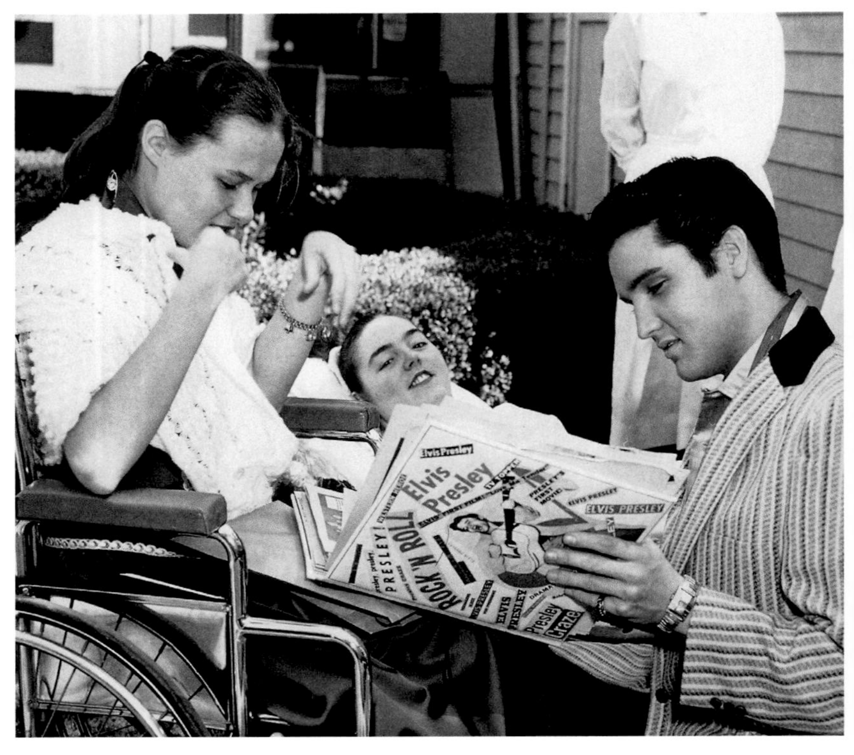

1957 JAILHOUSE ROCK Elvis looks at a scrapbook of his own memorabilia and talks to two disabled fans who were with a group on an arranged visit to the set of *Jailhouse Rock*. Elvis paid particular attention to those who were in difficult circumstances. This was also reflected in the extensive amount of charity work that he supported. He aided a variety of causes financially and, when his commitments allowed, he gave his time to appearing at many fund-raising events over the years.

1957 HAWAII Elvis hugs two fans during his visit to Hawaii. The two shows at Honolulu Stadium were witnessed by 14,000 fans, and Hawaii remained a favorite location with Elvis for movies in the 1960s as well as just for leisure.

1957 ELVIS DOLL The Elvis doll is an example of merchandise that purported to represent Elvis but did not even look remotely like him. So powerful was Elvis' name that if it was labeled an Elvis Presley doll, then fans would buy it.

1958 **NEW ORLEANS** During the location shooting for Elvis' fourth movie, *King Creole,* these fans in New Orleans, Louisiana, were lucky enough to get a glimpse—and autograph—of their idol, albeit through the railings of a cast iron fence.

1958 **NEW ORLEANS** The Colonel chats with fans who are awaiting Elvis' arrival, having been allowed onto the *King Creole* location set in New Orleans. For many fans, meeting the Colonel was the second best thing to meeting Elvis himself.

1958

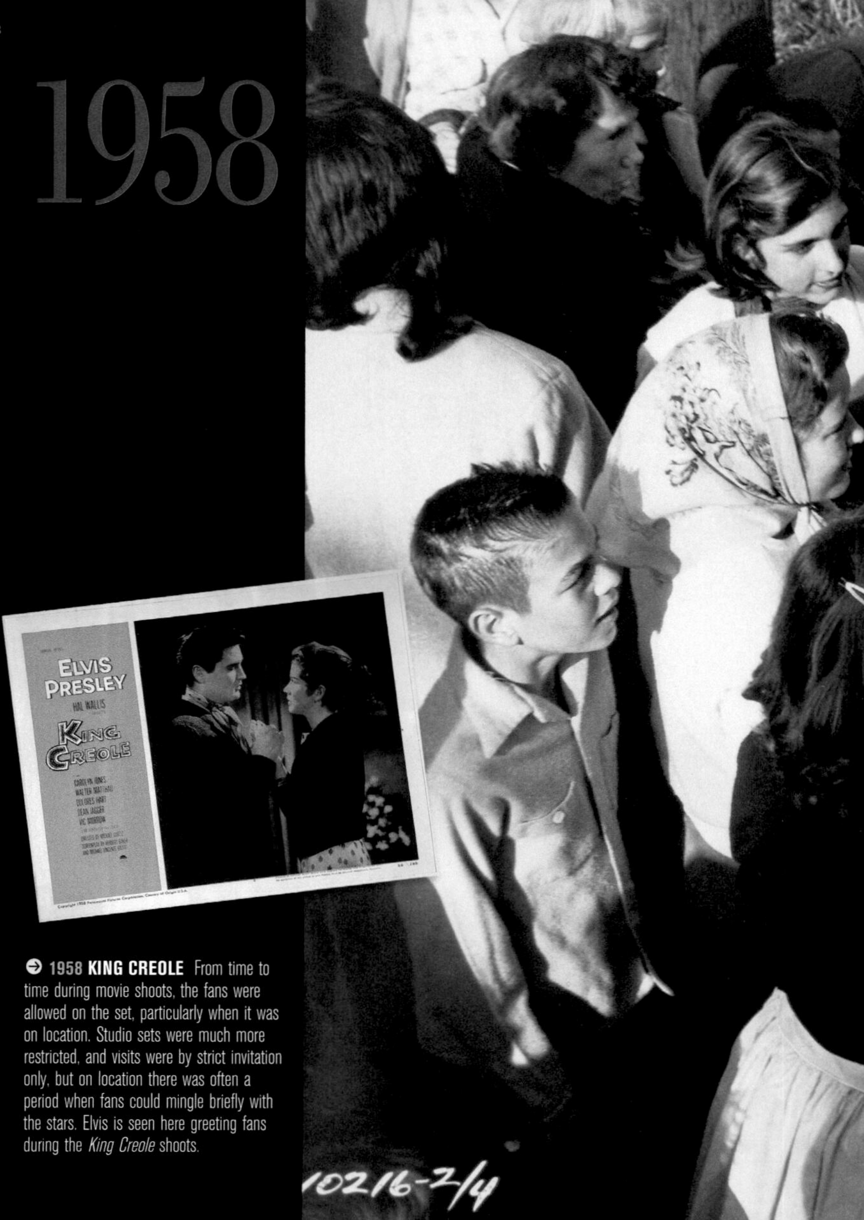

➔ **1958 KING CREOLE** From time to time during movie shoots, the fans were allowed on the set, particularly when it was on location. Studio sets were much more restricted, and visits were by strict invitation only, but on location there was often a period when fans could mingle briefly with the stars. Elvis is seen here greeting fans during the *King Creole* shoots.

1958 **KING CREOLE** Based on best-selling writer Harold Robbins' novel, *A Stone For Danny Fisher*, *King Creole* had some heavyweight credentials. It was directed by Michael Curtiz–whose long line of successes included *Casablanca*–and featured established names Carolyn Jones *(right)*, Walter Matthau, and Dolores Hart (*above*). Like *Jailhouse Rock* it was pitched as a serious drama by the Paramount studio. Despite this, Elvis managed to get through 11 songs during the course of the action!

1958

1958 PORTRAITS The portraits on these and the following four pages were part of the publicity that accompanied the release of *King Creole* and its associated records. The movie was shot between the end of January and early March. To make the picture Elvis had to request a special deferment from the Army draft board. The movie opened nationally across the United States on July 2, 1958. It was Elvis' first movie to be made on location—hence the attention paid to local fans visiting the sets.

10216-

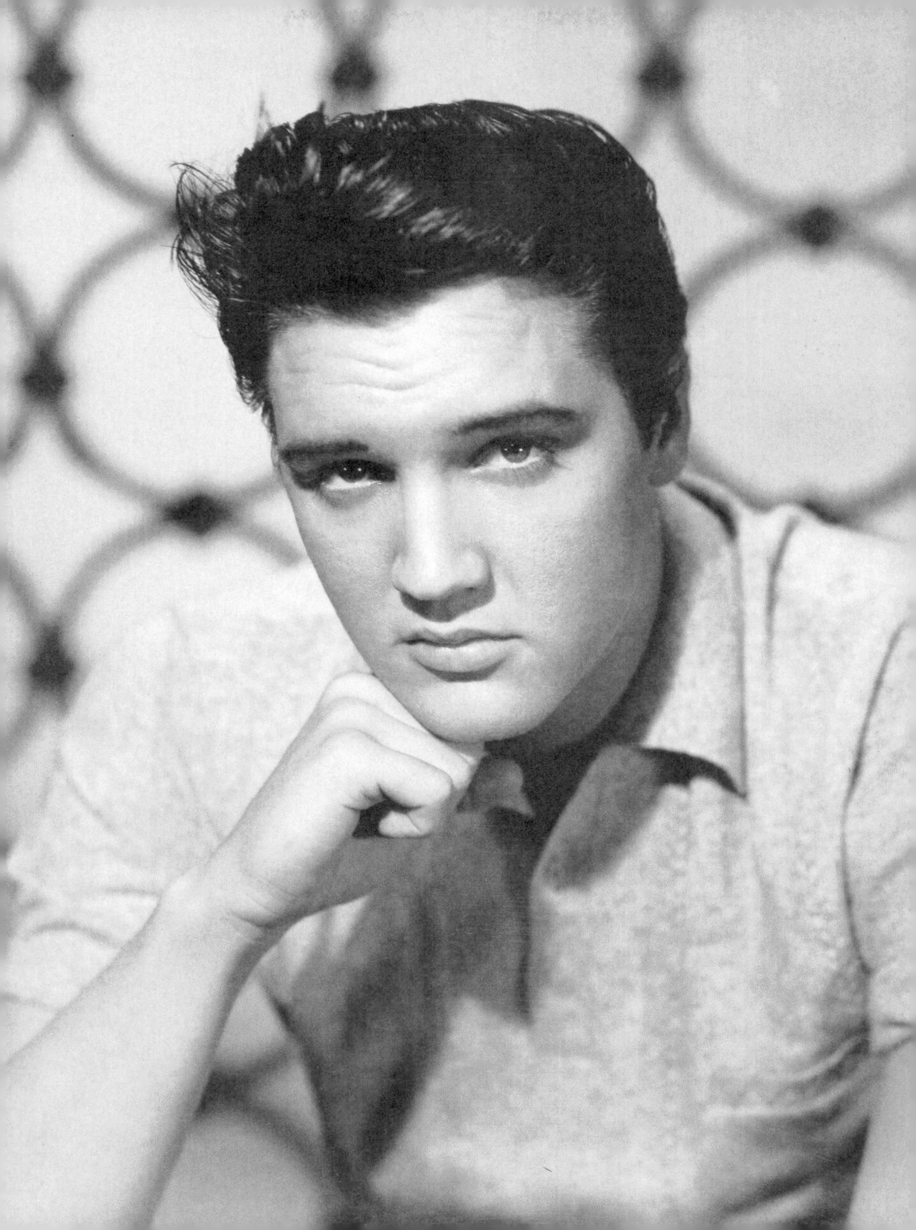

1957

➔ **1957 ARRIVING IN HAWAII**
November that year saw Elvis make one of several working trips to Hawaii, when he played at the Honolulu Stadium. The gig was followed by what was to be his last live date before being called up for the Army early the following year, when he appeared before service families at the Scholfield Barracks, Pearl Harbor.

1957 HAWAII Apart from his brief visits to Canada, the only nonmovie working trips that Elvis made outside the United States mainland were to Hawaii. Every time he arrived he was greeted in the traditional manner, with a *lei* hung round his neck. Elvis played several important dates there during his career, as well as making it the location of several movies and choosing it as the venue for his historic *Aloha* live satellite television link-up in 1973. He also spent leisure time in the islands

1957

1957

⊖ 1956 END OF THE DREAM?
This image from *Love Me Tender* must have become a distant dream for Elvis when, in December 1957, one Christmas present he probably thought he could have done without finally arrived. It was his draft papers for service in the US Army, the documents that were to herald his much-publicized tour of duty as America's most celebrated GI.

Elvis™

Serving Uncle Sam

ARMY DAYS & AFTER

[1958–1961]

← **1960 DISCHARGE** Elvis looks out onto a new future—in many ways an unknown future—in March 1960, as he leaves the United States Army after two years' service and contemplates life in the civilian fast lane once more.

March 1958 *March 1958* *August 1958*

1958–1961

The draft into the US Army could have been a disaster for Elvis Presley's career. But the combination of a backlog of material to keep the fans happy, and the positive press he would receive in "doing his duty" ensured that his time in the Army gave him an even higher public profile than before. When called up he was the world's number one entertainment personality; now his thousands of fans could watch their hero be a soldier.

The Colonel and RCA's publicity machine made sure that every aspect of the process was exploited for all it was worth—Elvis became a soldier in the full glare of publicity, from formalizing his induction to getting his first Army haircut. When he was shipped to a base in Germany, RCA even released an EP of interview material recorded prior to his departure called "Elvis Sails."

All the time he was in Germany, back home it was almost Elvis business as usual. The records were released, hit after hit; he was interviewed via transatlantic telephone (still a novelty in 1959) by Dick Clark on the *American Bandstand* TV show; and before you knew it, Elvis was back, with a new album aptly titled *Elvis Is Back* and a movie going into production called—again appropriately—*GI Blues*.

October 1958 *March 1960* *March 1961*

His homecoming was a media blowout, with a face-to-face interview in front of film and TV cameras, conducted in the office at Graceland, that revealed a confident, relaxed Elvis ready to get back to work. Finally, just to make sure that the message had sunk in that Elvis was indeed back, there was a "Welcome Home, Elvis" edition of Frank Sinatra's TV variety show.

Elvis was now not just a household name, but one with real family appeal. His service in the US Army had helped substantiate a wholesome image as an entertainer suitable for the whole family—one that fit the Colonel's long-term ambitions for his charge, and a million miles from the Hillbilly Cat who seemingly threatened to subvert the nation's youth just five years before.

As if to confirm this status as all-around regular guy, 1961 saw first a Memphis civic lunch in Elvis' honor, followed by two concerts at Ellis Auditorium in aid of over 30 local charities, and finally a benefit performance in Pearl Harbor, Hawaii, to raise money for the building of the USS *Arizona* Memorial. This last event was to be Elvis' final live, non-movie performance until his celebrated "comeback" seven years later.

1958 INDUCTION Elvis reported to the draft board office in Memphis on March 24, 1958. He was accompanied by his girlfriend Anita Wood and her parents, his parents, friends and relatives, dozens of fans (like Judy Spreckles in these pictures), and 20-plus reporters. The recruits were then bussed to the Kennedy Veterans Memorial Hospital, with the crowd in hot pursuit, where they underwent a physical, after which Elvis was given his Army serial number—53 301 761.

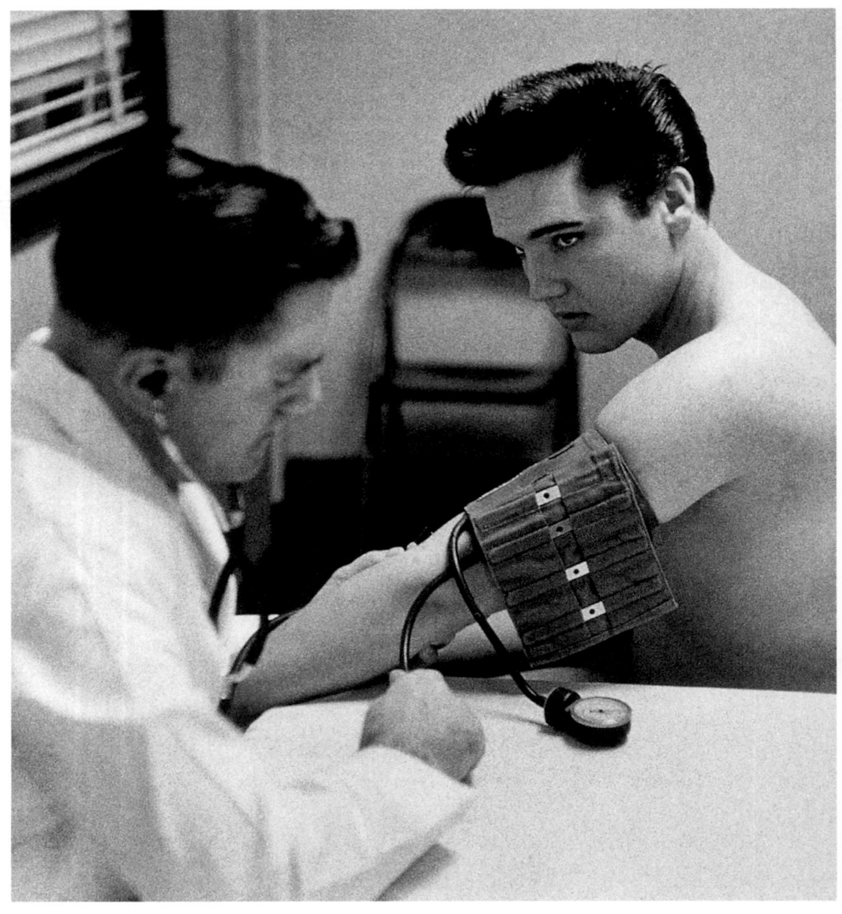

1958

⬆ ➡ **1958 INDUCTION** On the previous pages, Elvis sits with his fellow recruits awaiting his medical examination. Typically, the Colonel was handing out balloons promoting *King Creole* to the fans gathered there. Elvis' medical was well documented in the media, including the blood pressure test (*above*). More goodbyes ensued before Elvis and his new partners were taken to Fort Chaffee, 150 miles away. The following day Elvis received his first Army haircut.

U.S. ARMY

1958

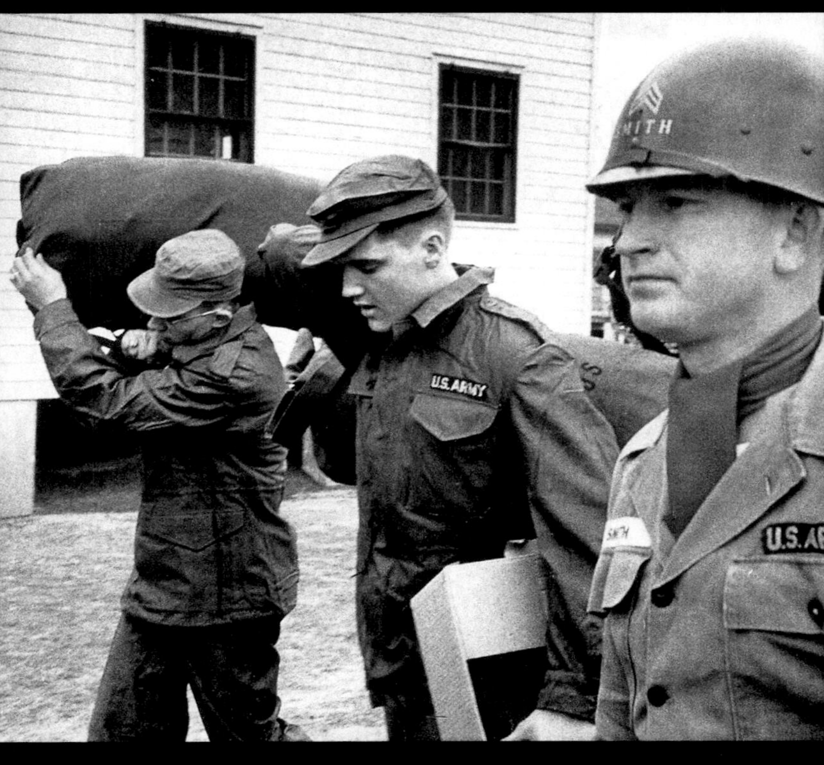

1958 FORT CHAFFEE Army life began with induction at Fort Chaffee in Arkansas, where Elvis and his group arrived on March 25 (*above*). The rigors of military life, including boot shining (*left*), became a daily routine. For his two-month basic training, Private Presley moved on to Fort Hood, Texas. Elvis was made acting assistant leader of his squad and gained a medal for marksmanship. He was to enjoy two weeks' furlough at home in Memphis before heading back to Fort Hood on June 14.

1958

ELVIS' MOM
in loving memory

...at he is, she made him. He'll never forget her,
...e'll never be quite the same as he was before.
...were Elvis' hours of tenderness—and torment.

got a job in a hospital. She emptied bedpans, mopped floors through long grey nights so that Elvis could be educated in peace.

Gladys Presley was a worrier. When Elvis played football, she was afraid he'd get hurt, and when Elvis rode a bike, she was afraid he'd get hurt; her concern never lessened even after her baby had grown up. The day he came home from the Army with a bruised knee and five stitches in his hand, she was ready to go to war with President Eisenhower. "What are they doing with you?" she cried, outraged.

When Elvis made his first record for a disc jockey in Memphis, Gladys sent him off to the movies; she and Vernon sweated out the results by themselves. The record was played, 1800 phone calls came in in less than an hour, and Gladys and Vernon took off for the theatre, went rushing down the aisles calling Elvis' name, the gorgeous news burning their tongues.

Gladys Presley babied her son, and he babied her right back. A relationship so sentimental it might have made other boys flinch was cherished by Elvis. At 23, he was still his mother's "good little boy" and he proved it a thousand different ways. He bought her a house, all air-conditioned, with jukeboxes and swimming pool and great carved gates...

By EUNICE FIELD

1958 GRIEF During the summer of 1958, while Elvis' family was living in temporary accommodation near the Fort Hood base, his mother Gladys became ill. His parents returned to Memphis to consult their physician, and Gladys was rushed from Graceland to the Methodist Hospital on August 9, suffering from an undiagnosed liver complaint. After much pleading (and a threat to go AWOL) Elvis obtained emergency leave on Tuesday, August 12, and rushed straight to the hospital having flown from Fort Worth to Memphis. Gladys died on the Thursday morning, and Elvis and his father were inconsolable. At the funeral they were on the point of collapse.

1958

1958 ON LEAVE At the end of May 1958 Elvis enjoyed his first leave from the Army. He spent most of the next two weeks relaxing, either at Graceland (as in these pictures) or around Memphis. He squeezed in one all-night recording session, at the RCA studios in Nashville, when he recorded five numbers, including the hit singles "Big Hunk O' Love" and "I Need Your Love Tonight." After returning to Fort Hood on June 14, he commenced a period of Advanced Tank Training.

2
HELL ON WHEELS

AND Elvis at home
t Graceland in full
ght in explaining
he insignia on his
ncluding the Armored
On Wheels"

1958 NASHVILLE During his first furlough Elvis attended a recording session at RCA's Studio B in Nashville. As well as regular accompanists, the session was to feature top session players including Chet Atkins on guitar and Floyd Cramer on piano

19

1958 **NASHVILLE** The recording session, Elvis' last for almost two years (*previous four pages*), took place overnight on June 10–11, including session men Hank Garland on guitar, Bob Moore on bass, and Buddy Harman on percussion.

1958 **NASHVILLE** Most of the tracks were up-tempo rockers—"I Need Your Love Tonight," "Big Hunk O' Love," and "I Got Stung," plus the rhythm and blues standard "Ain't That Lovin You Baby," and "(Now And Then There's) A Fool Such As I."

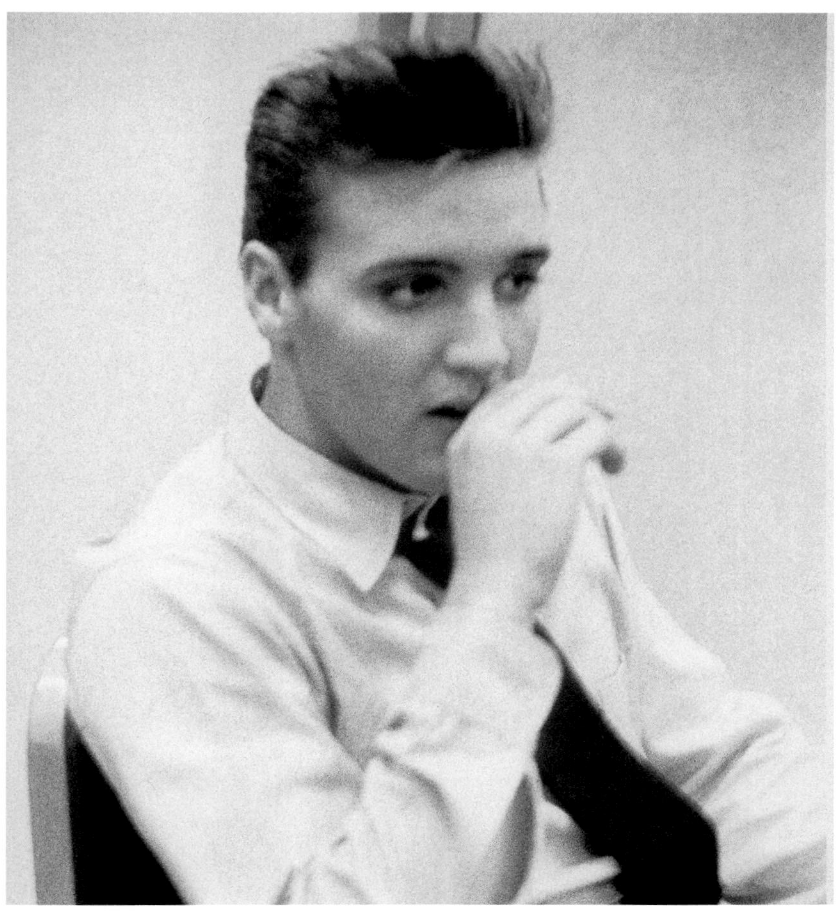

1958 NASHVILLE This brief opportunity to lay down some tracks was a rare window in a schedule dominated by Army commitment, as it would remain for nearly two years. Nevertheless, the singles that ultimately came from the session were not all immediately released. "I Got Stung" appeared as a B side later in 1958, while "Ain't That Lovin' You Baby" wasn't released until 1964, with the other three songs hitting the record stores through the following year.

HELL ON

1958 GRACELAND More photographs taken at Graceland during Elvis' first leave in June 1958. The picture in the car was to be used on the cover of the album *A Date With Elvis*. Released in August 1959, the album featured vintage tracks including some, such as "Blue Moon of Kentucky," "Milkcow Blues Boogie," and "Baby Let's Play House," that harked back to his earliest recordings on the Sun label. The Sam Phillips-produced songs had a raw energy that still sounds fresh today.

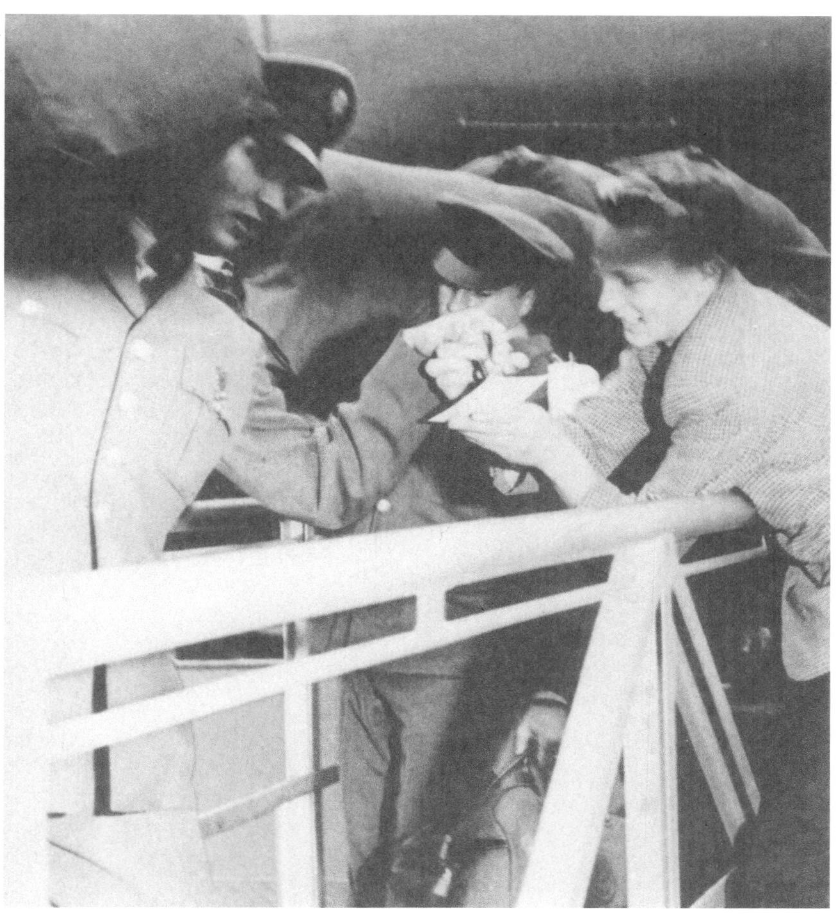

1958

1958 ELVIS SAILS In September 1958, Elvis was assigned to the 3rd Armored Division, based in West Germany. He left Fort Hood on September 19, on an overnight troop train to the Brooklyn Army Terminal in New York. From here he was to make his famous departure–after the obligatory press conference–on the USS *Randall.* The shots of screaming fans being held back by military police, and of Elvis signing autographs as he walked up the gangplank, form part of Elvis' visual history.

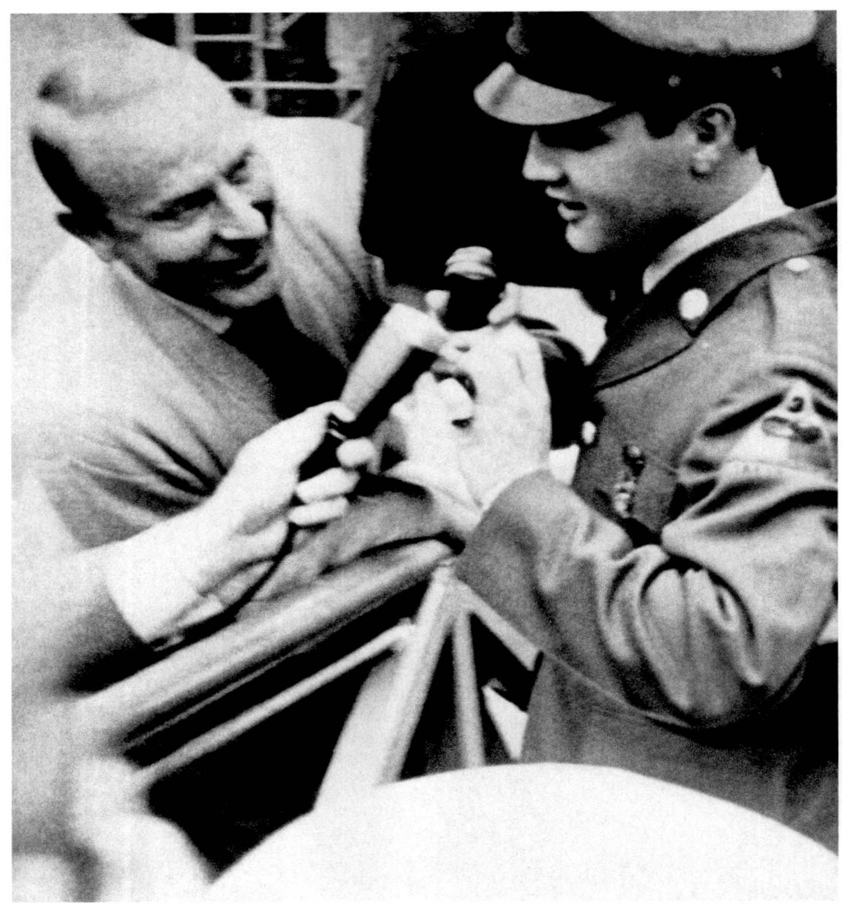

1958 FAREWELL Most of the interviews conducted immediately before and after the nine-day trip to Germany seemed to concentrate on matters concerning the opposite sex. Was he interested in German girls? Did he have a girlfriend back home? And would he like to get to know "the sex kitten" Brigitte Bardot? Elvis had already expressed an interest in meeting the French actress. Little were he or the press to anticipate that it was during his service in Germany that he would meet his future wife.

1958

1958

↑ 1958 **ON BOARD** On board Elvis got to know Charlie Hodge, another Southerner with a music background. The two were put in charge of organizing a talent show for the troops, with Charlie compering and Elvis playing piano in the ad-hoc backing group.

→→ 1958 **MEMPHIS** The train from Fort Hood refueled at Memphis, where Elvis was met by well-wishers (*above*), on its way to New York and the voyage to Germany. The troop ship arrived in Bremerhaven on October 1, 1958 (*overleaf*), after which Elvis—now a member of the 32nd Tank Battalion, 3rd Armored Division—boarded a train bound for Friedberg, near Frankfurt. From the start, he tried to blend in with his fellow servicemen as much as possible, but was thankful when his father and grandmother arrived.

U.S.

1958 NEW RECRUIT A picture of Elvis taken during basic training at Fort Hood. Such portraits were much sought after by fans, especially when he was transferred to Germany; many fans in the US felt they might never see him again.

1958 SNOW The relatively extreme German weather must have come as something of a shock to Elvis. The generally mild winters in the mid-South were a world away from the freezing temperatures and deep snow of central Germany in winter. Although this was an informal shot, it had the value of being yet another photo opportunity for Elvis, which would do no harm at all to his image with the fans back home, and indeed worldwide, awaiting his return to civilian life.

1958 MANEUVERS After a month or so in the Ray Keserne Barracks at the base in Friedberg, the Army company was transported to Grafenwohr, on the Czech border, for maneuvers. The press pictures were circulated and syndicated across the world, of course, and the public at large, and Elvis fans in particular, got an intriguing inside glimpse of their idol in action. After initially being allowed to cover Elvis on seriously active duty, the press was banned.

PRESLEY
U.S. ARMY

1958 PRIVATE PRESLEY Elvis during his basic training at Fort Hood, Texas, while still a private, before leaving for Germany (*left*), and later on maneuvers near the Czech border when he had gained his corporal's stripe. Shaving in the open air, fixing the engine on a jeep: this was Elvis the soldier as his day-to-day companions in the Army saw him. These latter pictures (*above*) were among those taken by the press corps before they were barred from the whole area.

1958 **32ND ARMORED** Elvis while still at Fort Hood (*above*). His basic training prepared him well for the rigors of the maneuvers (*right*) that were to follow. All in all, Elvis got to enjoy his time in the service, both the social experience of being treated as "normal" as far as possible, and the masculine culture of sports and military activity which was to remain a big part of his life from then on. His later interest both in martial arts and the collecting of firearms was evidence of this.

1959 BAD NAUHEIM Elvis got permission to live off base with his dependants, in his case his father and grandmother, so he initially arranged hotel accommodation for them and himself in Bad Nauheim, near the base. After a couple of such hotel arrangements, the Presleys moved to a rented three-story house in Goethestrasse, Bad Nauheim, where they lived for the remainder of Elvis' tour of duty in Germany. These pictures were taken there during February 1959.

SLEY
U.S. ARMY

1959

➔ **1959 GOETHESTRASSE** Elvis relaxes listening to records on a small portable record player, in the house at 14 Goethestrasse. He may have had the bonus of his own accommodation to alleviate Army life to a degree, but the modest record machine (and the tape recorder just visible in the foreground) show how life was a lot less luxurious than that to which he had become accustomed at Graceland.

1959

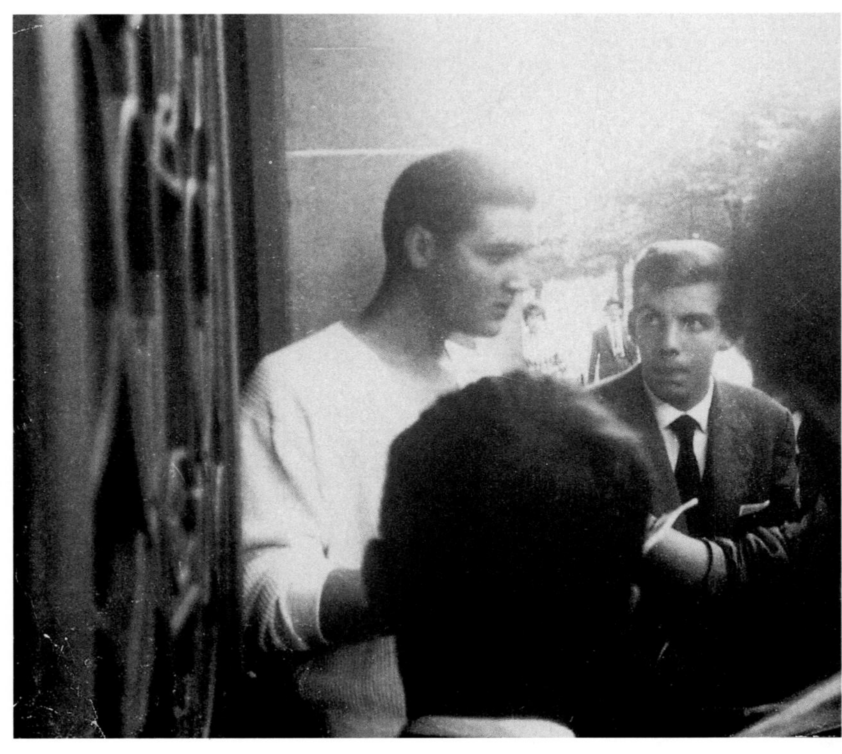

1959 PARIS On June 15, 1959, Elvis, along with Army buddies Charlie Hodge and Rex Mansfield, plus Lamar Fike, spent most of a two-week leave period in Paris. They traveled there by train, and were booked into the Prince of Wales Hotel, just off the then-fashionable Champs-Elysées. After a brief press conference, Elvis hit the streets, hoping to enjoy a welcome degree of anonymity. Within minutes, a couple of hundred people were mobbing the party, which retreated to the hotel. Thereafter, sightseeing was done by limousine, though Elvis was reported to be more interested in the Paris nightlife, visiting famous venues such as the Moulin Rouge and the Folies Bergère. These pictures were taken as Elvis met the press by his hotel.

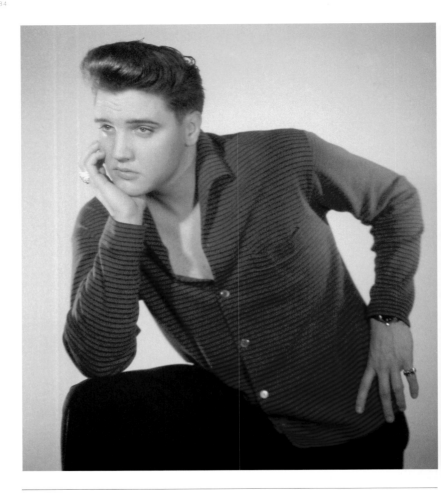

1959 PUBLICITY On this page and the two overleaf, another studio photo session staged during Elvis' time in the Army. The Colonel continually lobbied the military to allow his client to finish his tour of duty in the US, arguing that the photographs shot in Germany would make great publicity for the Army. The portrait on the right was taken later, during a publicity session for Elvis' collection of gospel songs *His Hand In Mine*, which was recorded in October 1960 and released in November.

U.S.ARMY

1960 MERCHANDISE The Army years provided more raw material for Elvis merchandising and promotion. As well as the trading cards featuring Elvis in various military poses (*left*), there was even an "Elvis Dog Tag" (*below*) similar to the nametag worn by all US service personnel (*bottom*), engraved with Elvis' picture and actual Army number.

Elvis Presley DOG TAG
Printed in U.S.A.
© 1956 ELVIS PRESLEY ENTERPRISES ALL RIGHTS RESERVED
I'M FOR ELVIS
NAME
STREET
CITY
© COPYRIGHT 1956 ELVIS PRESLEY ENTERPRISES
ALL RIGHTS RESERVED
VARI-VUE® PAT. APPL'D FOR • by PICTORIAL PRODUCTIONS, INC.
TUCKAHOE 7, NEW YORK, N. Y.
Elvis Presley

1960 PUBLICITY A large number of fan-oriented pictures continued to stream out of Elvis' and RCA Records' publicity departments. Among them was this example of Elvis in full Army fatigues atop a mountain peak. With the news pictures, in-uniform recording shots, and studio portraits like this, it was often hard to tell "Elvis in the Army" fact and fiction apart.

⬆ **1960 PUBLICITY** The Colonel and Elvis made sure that the publicity machine didn't grind to a halt while Elvis was in the army. As well as squeezing photo opportunities out of his military activity, there were also a number of studio photography sessions, as this portrait shows. The momentum generated by high-profile public relations meant that he remained in the public eye. With a major movie and record releases during that time, it was like he'd never been away.

➡ **1958 MIDGET FANS** At the Chicago convention of the Music Operators of America, the Colonel assembled an Elvis Presley Midget Fan Club to provide a photo opportunity for the press, eager to seize on any new angle on the Elvis phenomenon.

WELCOME!
MUSIC OPERATORS OF AMERICA
ELVIS PRESLEY'S MIDGET FAN CLUB
ELVIS & THE COLONEL
Let's Don't Forget
ELVIS

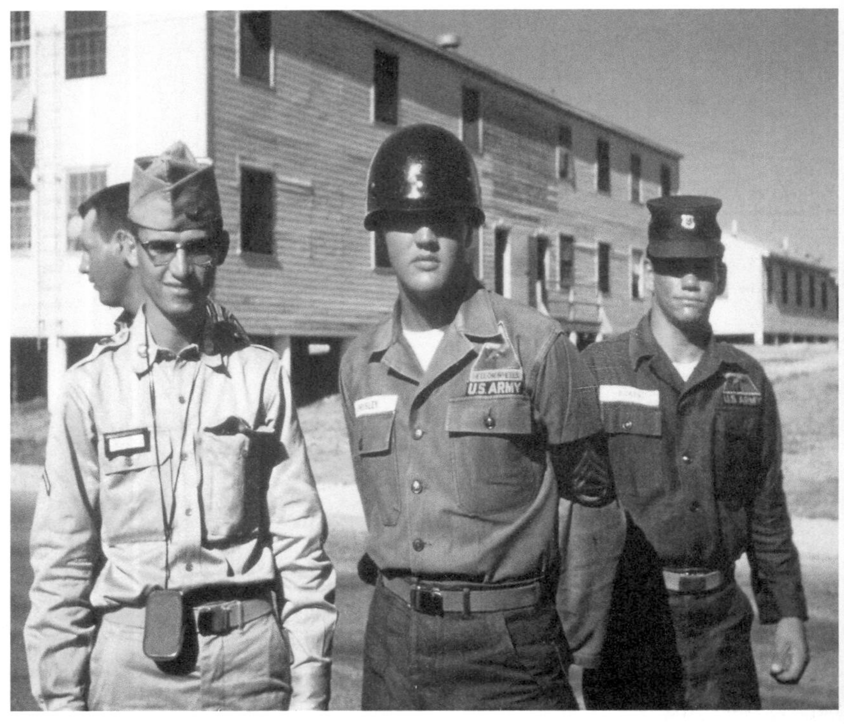

1959

1959 **BAD NAUHEIM** Elvis poses in a rare color photo taken at the base in Bad Nauheim. Army service allowed the star to allow him to rub shoulders, albeit in a limited way, with "ordinary" guys. He was discovering for the first time in his adult years the kind of relationships with work and leisure acquaintances that don't all bond into close friendships, but are nevertheless a part of normal, everyday life. That was probably the greatest legacy of his Army years.

1960 GI JOES Elvis and some of his Army buddies on winter maneuvers in Grafenwohr, January 1960. The picture is inscribed on the back "Ed–Elvis–Al Ha Ha Velsect 1960, to Elvis, Eddie." One can assume that Al's nickname was Ha Ha and Elvis was dubbed "The Twist," by these guys at least. He seems to be doing a joke mime of the Twist dance craze, which was just becoming popular via hits by Hank Ballard, Joey Dee. Not one to jump on bandwagons, Elvis never made a Twist record

1960

1960 GOETHESTRASSE Relaxing at home in Germany. Very few draftees, indeed probably none other, were in a position to bring over to Germany two members of their family plus friends, and to rent an entire house for them to live in. As in Texas, it enabled (maneuvers apart) Elvis to travel to work every morning, almost as if it was another day at the office. But even that daily routine would of course have been a radical change of lifestyle for the superstar.

1960 BREAKFAST Grandmother Minnie Presley stops for the camera as she serves breakfast for Vernon and Elvis at 14 Goethestrasse, Bad Nauheim. Perhaps surprisingly, the picture has ended up on postcards.

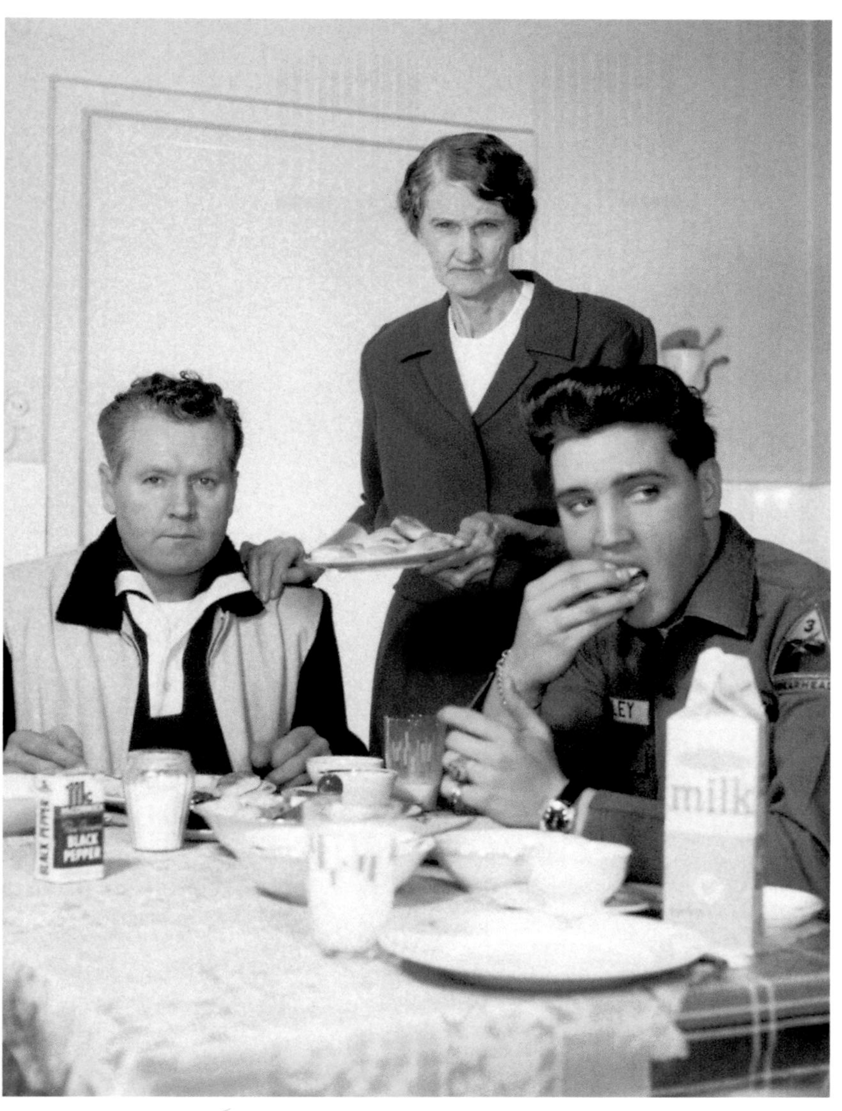
BLACK PEPPER
milk

1960

➔ **1960 PRISCILLA** Priscilla Beaulieu was only 14 when she met Elvis in the house in Bad Nauheim on September 13, 1959. The daughter of a full-time Air Force captain, she had arrived in Wiesbaden, another small town near Frankfurt, a month earlier. A mutual acquaintance had brought her around to the Presley family home in Goethestrasse, and she and Elvis immediately struck up a rapport. After just four dates he met her parents, and from then on in they saw each other constantly. The picture at right was taken as Priscilla bade farewell when Elvis left Germany from the Rhein-Main airbase on March 2, 1960.

1960

1960 HOME On March 3, 1960, Elvis left Germany. He landed at McGuire Air Force Base near Fort Dix, New Jersey, clutching his official separation papers. He flew into a heavy snowstorm, something he'd started to get used to in Germany.

1960 HOMECOMING The Colonel staged a press conference on Elvis' return to Graceland. The filmed session can still be viewed by visitors to the mansion. During the very relaxed interview Elvis articulated his feelings about his time in the Army and his return to civilian life. At least one questioner raised the issue of whether he'd had a regular girlfriend in Germany, to which Elvis coyly replied that there *was* someone he'd been seeing, but would give away no more.

1960

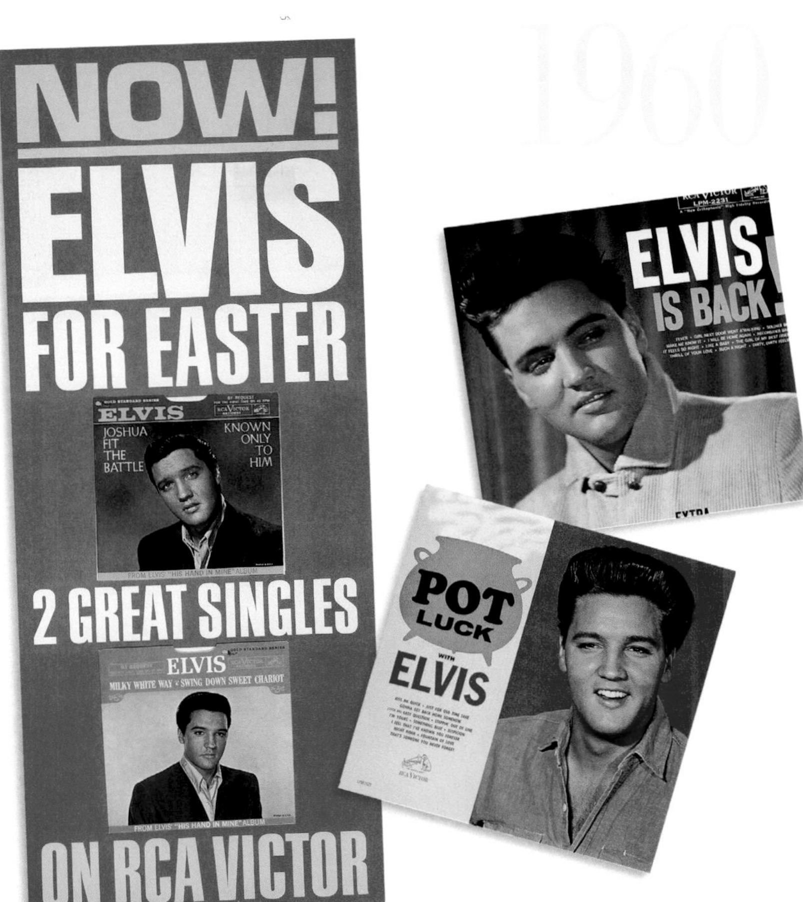

1960 50 MILLION RECORDS Soon after his return, Elvis' record company, RCA, delivered a huge state-of-the-art TV and record player console to commemorate the sale of more than 50 million records worldwide (*left*, Elvis greets its arrival).

1960 RECORDS April 1960 saw the release of the aptly titled *Elvis Is Back!* RCA Records was to release another five LPs over the next two years. One of the most important releases was the collection of gospel songs, *His Hand In Mine*, which appeared in November 1960. Two singles taken from the album were to appear six years later in February 1966, "Joshua Fit The Battle"/"Know Only To Him" and "Milky White Way"/"Swing Low Sweet Chariot," this time being pitched as "Elvis For Easter."

Copyright © 1960 by Hal B. Wallis and Joseph H. Hazen. Permission granted for newspaper and magazine reproduction. (Made in U.S.A.)
"G.I. BLUES"
A Hal Wallis Production A Paramount Picture Technicolor®

1960 GI BLUES The movie *GI Blues* was set in a US Army unit stationed n West Germany. The songs proved fairly ightweight in terms of memorable hits, and a scene in a club where Elvis sings "Doin' The Best I Can" is eclipsed musically by someone playing "Blue Suede Shoes" on the jukebox! The biggest hit from the picture was the somewhat sentimental "Wooden Heart." Nonetheless, the film did well at the box office, and was among the 15 top-grossing movies of 1960.

HAPPY

⊖ ⊕ **1960 GI BLUES** Filming ran through May and June. Elvis did all his scenes in the Paramount studios, while the cameras went to Germany for some authentic atmosphere photography. It was one of Elvis' most successful movies in commercial terms, taking more than $4 million in the last six weeks of 1960. His costar was Juliet Prowse, who was being acclaimed as a bright new singing-and-dancing Hollywood talent. The allusions to Elvis' own recent tour of duty in the Army were reinforced by the inclusion of a song called "Frankfort Special," during which Elvis and the Jordanaires are seen singing on a train heading for "Frankfort," which was presumably a veiled reference to his own Army location near Frankfurt.

1960 SINATRA TV SPECIAL The biggest "welcome back" event the Colonel negotiated to mark Elvis' return to civilian life was the Frank Sinatra TV special. The show, for which Elvis received $125,000, a record then for a TV guest spot, was recorded on March 26, 1960. For Frank Sinatra it was an about-face as far as his attitude to rock'n'roll was concerned. The crooner had famously criticized the music in 1957 as being "sung, played, and written for the most part by cretionous goons," yet now he was accommodating in no uncertain terms its biggest figurehead. When the show was broadcast on May 12, it captured nearly 70% of the audience share. Elvis was certainly back, and everyone knew it.

1960 HIS HAND IN MINE Two publicity pictures, one used on the cover of the album *His Hand In Mine*. Recorded in RCA's studios in Nashville on October 30, 1960, it featured such traditional religious items as "Swing Low Sweet Chariot," and the musicians included Scotty Moore, D. J. Fontana, the "Yaketty Sax" man Boots Randolph on tenor saxophone, and, as well as Elvis and the Jordanaires, Millie Kirkham on vocals. Interestingly, Elvis' only Grammy awards were for gospel recordings.

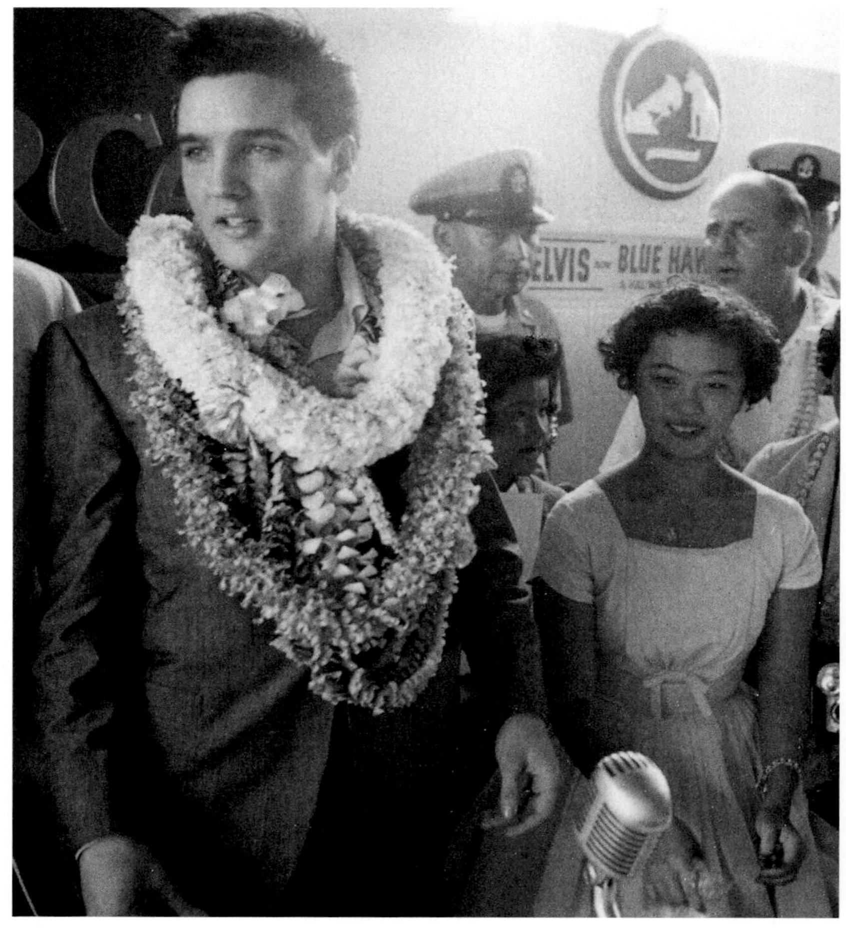

1961

1961 HONOLULU On March 15, 1961, Elvis played a benefit to raise money for a memorial to the 1,102 men entombed in the World War II battleship USS *Arizona*, sunk at Pearl Harbor 20 years before. It was promoted by the Pacific War Memorial Commission and held at the Bloch Arena in Honolulu, Hawaii. Elvis waived his $150,000 fee for the cause, and his participation was invaluable as a means of generating publicity and raising public awareness of the proposed memorial.

1961 HONOLULU More than 3,000 fans and 75 police greeted Elvis at Honolulu airport. It was mayhem. Second-on-the-bill star, country singer Minnie Pearl, later described it: "We got off the plane, girls were screaming. He walked over to sign autographs, I'd never seen anything like it before, I was just horrified . . . I thought they were going to kill him . . ."

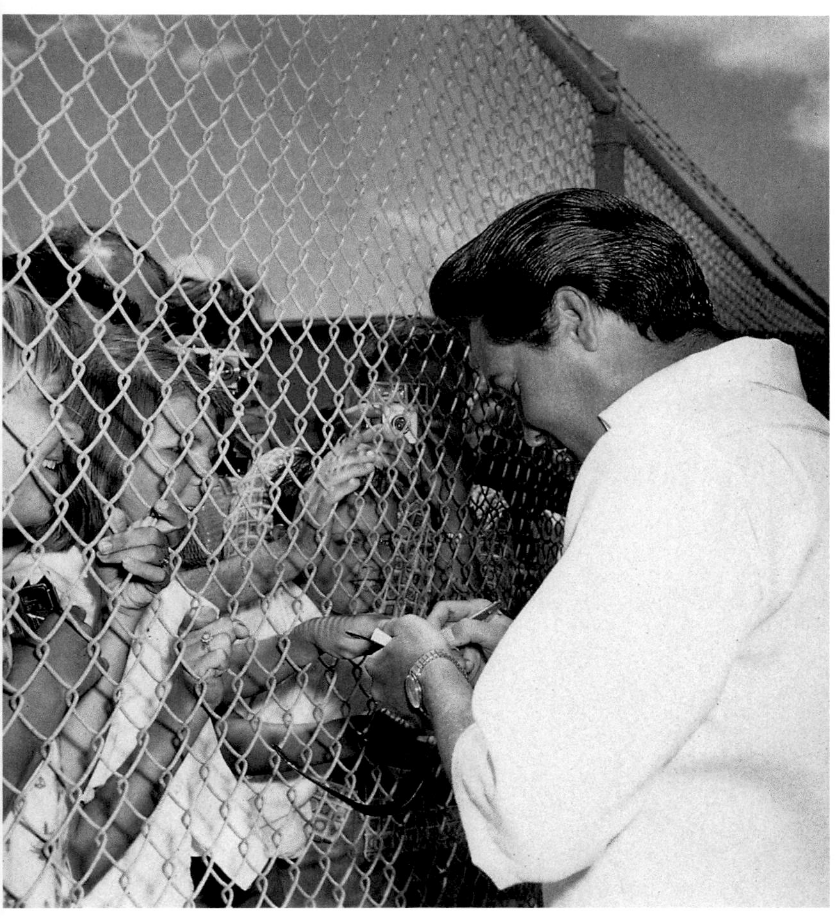

← **1961 HONOLULU** The USS *Arizona* benefit concert raised more than $62,000. The Hawaii House of Representatives formally thanked Elvis and the Colonel and many accolades were received from the US Navy.

↑ **1965 HONOLULU** Elvis visits the USS *Arizona* Memorial. The Colonel wrote to Vice President Lyndon Johnson in 1961, offering his and Elvis' services to their country "in any capacity, whether it is to use our talents or help load the trucks."

1961

1961

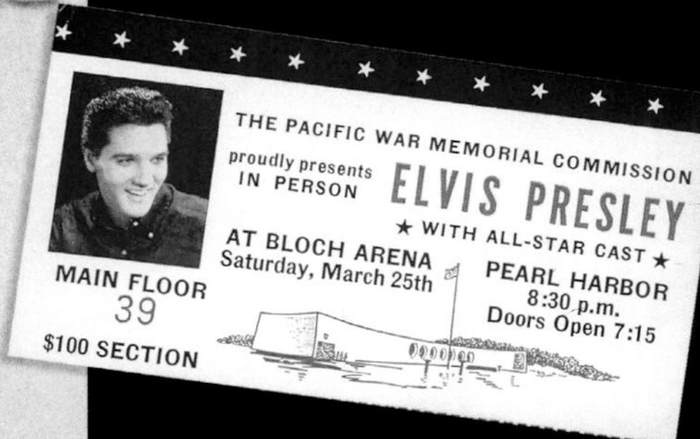

THE PACIFIC WAR MEMORIAL COMMISSION
proudly presents
IN PERSON
ELVIS PRESLEY
★ WITH ALL-STAR CAST ★
AT BLOCH ARENA
Saturday, March 25th
PEARL HARBOR
8:30 p.m.
Doors Open 7:15
MAIN FLOOR
39
$100 SECTION

1961 HONOLULU Elvis contemplates Honolulu harbor from the balcony of the Hawaiian Village Hotel. The Colonel and Elvis stayed on in Hawaii to commence shooting on the movie *Blue Hawaii*, which was to mark the beginning of his movie-only career through the next seven years.

ELVIS PRESLEY

Elvis™ Hollywood Calls

IN THE MOVIES

[1960–1969]

← **1965 PARADISE, HAWAIIAN STYLE** Elvis relaxes on the exotic location set in Hanauma Bay, Hawaii, during the filming of his 21st movie, which was released worldwide in July 1966.

December 1960

August 1968

April 1961

April 1967

From early on in his career, Elvis' name was suggested for roles in a number of "serious" movies, including *The Defiant Ones*, *Cat On A Hot Tin Roof*, and the late-Seventies remake of *A Star Is Born*. But despite encouraging early performances in *Love Me Tender*, *Jailhouse Rock,* and *King Creole*, his potential as a dramatic actor was never to be realized.

Most of Elvis' activity through the 1960s was centered on a plethora of (mainly lightweight) movies that by and large presented an increasingly anodyne image of the singer. There were some exceptions. In *Flaming Star* and *Charro!* (both Westerns) he played parts that stretched him as an actor, giving him plots that didn't require him to burst into song. But mostly the audiences saw an Elvis with immaculate hair, and clothes to match, in a variety of contrived situations, and always with glamorous female costars.

There were "travelog" movies, with romantic locations as backdrops to song-and-dance routines with interchangeable Sixties starlets. Likewise, there were Elvis-on-wheels plots, in roles that again were an excuse for him to pursue, be pursued by, and serenade a seemingly never-ending line of Hollywood lovelies.

December 1961 August 1963 April 1961

Nevertheless, within the confines of this quickly-established formula, there were still some memorable moments: the double part he played in *Kissin' Cousins,* the raunchy dance sequences with Ann-Margret in *Viva Las Vegas!,* and the boxing scenes (in which Elvis didn't use a stand-in) in *Kid Galahad.*

Interestingly, Elvis came to work with a surprising number of Hollywood greats, alongside the newer names who dominated the cast lists of most of the movies. *Blue Hawaii* featured Angela Lansbury, who was first nominated for an Oscar for *Gaslight* in 1944. Gig Young, who appeared in *Kid Galahad,* was nominated three times. Hollywood veteran Barbara Stanwyck shared the honors for *Roustabout,* while 1967's *Easy Come, Easy Go* featured Elsa Lanchester, who was twice nominated for an Oscar.

What the Hollywood years established was Elvis' prime position in the upper echelons of the showbusiness élite, evidenced by the many celebrities who visited him during his sojourns in California. Whether legendary names like Jimmy Durante and Mahalia Jackson, or pop-chart stars (from Tom Jones to the Beatles), they all came to pay homage to the King of Rock'n'Roll.

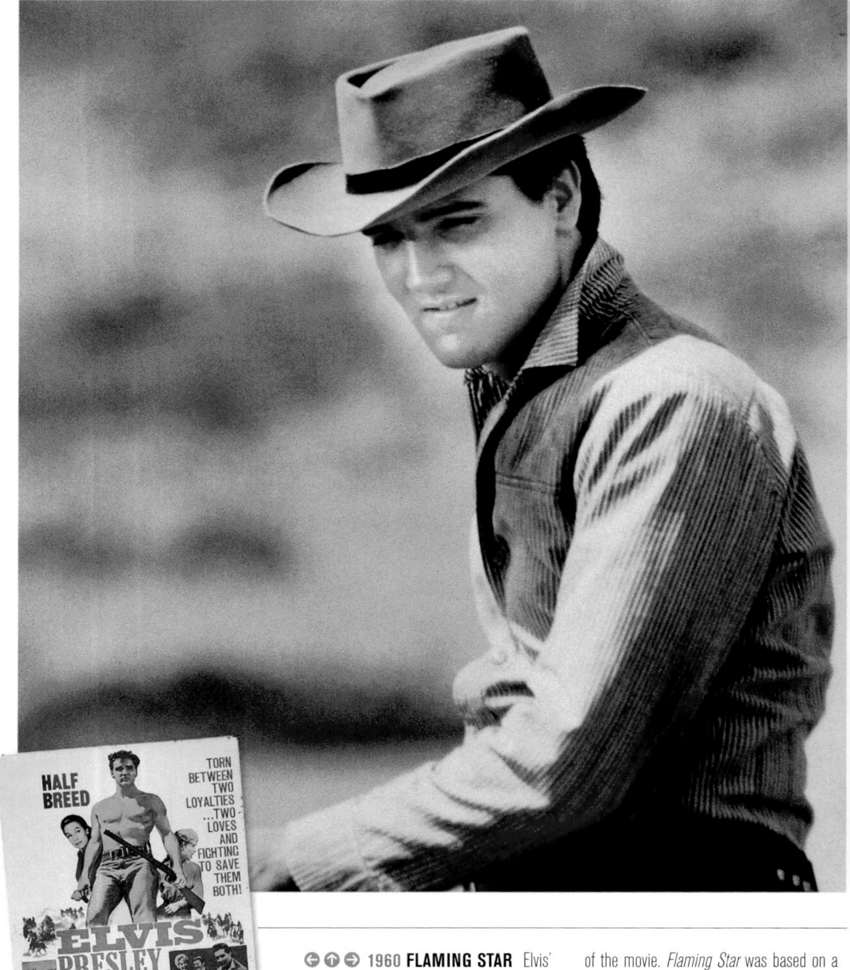

1960 FLAMING STAR Elvis' sixth film was, with the exception of *Charro!* later in the decade, the nearest he got to a nonsinging role. It features only the title song (over the credits) and "A Cane and a High Stitched Collar" in the opening minutes of the movie. *Flaming Star* was based on a book called *The Brothers of Broken Lance* by Claire Huiffaker, and was originally going to be filmed in 1958 as *The Brothers of Flaming Arrow* with Marlon Brando and Frank Sinatra as the two brothers.

A Scene from the 20th Century-Fox Production
"FLAMING STAR"
In CinemaScope
Printed in the U.S.A.

1960 FLAMING STAR Elvis' role in *Flaming Star*, as the mixed-ethnicity Native American Pacer Burton, was a serious if not exactly controversial one, dealing with a clash of cultures, and therefore a clash of loyalties facing the hero.

1960 FLAMING STAR This publicity photograph for *Flaming Star* was one of the many images of Elvis that were to become pure iconography, especially when it was later the subject of a 1964 painting, *Single Elvis*, by the pop artist Andy Warhol.

FLAMING STAR Elvis on a
during the filming of *Flaming*
of the movie was shot on three
he San Fernando Valley near
. It was directed by Don Siegel,
many cult classics.

1961 BLUE HAWAII On location shooting the early scenes of *Blue Hawaii*, in which he played a serviceman, Elvis shares a joke with the film's producer Hal Wallis. Wallis was a Hollywood veteran whose productions included *Casablanca*

1960

1961

1961 BLUE HAWAII This was the first in Elvis' trilogy of "South Seas" movies and first of the lighthearted genre of films that became the stereotype for much of his subsequent Hollywood output (*here* and *overleaf*). The trite plot served as a backcloth for no fewer than 14 songs, and the film grossed over $4 million at the box office, not to mention the tie-in soundtrack album, which went gold immediately on release. It costarred Joan Blackman and also featured Angela Lansbury.

Copyright © 1961 by Hal B. Wallis and Joseph H. Hazen. Permission granted for newspaper and magazine reproduction. (Made in U.S.A.)
"BLUE HAWAII"
A Hal Wallis Production A Paramount Picture Panavision® Technicolor®

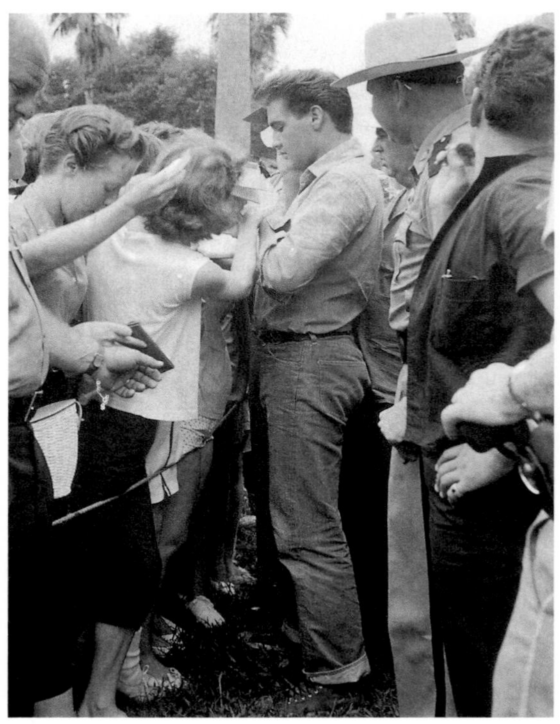

1961

1961 FOLLOW THAT DREAM
Location shooting for Elvis' films often provided lucky fans with a rare chance to get close to their idol. Florida was the chosen site for *Follow That Dream*. Here, eager kids get their autographs from Elvis.

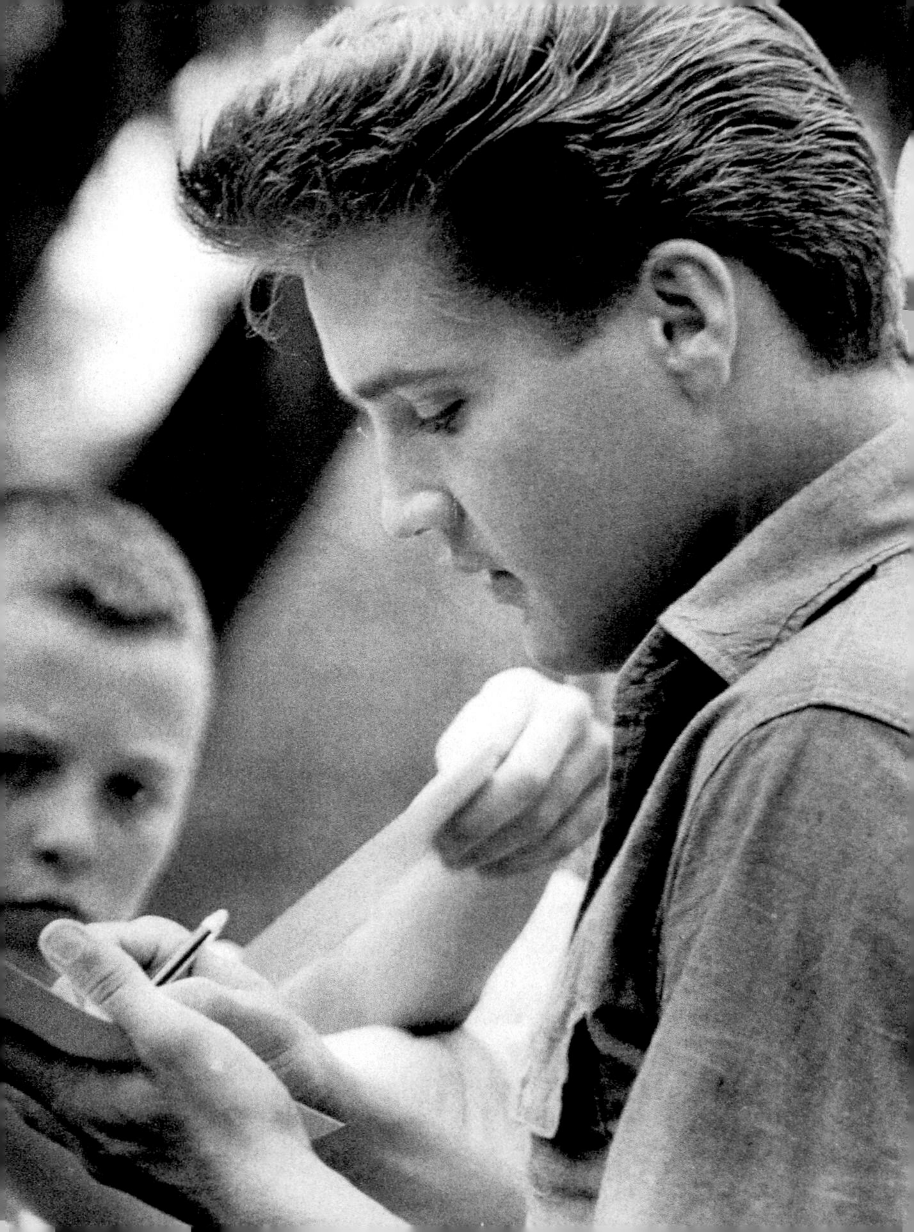

1962 FOLLOW THAT DREAM
This film was distinguished by a well-received stab at comedy on Elvis' part. Based on a novel entitled *Pioneer Go Home!* by Richard Powell, the plot followed the adventures of a family down on their luck. The premiere was staged in Ocala, Florida, on April 11, 1962, and it was released nationally–and worldwide–at the end of May. With only five complete songs, the disc spin-off was restricted to a 45 that got to number 15 in the US singles chart.

1961 FOLLOW THAT DREAM
Principal photography on *Follow That Dream* took place in July 1961. Here, Elvis plays with one of his costars on the set, child actress Pam Ogles, who played the youngest member of the family, Ariadne.

1961 FOLLOW THAT DREAM
Elvis had a good time while shooting *Follow That Dream*. Arriving at the Florida set in a privately-rented bus, he brought along with him—for recreation purposes only—a speedboat, a motorcycle, and two cars.

1961

ORTH
SY. 6-7173

1961 KID GALAHAD The outdoor locations for the boxing movie *Kid Galahad* were shot primarily in Idylwild, California. The film, costarring Lola Albright, Gig Young, and Charles Bronson, was shot in the winter of 1961 and released the following August.

1961 FOLLOW THAT DREAM Filming away from the studio on location always provided an excuse for Elvis to indulge in his passion for various forms of outdoor activity, particularly his love of high-powered motorcycles.

1961

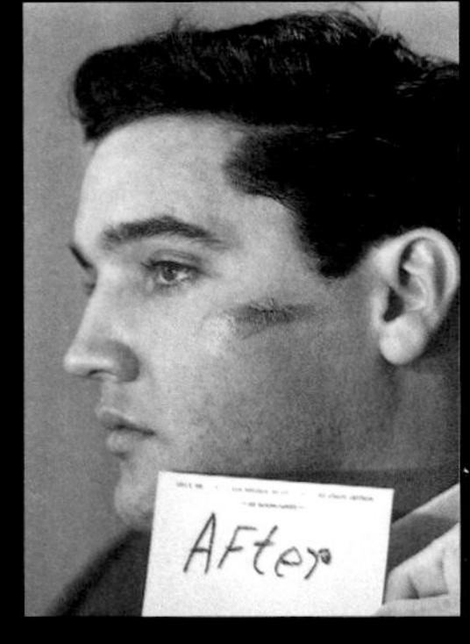

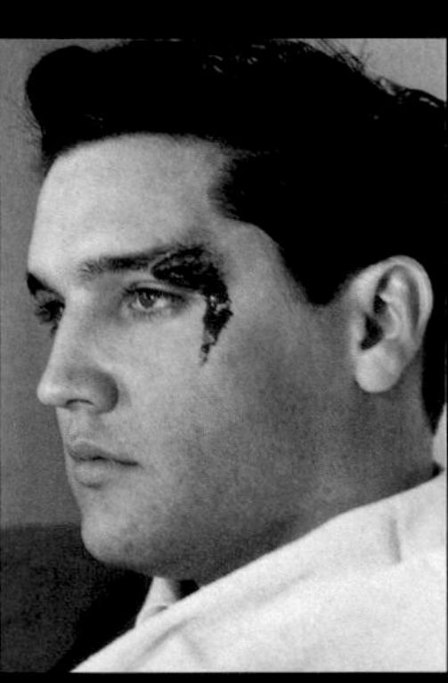

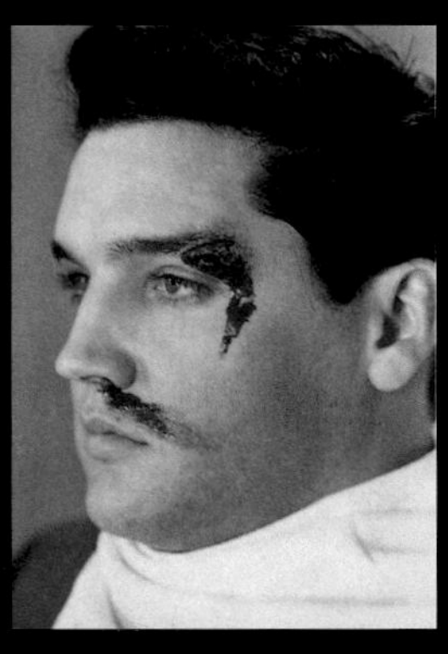

962

1962 **KID GALAHAD** Some of the most sensational images in this boxing movie, based on a 1930s story, are those of Elvis with fight wounds. These were also captured in a series of snaps taken in the makeup unit before shooting. Elvis declined to have a stand-in for the actual fight sequences; instead, he was coached by the former world junior welterweight champion Mushy Callahan, and Al Silvani trainer of such boxing luminaries as Floyd Patterson and Rocky Graziano.

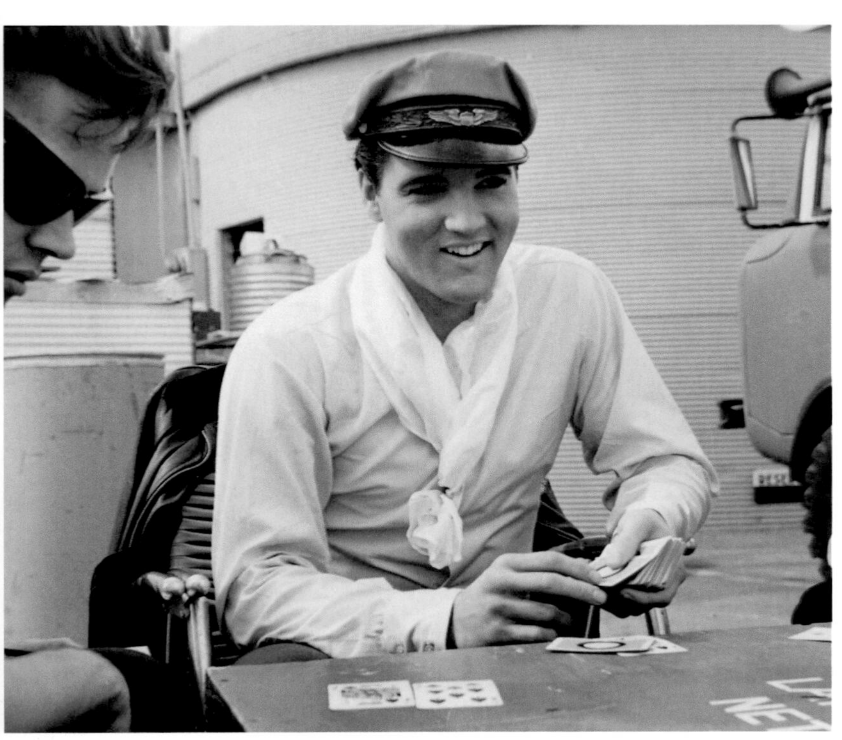

1962 GIRLS! GIRLS! GIRLS! Archetypal of Elvis' "all-singin', all-lovin'" vehicles, he plays a charter fisherman who sings in a nightclub to raise money for a boat, torn between the affections of Stella Stevens and Laurel Goodwin.

1962 WORLD'S FAIR Elvis relaxing on set during filming at the Seattle World's Fair for his 12th film. Shooting for *It Happened At The World's Fair* began in September 1962, and the movie was released the following April.

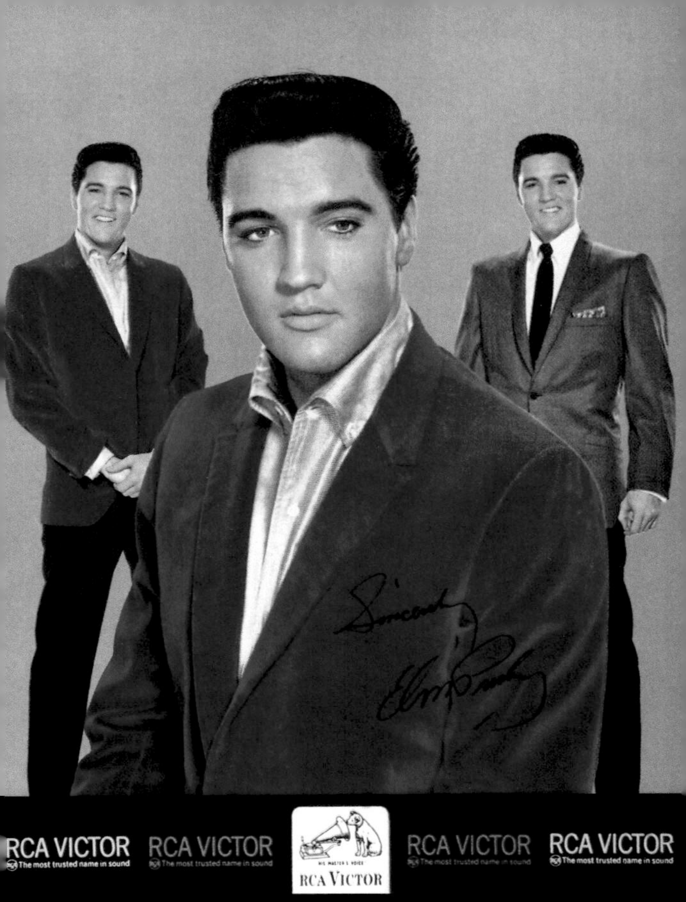

RCA VICTOR The most trusted name in sound
RCA VICTOR The most trusted name in sound

RCA VICTOR The most trusted name in sound
RCA VICTOR The most trusted name in sound

ALENDAR During the years s made movies, he still made publicity machines of film Records, and Colonel Tom pt his image prominent on s and merchandise

1964 RCA PUBLICITY RCA Records couldn't go wrong with Elvis. As well as albums that were produced to accompany the movies, there were also studio albums and his huge back catalog—a treasure trove in terms of quality as well as quantity.

196

1963

↑ 1963 WORLD'S FAIR For his role in *It Happened At The World's Fair*, Elvis portrays a crop-dusting pilot, who, along with his partner (played by Gary Lockwood), gets involved at the Fair with Joan O'Brian and Vicky Tiu.

→ 1963 WORLD'S FAIR As well as the World's Fair security organizations and the Seattle police, MGM hired 100 policemen to protect Elvis during filming, and six Pinkerton plainclothes detectives at other times.

MIKE EDWARDS

1962

1962 WORLD'S FAIR The movie appeared to be an excuse for a conducted tour of the Seattle World's Fair of 1962, and, of course, for Elvis to run through a collection of songs. Shooting proved difficult, as the actors and crew were hampered by genuine visitors to the Fair who suddenly realized that Elvis was there too. Unlike other Elvis shoots, at which fans could be strictly monitored and kept away from the set if necessary, the crowds were there anyway.

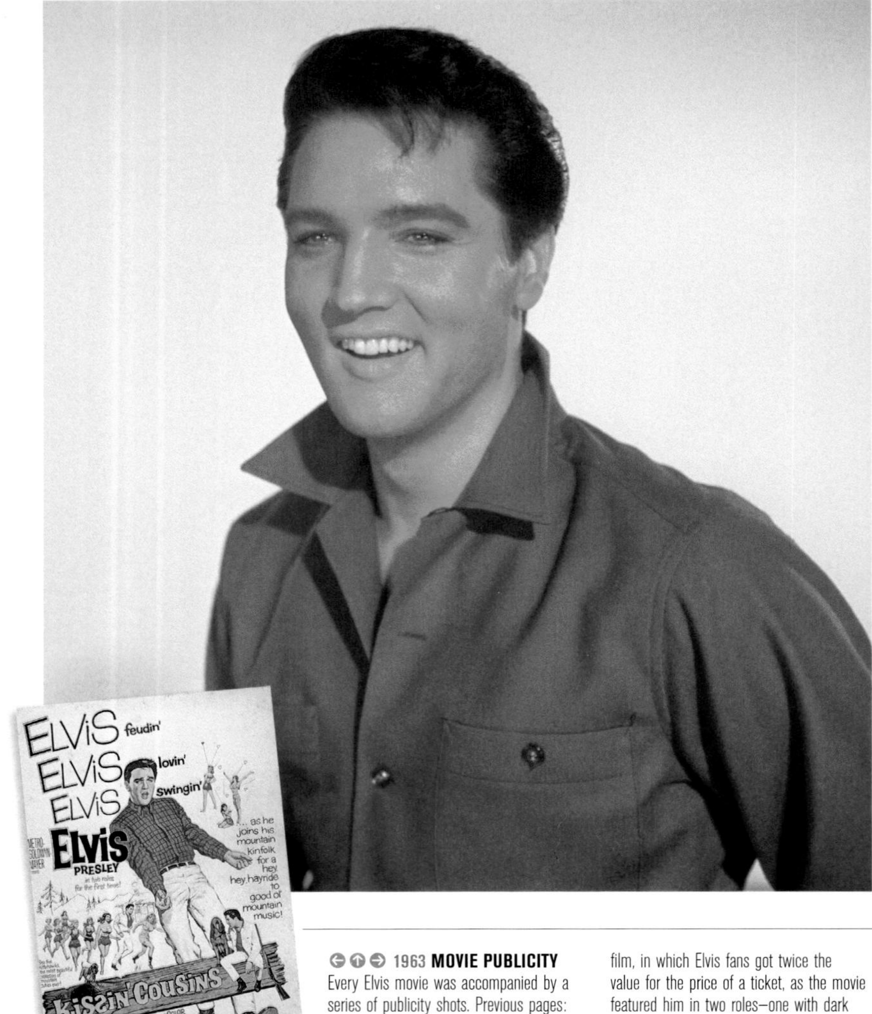

1963 MOVIE PUBLICITY Every Elvis movie was accompanied by a series of publicity shots. Previous pages: a portrait *(left)* from *Fun In Acapulco*, this time set in Mexico; and *(right)* *Kissin' Cousins*. The shot above is also from this film, in which Elvis fans got twice the value for the price of a ticket, as the movie featured him in two roles–one with dark hair, one blonde–as long-lost cousins. The picture opposite, with Elvis in race-driver gear, was posed for *Viva Las Vegas*.

JACKSO

1963 VIVA LAS VEGAS The stand-out features of *Viva Las Vegas*, released in 1964, are Elvis' song-and-dance routines with his vivacious costar, the Swedish-American actress Ann-Margret. The film's success was helped in no small way by the director George Sidney, whose achievements included the classic MGM musicals *Annie Get Your Gun* and *Show Boat*. Ann-Margret, who was romantically linked to Elvis during shooting, had had a single in the US Top Twenty chart in 1961.

1964 ROUSTABOUT In *Roustabout* Elvis played a wandering singer whose musical contribution rescues a traveling carnival from bankruptcy. The carnival proprietor was played by Barbara Stanwyck (*above*), a Hollywood veteran with four Oscar nominations behind her. The best musical number was undoubtedly "Little Egypt." The film also featured Sue Ane Langdon—best known for a number of popular American TV series, and pictured (*right*) with Elvis on set.

1965 GIRL HAPPY Elvis' costar n *Girl Happy* was Shelley Fabares, an early ixties pop star who had had a number one ecord in the US singles chart with "Johnny ngel" in 1962. She went on to star with lvis in two more movies. His other romantic interest in the film was played by a former Miss America, Mary Ann Mobley; they are seen here together in an on-screen clinch. She also appeared opposite Elvis in *Harum Scarum*. The portraits overleaf were publicity material for the film.

1965

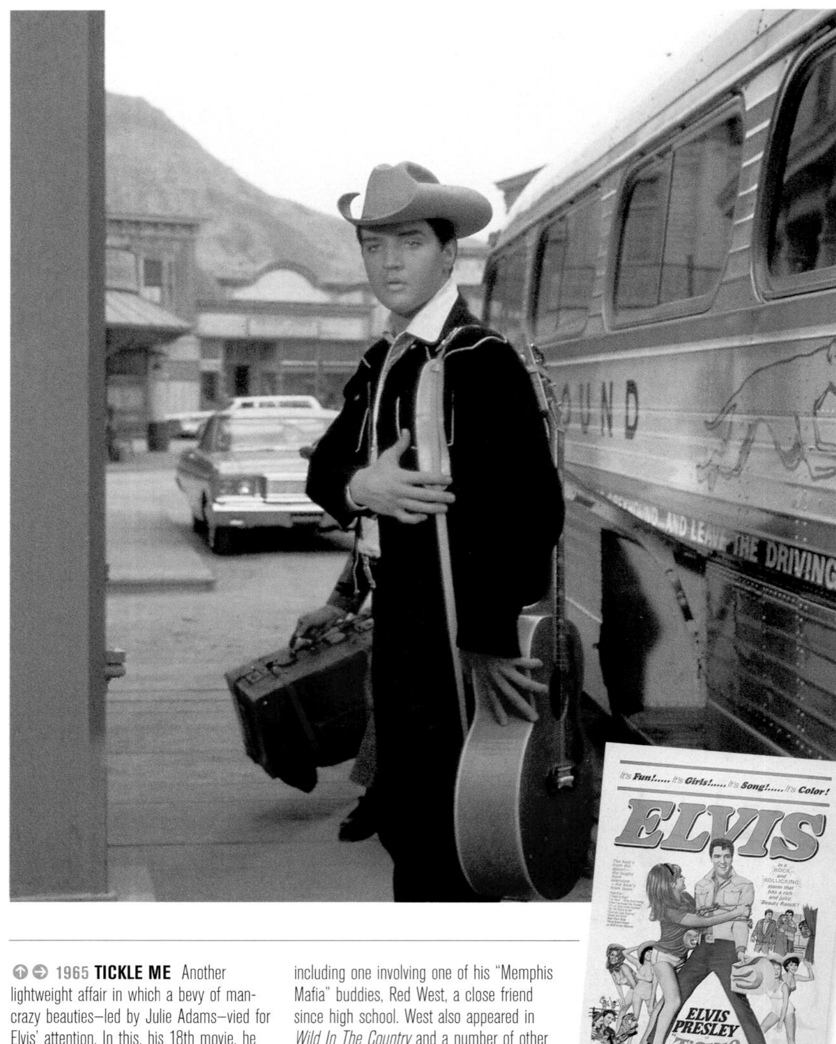

1965 TICKLE ME Another lightweight affair in which a bevy of man-crazy beauties—led by Julie Adams—vied for Elvis' attention. In this, his 18th movie, he played a rodeo rider—he got to ride a lot, and also engage in fistfight scenes, including one involving one of his "Memphis Mafia" buddies, Red West, a close friend since high school. West also appeared in *Wild In The Country* and a number of other Elvis films. The film is said to have saved its studio, Allied Artists, from financial ruin.

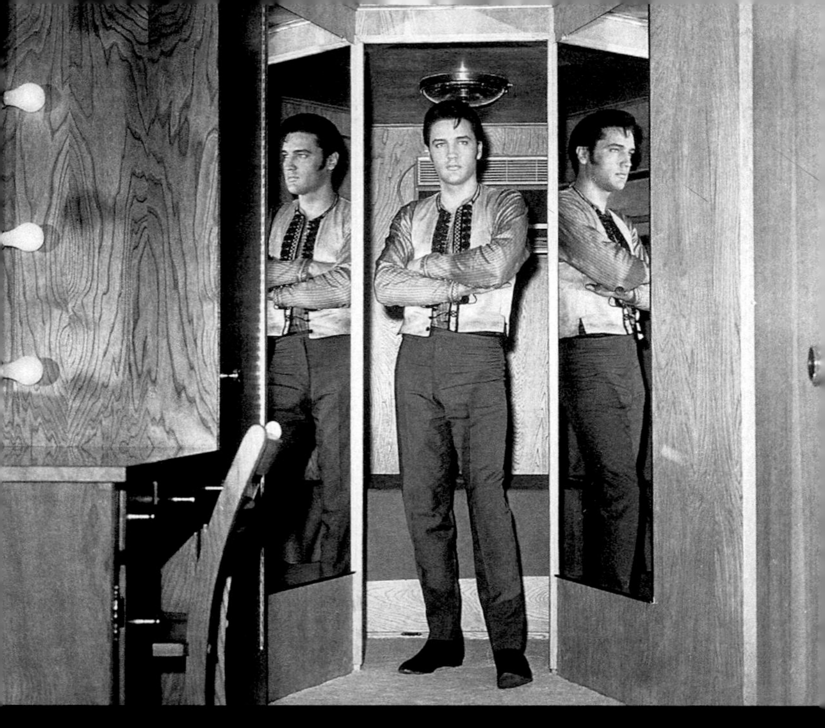

1965

1965 HARUM SCARUM
Without doubt the most ludicrous setting for a Presley film, the fantasy-land of Lunakahn is visited by American actor Johnny Tyronne (played by Elvis), who is on a tour of the Middle East promoting his movie, *Sands Of The Desert*. Predictable adventures ensue, involving every "Arabian Nights" character stereotype known to Hollywood. The shots here were taken in Elvis' studio dressing room, while the stills overleaf show Elvis in full "Rudolph Valentino" sheik mode.

ELVIS PRESLEY

1966 PARADISE IN HAWAII

Given that he was not performing live in the mid-1960s, films shot on location afforded the only opportunity, in his working life at least, for Elvis to get in touch with the "real" world. While on location in Hawaii in August 1965, he was interviewed for a local radio station by Peter Noone, the lead singer with the successful UK beat group, Herman's Hermits. The interview has since appeared on a number of bootleg releases over the years.

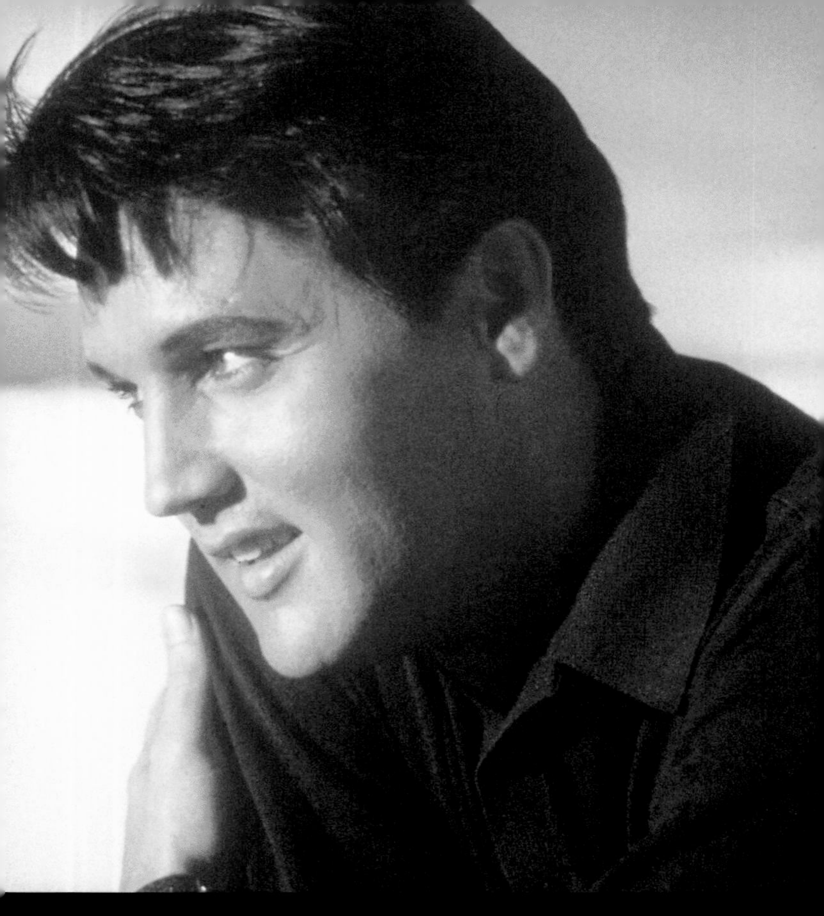

1966 EASY COME, EASY GO
his 1967 release was the only Elvis movie o contain references to hippies. In the film, Hollywood legend Elsa Lanchester–the riginal *Bride of Frankenstein* in 1935–runs yoga class. The pictures here were taken during the shoot in October 1966, which took place in Hollywood and at Long Beach Naval Station. Elvis played a naval frogman, Ted Jackson, who becomes involved in a hunt for sunken treasure–a quest that, bizarrely, leads him into the yoga class.

1966

1966 SPINOUT Another movie in which Elvis plays a race-car driver. MGM studios mounted a huge publicity campaign for *Spinout* to mark Elvis' tenth year in the movie business. The literature included press kits, theater competitions, and advertisements. The on-set picture *(right)* shows him with a costar, Deborah Whalley. The female lead was played by Shelley Fabares, and two members of the race-track pit crew were played by Elvis' buddies Red West and Joe Esposito.

222-1
222-5
222-2
222-6
222-3
222-7

1967 STAY AWAY JOE During the location shooting for his 26th film, *Stay Away Joe*, which took place in Sedona, Arizona, Elvis was interviewed by *Cosmopolitan* magazine. He put a modest spin on his acting ability, insisting that he had learned most of what he knew from more seasoned professionals. In the case of *Stay Away Joe*, these included the great Burgess Meredith, whose track record involved dozens of films and, at the time, the *Batman* television series.

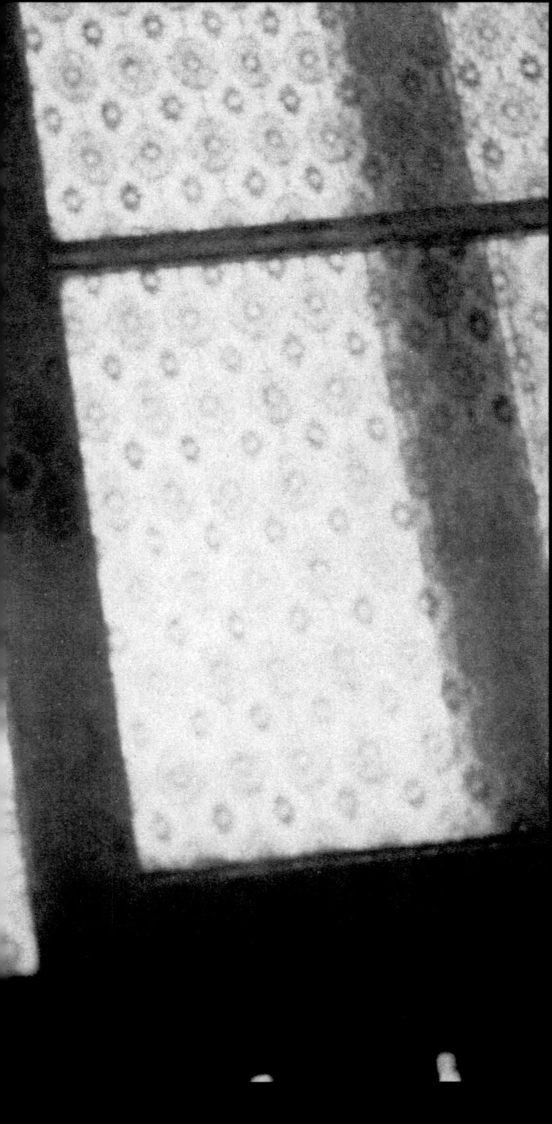

1968

←↑ 1967 **STAY AWAY JOE** As the hard-drinking Native American Joe Lightcloud, Elvis was back in almost dramatic territory with *Stay Away Joe*, a 1968 release, which featured only three songs. The location was Arizona, with plenty of horse riding to enjoy.

1969

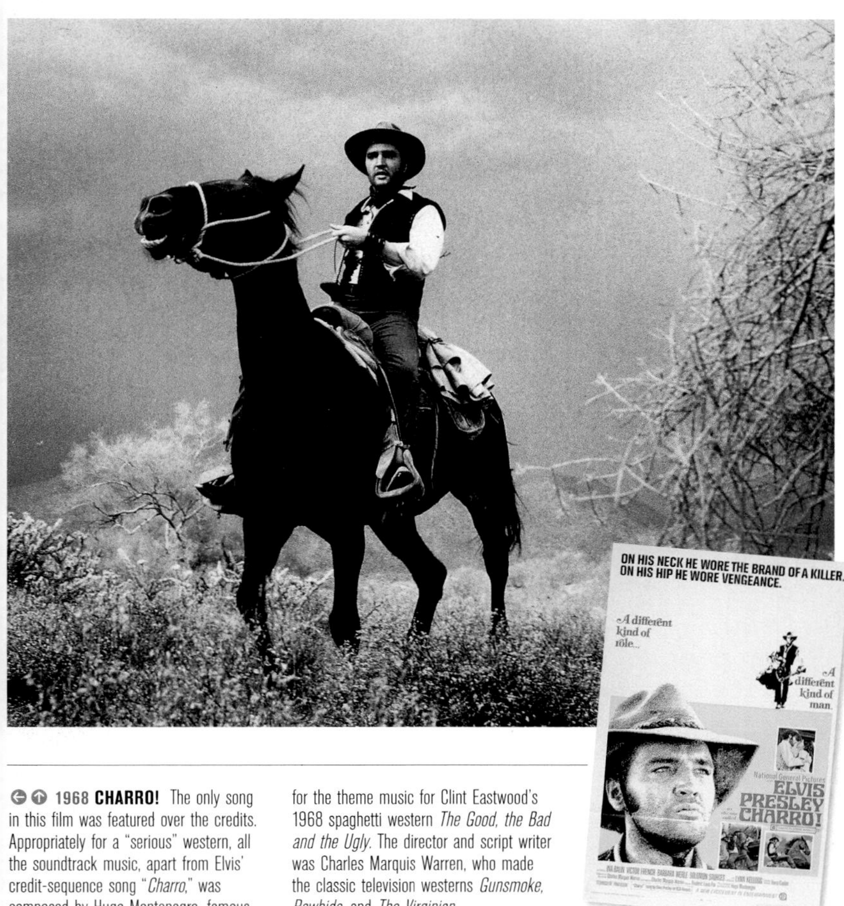

ON HIS NECK HE WORE THE BRAND OF A KILLER.
ON HIS HIP HE WORE VENGEANCE.
A different kind of rôle...
A different kind of man.
National General Pictures
ELVIS PRESLEY
CHARRO!

1968 CHARRO! The only song in this film was featured over the credits. Appropriately for a "serious" western, all the soundtrack music, apart from Elvis' credit-sequence song "*Charro*," was composed by Hugo Montenegro, famous for the theme music for Clint Eastwood's 1968 spaghetti western *The Good, the Bad and the Ugly*. The director and script writer was Charles Marquis Warren, who made the classic television westerns *Gunsmoke, Rawhide*, and *The Virginian*.

1969 TROUBLE WITH GIRLS
Set in the late 1920s, Elvis' penultimate fiction movie had him playing the manager of a traveling tent show. Undoubtedly to Elvis' delight, there was a football sequence in the movie, in which he was able to indulge in his favorite sport, albeit wearing an antiquated helmet and shirt. The full title of the film was *The Trouble With Girls (And How to Get Into It)*, and it was directed by the man who had made *Stay Away Joe,* Peter Tewksbury.

1969

1969

1969 THE TROUBLE WITH GIRLS Elvis completed shooting *The Trouble With Girls* in December 1968, by which time he had already completed the TV special for NBC. Aired on December 3, it was to represent his comeback to live performance.

1969 CHANGE OF HABIT In Elvis' final fictional picture (poster, *bottom right*) he plays a doctor in an inner-city clinic who accepts the help of Mary Tyler Moore and her two friends, not knowing they are novice nuns in "civilian" clothes. After enjoying huge success in *The Dick Van Dyke Show* in the 1960s, Mary Tyler Moore had her own successful series in the early Seventies. Other movies in Elvis' total of 31 included *Clambake* in 1967, and *Speedway* and *Live A Little, Love A Little*, both 1968.

Elvis™

Intermission

RELAXING

[1967–1976]

← **1968 HAWAII** Priscilla and Elvis relaxing in Hawaii, the island paradise where he had performed and filmed throughout his career. The couple spent a two-week vacation there in May 1968 with their daughter Lisa Marie and five friends.

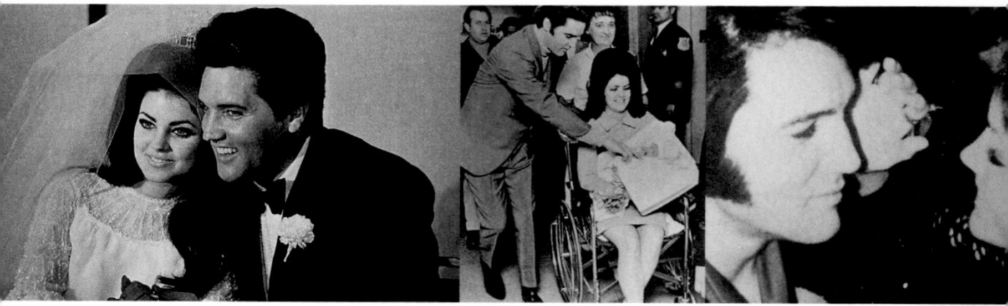

May 1967 *February 1968* *February 1970*

1967–1973

Movie making, by its very nature, involves a lot of spare time between shoots for those involved. Consequently, although he was taking part in feature films at a rate of two or three a year in the mid-1960s, Elvis had more leisure time on his hands than when he was touring concert venues across America for live performances. Pictures from home, fan shots, newspaper paparazzi photographs—a variety of candid pictures allows us a peek into the Presley private life during a period when he was sharing his domestic time between homes in California and Memphis, Tennessee.

The most significant change in his family arrangements, of course, was his marriage in May 1967 to Priscilla Beaulieu, whom he had met during his draft duty in 1959, when he was stationed in Germany. Significantly, the wedding ceremony was held in the showbiz capital of Las Vegas, not Memphis.

There were few guests invited to the ceremony, but among them, acting as best men, were Joe Esposito and Marty Lacker, two of a small group of the so-called "Memphis Mafia" in attendance. The Colonel, however, arranged a post-ceremony press conference to make the event headline news around the world.

February 1970 *February 1969* *February 1967*

At the same time that he was dividing his residence between Palm Springs and Graceland, Elvis purchased a 163-acre cattle ranch near Walls, Mississippi, cutely called Twinkletown Farm, to indulge his passion for horses. He renamed the property the Circle G (for Graceland) and adopted a cowboy lifestyle for himself and his entourage whenever he was there. Elvis added "Flying" to the name when he discovered a ranch called the Circle G already existed.

Another leisure activity which was occupying Elvis more and more was karate. He had developed basic skills during his time in the Army, and at his "welcome home" press conference after his service ended, he offered to demonstrate if someone could find a piece of wood! By the end of the decade, karate had become so much a part of Elvis' lifestyle that he began to incorporate the moves into his stage act when he resumed live performances.

In February 1968, Priscilla gave birth to a baby girl, Lisa Marie, and for the rest of the 1960s, the family album photographs invariably featured the three of them—Elvis at ease and relaxed, in a "normal" home life that was in stark contrast to the professional pressures that persisted in the world outside.

1967

1967 MARRIAGE May 1,1967, at 11.45 AM Elvis and Priscilla are married by Nevada Supreme Court Chief Justice David Zenoff at the Aladdin Hotel in Las Vegas. Though called at short notice, the wedding announcement came as no surprise, for the couple had been engaged since the previous Christmas. Elvis had presented Priscilla with a ring purchased from Memphis jeweler Harry Levitch. Harry was one of a select group of non-family guests at the ceremony.

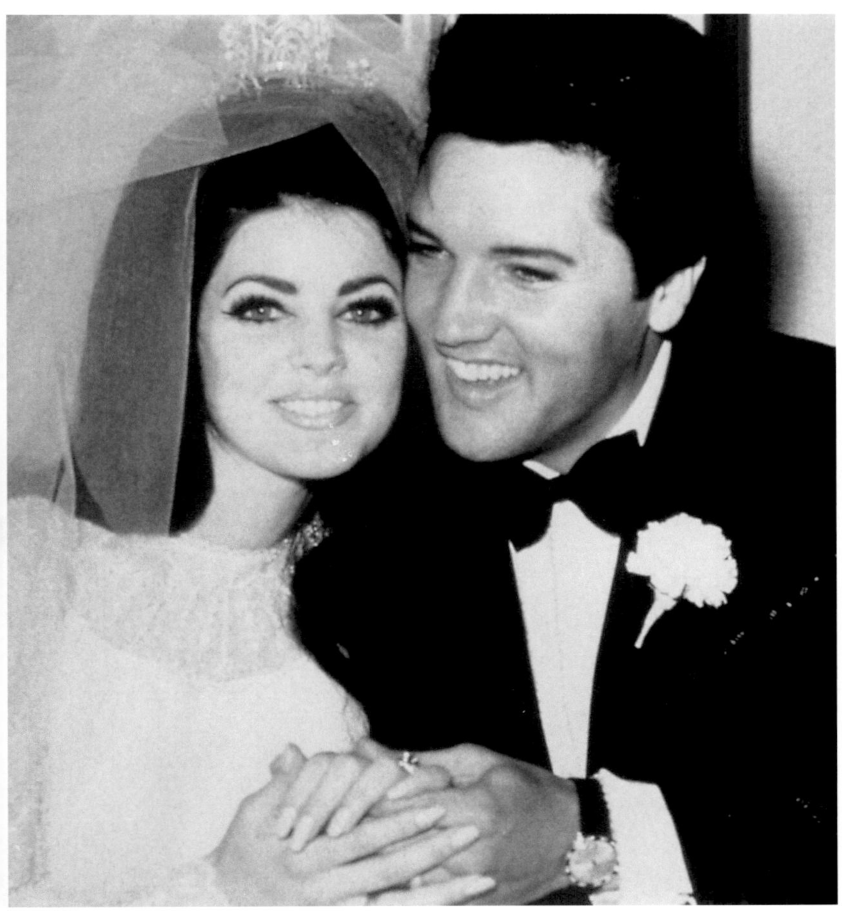

1967 **RECEPTION** The wedding rites were followed by a brief press conference that the Colonel had arranged. There was a lavish reception in the hotel, attended by about 100 people. They included family, many of the Memphis entourage, their wives and at least one celebrity, comedian Redd Foxx. The buffet banquet at the reception was said to have cost over $10,000. The guests enjoyed salmon, oysters, and champagne, as well as more traditional Southern fare.

1967

➔ **1967 WEDDING CAKE** The bride and groom sample the wedding cake at the reception. They then spent two days in Palm Springs, California, at the house that Elvis had leased at 1350 Ladera Circle. A quick visit to Memphis was followed by a more extended vacation at their Circle G ranch in Mississippi, though it could hardly be called a honeymoon as all the Memphis guys also went along.

Jo Ann Castle: "How the Lennon Sisters made me get married..."

Tommy Smothers explains: "Why I stay away from my own son..."

PHOTOPLAY

MAY 50¢

MINUTE BY MINUTE...

the birth of Lisa Marie Presley

EDDIE HUMILIATES POOR CONNIE!

✓His shocking ideas against getting married

✓More about the wedding nobody witnessed

✓Why Eddie's servants call Connie Miss Stevens

✓Did Sinatra punch Eddie in the mouth?

1968 LISA MARIE On February 1, 1968, just after 5.00 AM, Priscilla Presley gave birth to a baby girl, Lisa Marie, at the Baptist Hospital in Memphis. Their departure four days later was an unprecedented event for the hospital. While student nurses and fans crowded outside, the staff and patients waved from the windows as the Presleys were whisked away by car. Over the next few months an avid press worldwide followed the progress of the baby and her proud parents. Elvis, once a symbol of rebellious youth, was now truly the family man.

1968 HAWAII Elvis and Priscilla on the beach (*above*), and in the water (*right*), while relaxing in Hawaii in May 1968. Elvis enjoyed the sea and sunshine of both the Hawaiian islands and California, and by the end of the 1960s he had rented or purchased a string of properties on the West Coast. These included a house designed by Frank Lloyd Wright (the former home of the actress Rita Hayworth) in Bel Air, two more homes in Bel Air, and two locations in the Los Angeles suburbs.

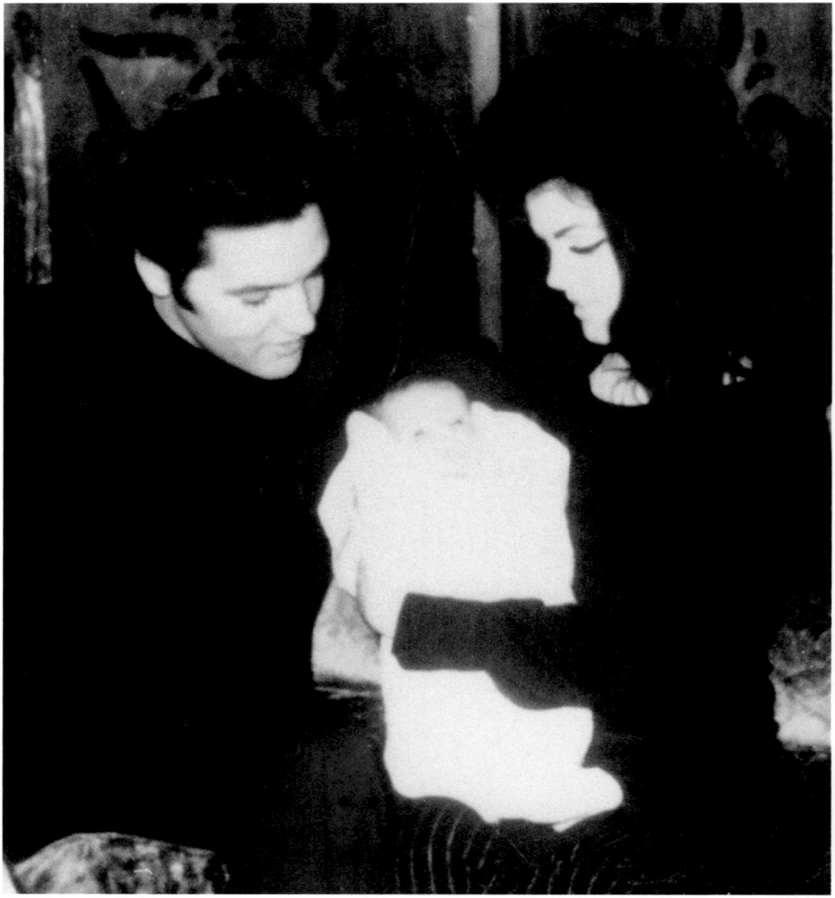

1968 MEMPHIS Father and mother with the newborn Lisa Marie. It was still a convention in the 1960s for pop stars with a large following of the opposite sex to avoid marriage. But by the time Elvis finally got married, it was in the context of the "family entertainer" image that the Colonel had fostered over the years. So when he became a father, it fitted perfectly with his "mature" persona as a regular family man. And, of course, for the media it was another stage in the Presley saga.

1969 GRACELAND Elvis and Priscilla play with one-year-old Lisa Marie at Graceland. It was the time of the comeback in Elvis' career as a live performer, and also a period when the strain was starting to show in the marriage.

1970 **FAMILY PICTURES** Lisa Marie not long before her third birthday, in more family pictures, taken at one of their homes in California. When photographs like these (*above* and *following pages*) were released, the Presleys' obvious delight in their daughter was shared by Elvis' legions of fans worldwide. During the 1970s Elvis would name his private jet (which now stands across the highway from Graceland) the *Lisa Marie* after his daughter, who was to be his only child and heir to his estate.

1970

1970 ROYALTY To the outside world, not yet aware of the difficulties besetting their marriage, Elvis and Priscilla were the royal couple of show business. She was a natural beauty, later to succeed as both a model and actress. Elvis was reemerging from what many considered his Hollywood exile to establish himself once again as the undisputed King of Rock'n'Roll.

1970 **CLOSE-UP** A close-up shot of Mr. and Mrs. Presley. The couple spent as much time as possible together, given the responsibilities of parenthood and Elvis' career. In 1969 they even planned a trip to Europe. However, the Colonel dissuaded them on the grounds that it would be bad for Elvis' image to be seen visiting the Continent as a tourist rather than in a professional capacity. In the event, Elvis Presley never did get to perform live in front of his millions of loyal European fans.

1971 "JAYCEE" AWARD A prayer breakfast preceding the "Jaycee" Award for the nation's Ten Outstanding Men of the Year for 1970, selected by the Junior Chamber of Commerce—on this occasion presented in Memphis in January, 1971.

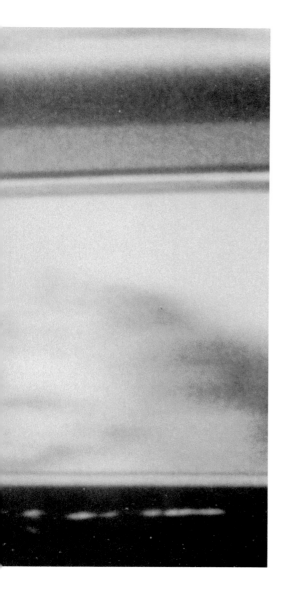

1967

1967 PRIVACY Elvis in a car, somewhere, 1967. The privacy that most of us take for granted was not to be enjoyed by Elvis very often. Even in the chauffeured security of the back seat of a limousine, passersby would rubberneck, the cameras would intrude, and the curious gawp. That was the price of ultimate fame, and he paid dearly. There is a picture that could be constructed which describes his fame, his absolute celebrity, purely from the myriad candid camera shots of him getting in and out of cars, traveling in cars, sometimes in the back, sometimes driving up front.

1964

1964 ESCAPE By 1964, the touring was over for a while. It should have been easier to escape for a while but it would never happen. There were the furtive excursions to favored hamburger joints in the middle of the Memphis night, and rented movie theaters for private showings of the latest releases. Entire amusement parks were reserved for his pleasure, and stores opened specially so he could browse uninterrupted, like anyone else. But he was Elvis, he simply wasn't like anyone else.

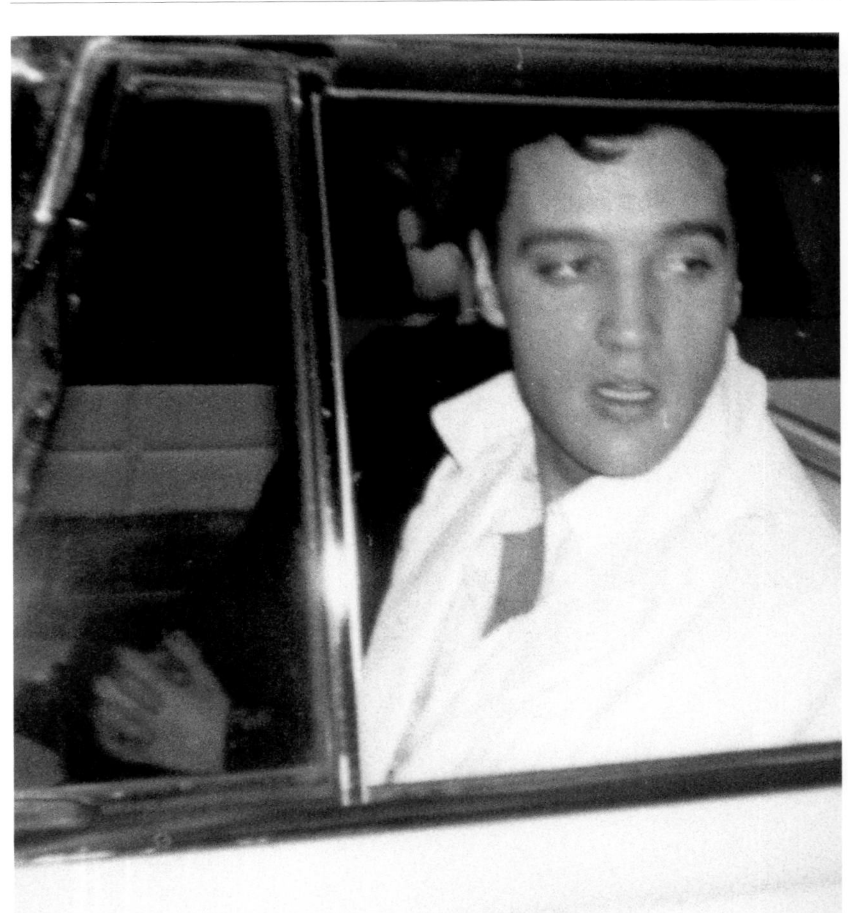

1968 GRACELAND The mansion on the hill overlooking Highway 51 was his sanctuary, the one place where he could rely on being alone, or not alone, as he wished. But he only had to venture out of the gates (*below*) and the world outside was waiting for his every appearance. As his car halted at the bottom of the driveway, there would be the inevitable tap on the window, the smiling face, that he couldn't—and certainly wouldn't—ignore. He was the star, and these were his public.

1968

X When Elvis
eback to live
a return to an
tyle. From here
d be more hectic
s.

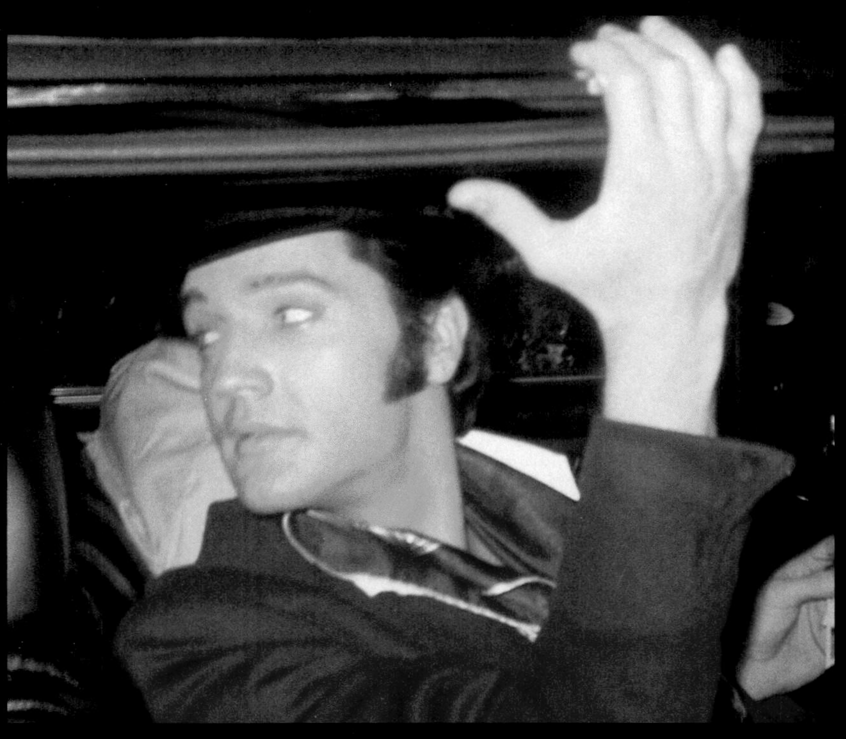

↑ **1969 MEMPHIS** Before he embarked on live recordings from his new performance base of Las Vegas, Elvis was working on his first significant studio recordings in years. He used American Studios in Memphis, and session players that included the Memphis Horns. Elvis created a fresh sound in February 1969 that ended up as the album *From Elvis In Memphis*, recognized to be as much of a comeback as his recent TV show. *Above*, Elvis leaves American Studios.

1969

1967

1967 HORSES The early months of 1967 saw Elvis indulging in another of his favorite pastimes, horse riding. Between Christmas 1966 and the end of February 1967, he purchased no fewer than 25 horses, making room for them at Graceland. In the early months of that year he took on a totally "western" persona, even turning up to a recording session in cowboy attire, complete with chaps! In the picture above, Elvis is seen riding at Graceland on his favorite horse, a golden palomino called Rising Sun, which he had bought in January 1967. The stable had written on its front door "The House of the Rising Sun" (like the song) and when the horse died he was buried in the pasture outside, facing the rising sun.

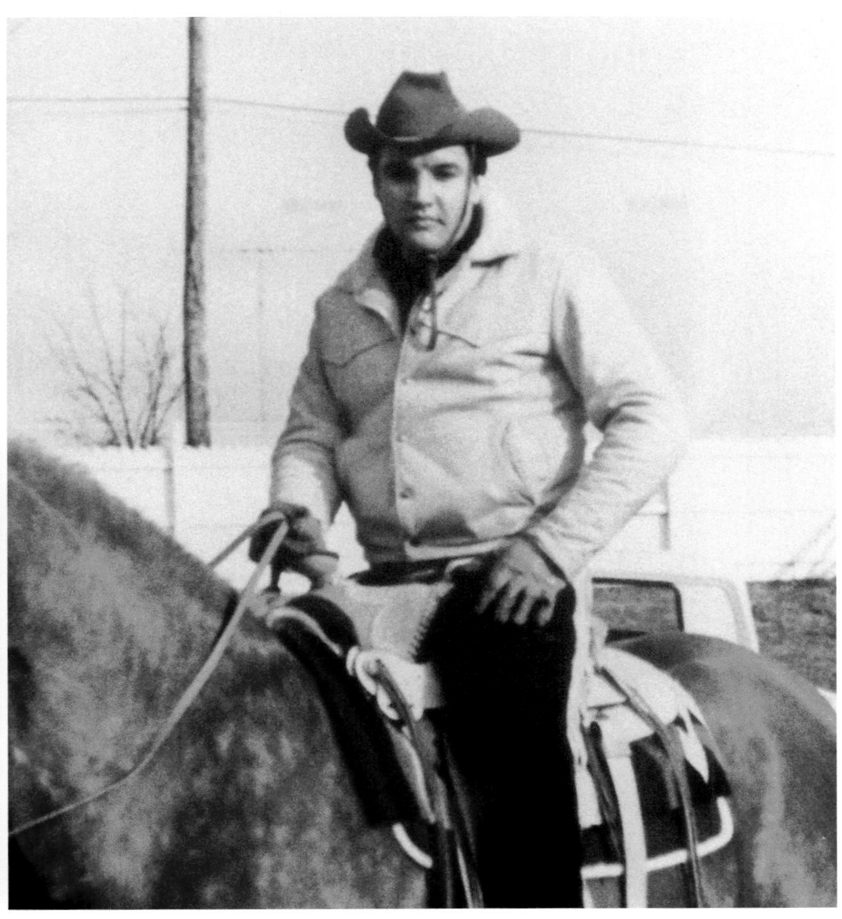

1967 CIRCLE G RANCH During this period Elvis bought what was later to become known as the Flying Circle G ranch–the G standing for Graceland–primarily in order to accommodate his growing herd of four-legged friends. The ranch rapidly became a new playground for him and his (two-legged) friends, and for a time it threatened to become a serious distraction from his professional work. He eventually, and reluctantly, sold the ranch two years later in May 1969.

1967

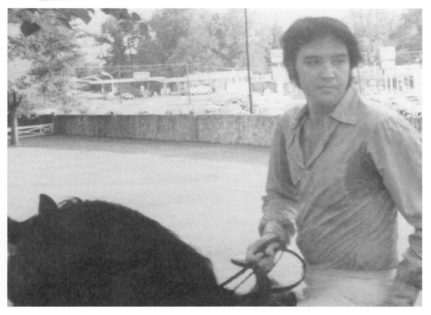

⊖ ⊕ 1969–70 **HORSES** Elvis riding in the grounds at Graceland. Elvis bought Priscilla a quarterhorse for Christmas 1966, which they named Domino. In the picture *left* Elvis is riding Rising Sun, and *above* another favorite, Bear. In the stables at Graceland, Elvis personally supervised where everybody's tack and gear would be hanging in the barn. It is his writing that is still to be seen in the back "tack room," indicating whose riding equipment was to be hung where.

⊕ 1970 **CHRISTMAS CARD** A handmade Christmas card to Elvis with a photo taken outside Elvis' Hillcrest home in California. Christmas was a favorite time of year for Elvis, and Graceland was decorated in spectacular fashion.

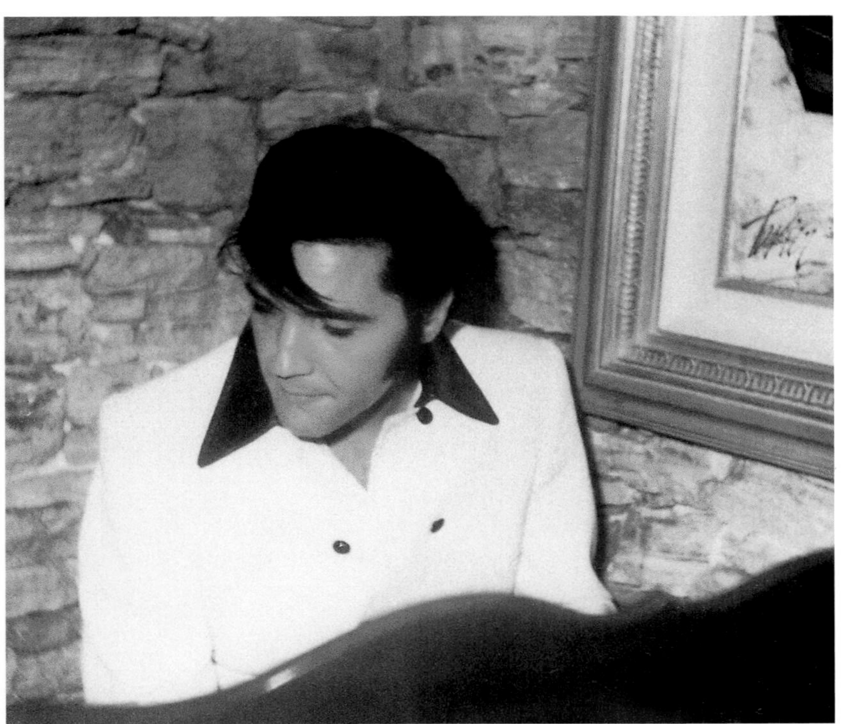

1969 HILLCREST Elvis outside his Hillcrest house in California, wearing the suit in which he performed "If I Can Dream" during the 1968 TV special. The month-long run at the Showroom of the International Hotel grossed in excess of $1,500,000.

1969 RELAXING Elvis is not thought of as a pianist, yet one of his favorite forms of relaxation was to play the piano. Many anecdotes of Elvis backstage involve him "jamming" at the piano with other artists. Similarly, people remember private parties when he would find the nearest keyboard and just play along. And of course there was the "Million Dollar Quartet" session in 1956, in which he accompanied Jerry Lee Lewis, Carl Perkins, and Johnny Cash in an impromptu musical get-together.

1974

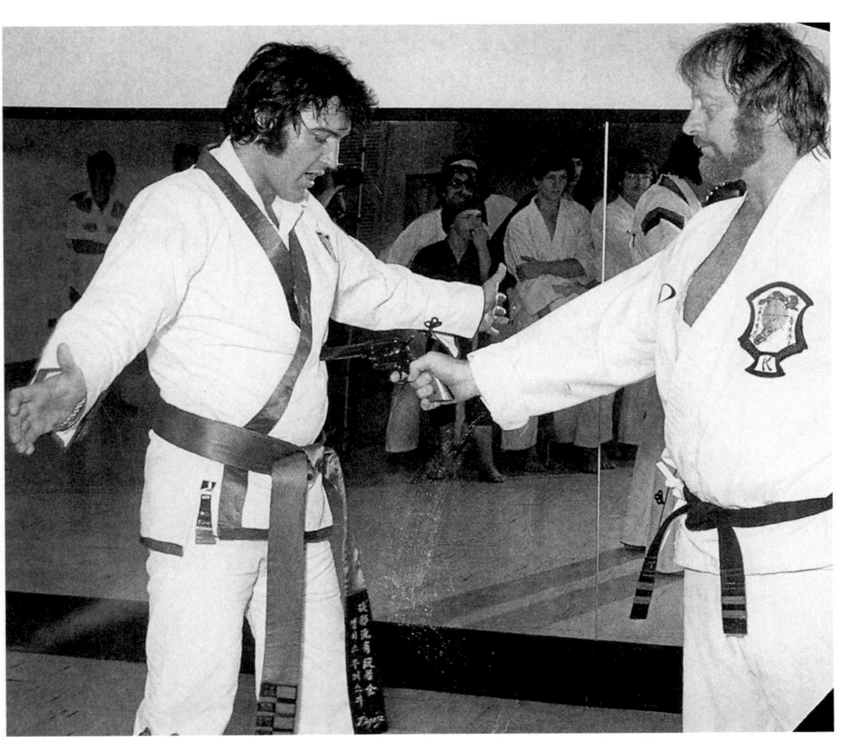

⊖ ⊕ 1974 **FAVORITE HOBBY** By the 1970s, Elvis was even more involved with his favorite hobby of karate, using a lot of the poses in his flamboyant stage act. Here (*left*) he strikes a characteristic pose, while (*above*) Red West points a pistol at him in a mock fight. Elvis received his black belt in 1960 and went on to get an eighth degree–making him a "master of the art." He used the skill for fight sequences in some of his movies, including *GI Blues*, *Blue Hawaii*, and *Kid Galahad*.

1974

1976

← **1974 LINDA THOMPSON** Crowned Miss Memphis State and then Miss Tennessee in 1972, Linda Thompson was 22 when she started dating Elvis in July of that year, not long after his separation from Priscilla was formalized. By the time this romantic vignette was taken, the couple were involved in a regular relationship. Linda accompanied Elvis on most of his concert dates and moved into Graceland. She became what the guys in the entourage called themselves–a "lifer."

↑ **1976 ELVIS AND LINDA** Linda and Elvis boarding his private jet, the *Lisa Marie*. By 1976 his health was becoming more of a problem. Linda was seen by all as providing great support and security during a period of real crisis in Elvis' life and career.

1970

1970 CALIFORNIA Elvis takes in the sun in the grounds of one of of his California homes. Much of the visual record of Elvis, his family, and close friends at leisure, has survived either from personal snapshots, home movies, or "paparazzi"-style photos. The latter in most cases were not taken by an intrusive media trying to grab an exclusive picture of Elvis' private life, but more often by well-meaning fans who were lucky enough to grab a "personal" picture of their idol. Elvis appreciated this, and over the years treasured hundreds of such shots which fans sent to him at Graceland.

TV & Vegas

THE COMEBACK

[1968–1969]

1968 NBC SPECIAL Elvis in a big production number on the comeback TV special; the historic program was taped before a live audience on June 27 and 29, 1968, at NBC Studio 4 in Burbank, California, and broadcast across America on December 3.

June 1968 *August 1969* *June 1968*

1968–69

Just when the world thought Elvis was consigned to only appearing in front of the movie cameras, he made a sensational comeback to live performance in December of 1968. It took the form of an NBC TV spectacular that would be seen worldwide, in which he reestablished himself as a classic rock'n'roll singer, a stereotype that he himself had created a decade and a half earlier.

The original plan—at least as far as the Colonel was concerned—was to make it a Christmas special, typical of the ones seen on television during that period. But the show's director, a TV whizz-kid called Steve Binder, who at the age of 23 had already produced the top rock TV show *Hullabaloo*, had other ideas. Binder wanted a show that would reveal to the audience the various sides to Elvis' music in a loosely biographical way; he envisaged including a rock'n'roll section, a gospel section, a big production number, and so on.

Months of preparation included, in June, the taping of various segments of music, starting with the big "Guitar Man" production number and the show-closer "If I Can Dream" that featured a backing outfit of the very best studio session musicians. But it was the rock'n'roll era of the Fifties that was

June 1968 *August 1969* *August 1969* *August 1969*

acknowledged most potently. Dressed in black leather, Elvis went through his great rock hits of the period with his old buddies (including Scotty Moore on guitar and D. J. Fontana on drums, the two surviving members of the original touring quartet), in an "informal" session surrounded by a live audience, Elvis and the boys performing "in the round."

The show, when broadcast across America on December 3, confirmed him once more as a live (albeit in a recorded program) performer without equal.

He even made it to the front cover of *Rolling Stone*, which in the late Sixties was considered the mouthpiece of the new "alternative" youth culture. This wasn't as surprising as it might seem; the movement the magazine represented identified strongly with rock, and after the TV special Elvis was again recognized as being a prime force in that musical constituency.

And never one to let the grass grow under his charge's feet, the Colonel followed the public (and critical) acclaim for the TV Special—which was simply entitled *Elvis*—with a series of live dates in Las Vegas that created a template for much of Elvis' live performances for the remainder of his career.

More women
age 18 to 49
watched
his TV special
than any other
in '68
According to Advertising Age, Network
TV Program Popularity Poll,
January 13, 1969.
See "SINGER presents ELVIS"
Sunday Night, August 17th,
on NBC-TV in Color!
Hear Elvis Presley exclusively on RCA Records.
What's new for tomorrow is at SINGER today!*
*A Trademark of THE SINGER COMPANY

1969 SINGER "Singer Presents Elvis" was the highest-rated TV program in America for the week it was broadcast. The prepublicity for the repeat, shown on August 17, 1969, focused on female viewers to connect with the sponsor's target market.

1968 GOSPEL Rehearsals for the show took place in June. In some of the numbers, as in the gospel segment (*above*), Elvis lip-synched to prerecorded tracks, while in the "jam session" segment everything was recorded "as live" in front of an audience.

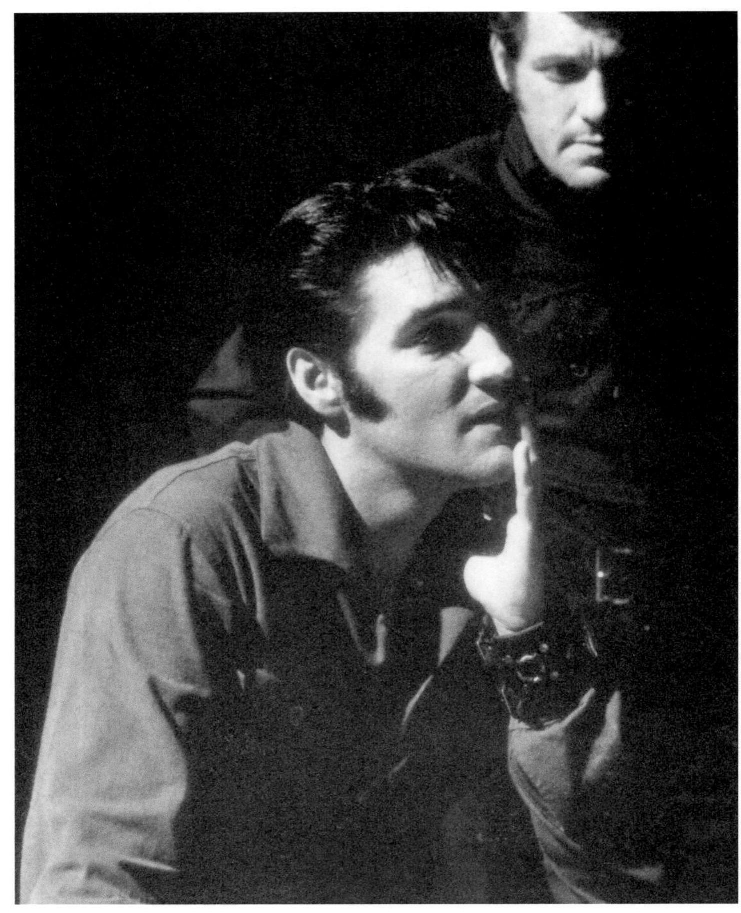

1968

1968 **INFORMAL SET** Elvis discusses the "informal" segment of the show with ex-Army buddy Charlie Hodge (*above*). Charlie played guitar on the set, along with Scotty Moore and D. J. Fontana. Also involved in the "jam" were "Memphis Mafia" road manager Alan Fortas, tapping the back of a guitar case, and Lance LeGault, who had doubled for Elvis in many of his movies, playing tambourine. It was this set that delighted fans and critics more than any other part of the show.

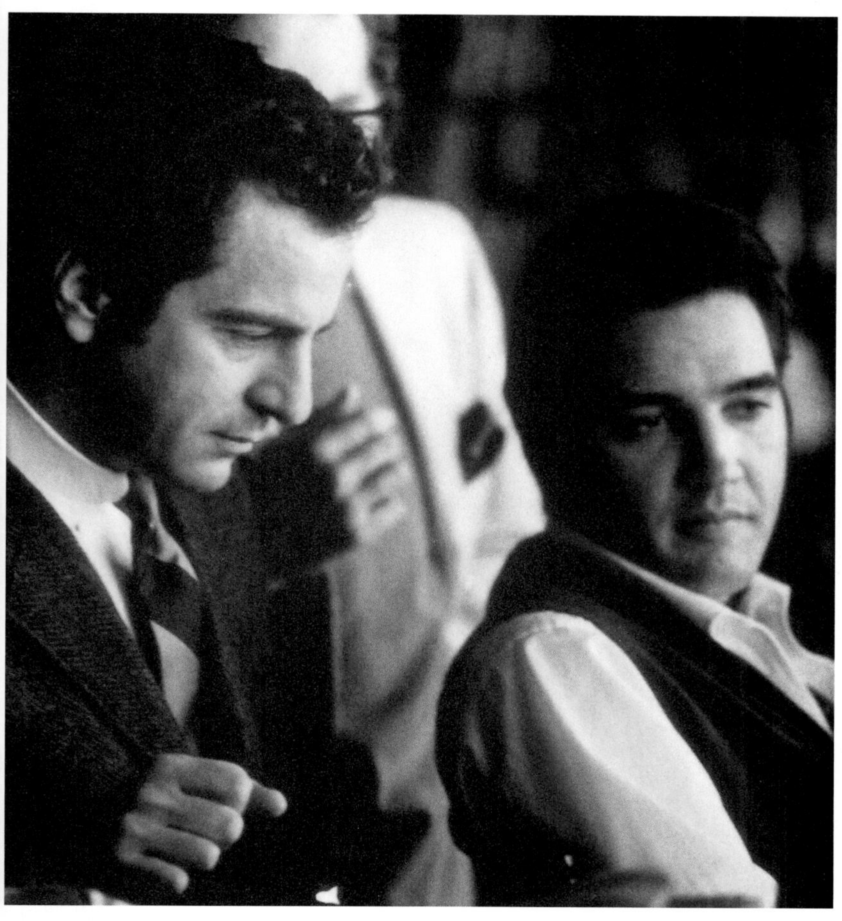

1968 BOB FINKEL Rehearsals were supervised by director Steve Binder and NBC executive producer Bob Finkel (seen *above* with Elvis). It was Binder who persuaded Elvis to make a program that featured all aspects of his music.

1968

1968 TV STUDIOS The days leading up to the actual recording of the TV special included a press conference in which Elvis and the Colonel came over as a skilled double act. Elvis informed the press he would be "singing the songs I'm known for" to which the Colonel commented, "If he sang the songs he's known for, that would take a couple of hours." Asked whether his audience had changed much, Elvis observed, "Well, they don't move as fast as they used to."

1968

1968

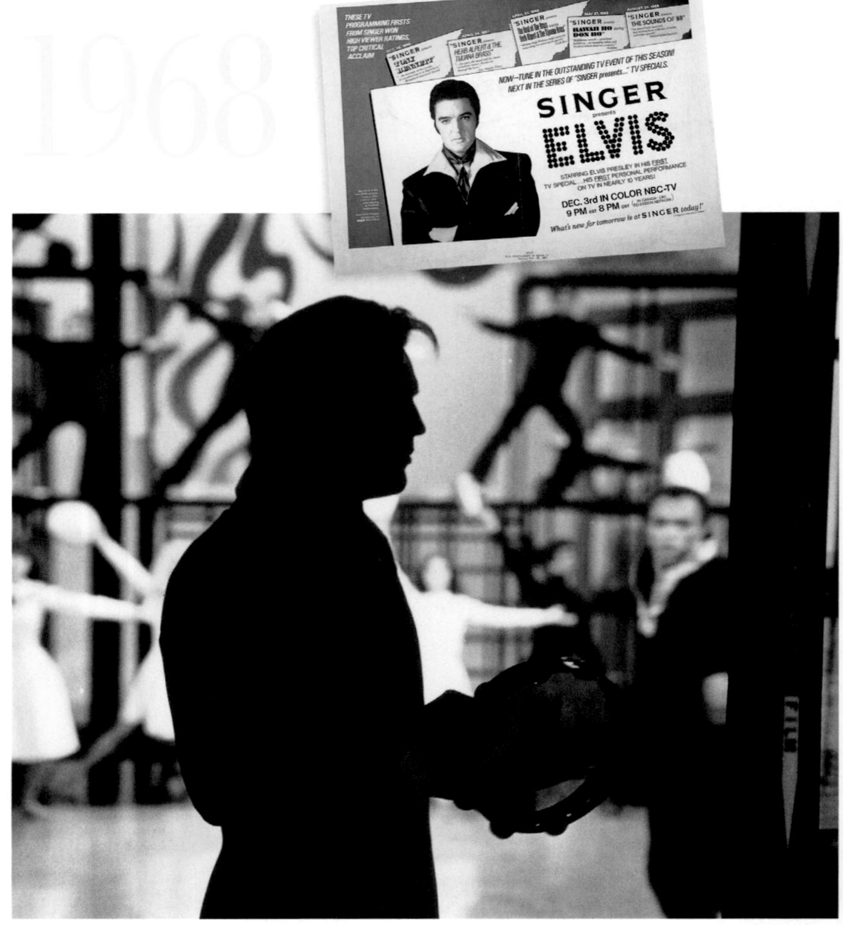

1968 SESSION Taping the big gospel production number for the TV special, in which Elvis is backed by a band of top session players including Tommy Tedesco and Al Casey on guitars, Larry Knechtal on keyboards, and Hal Blaine on drums. He also had a backup vocal group, the Blossoms, and a full orchestra. He was accompanied by male and female dancers too. The show's director, Steve Binder, was quoted as saying: "This show is a matter of video history significance . . ."

1968

➔ **1968 "STAND UP"** Throughout the show, with various changes of set and costume, Elvis had the studio audience—and millions at home—in the palm of his hand. But the highlight was undoubtedly the second section, when, clad in black leather, he ran through his old rock'n'roll classics with long-time colleagues Scotty Moore, Charlie Hodge, and D. J. Fontana. This has come to be referred to as the "sit down" show, and was recorded on June 27, followed by a "stand up" segment (*right*) on June 29, in which he also ran though his hits in a live environment, in the same "boxing ring" arena with the audience all around, but this time backed by the full studio band, orchestra, and vocal group.

ROLLING STONE

ACME No. 37 JULY 12, 1969 UK: 2/6 35 CENTS

ELVIS IN HOLLYWOOD

TOWNSHEND ON TOMMY

BEATLES NEW LP

1968 "STAND-UP" In the "stand up" show, Elvis went though a selection of his greatest hits including "Heartbreak Hotel," "Hound Dog," "All Shook Up," "Jailhouse Rock," and "Blue Suede Shoes." A still from the show was used on a 1969 cover of counterculture magazine, *Rolling Stone.* Although youth culture had moved a long way from the mainstream that Elvis seemed to represent in most of his movies, rock music was at its center. This showed that Elvis was back as a potent force.

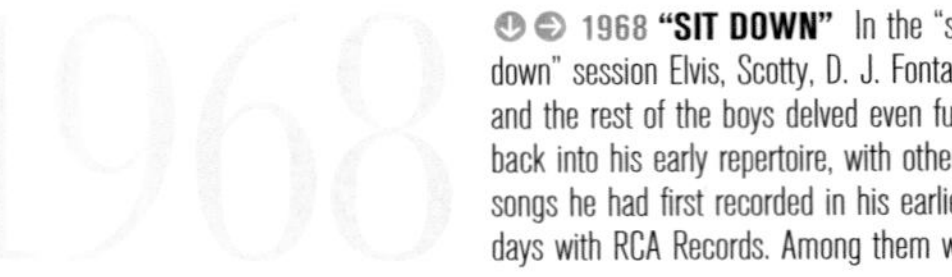

1968 "SIT DOWN" In the "sit down" session Elvis, Scotty, D. J. Fontana, and the rest of the boys delved even further back into his early repertoire, with other songs he had first recorded in his earliest days with RCA Records. Among them were "Lawdy Miss Clawdy," "Trying To Get To You," and "When My Blue Moon Turns to Gold Again." He began the first of the two evening sessions with the very first title he had released on the Sun label back in July 1954, "That's All Right."

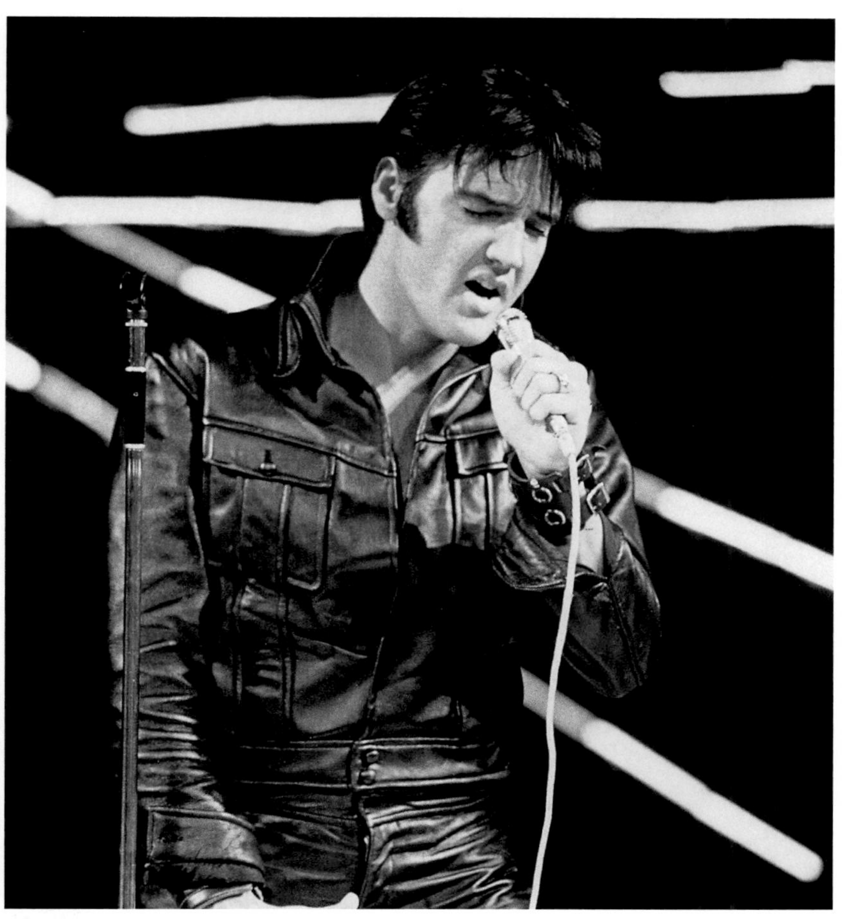

1968 BLACK LEATHER All Elvis' outfits (*see also overleaf*) on the program were made for him by the show's costume designer, Bill Belew. That included the black leather suit for the "informal" sessions. Elvis was sweating so much after the first "sit down" set that Belew had to get the leathers cleaned and pressed before he went on again an hour later. Wearing black leather for these most intimate segments of the show was a shrewd move; it was a look that personified rebellious youth.

1968

1968

1968 **FINALE** The show concluded with one of the most spectacular and enduring images of Elvis, with a white suit and red scarf standing in front of the vast ELVIS in red lights, which has become part of Presley iconography. The final song in the special was "If I Can Dream," after which he raised his arms in triumph, and bade his audience, through the lens of the TV camera, a simple "Thank you, good night."

←↑ **1968 IF I CAN DREAM** Despite Colonel Parker's insistence that there should be at least one Christmas number in the show, the proposed notion to end on a seasonal note was rejected by Steve Binder. He favored something that reflected the feeling of optimism that he wanted to run through the whole program. The show's vocal arranger, Earl Brown, came up with "If I Can Dream" (*see also overleaf*). Binder and Elvis loved it, and the song was in as the closer.

1968

1968

1968 **BREAKTHROUGH** The biggest influence of the show was on the public perception of Elvis as a performer of hit popular music. After "Return To Sender" in 1962, the subsequent movie-dominated years had only yielded a few really big chart singles. The TV show, despite all its showbiz trappings of long-legged dancing girls and fight sequences, represented a tangible breakthrough for Elvis' credibility. He was seen by the world to be able to cut it on stage as dynamically as ever.

1969 CHANGES Elvis during the time of his Las Vegas comeback at the end of July 1969. Months before this live debut, he had told a UPI journalist that he was considering a return to live concerts: "I'm planning a lot of changes. You can't go on doing the same thing year after year . . . Before long I'm going to make some personal appearance tours. I'll probably start out here in this country and after that play some concerts abroad . . . I miss the personal contact with audiences . . . "

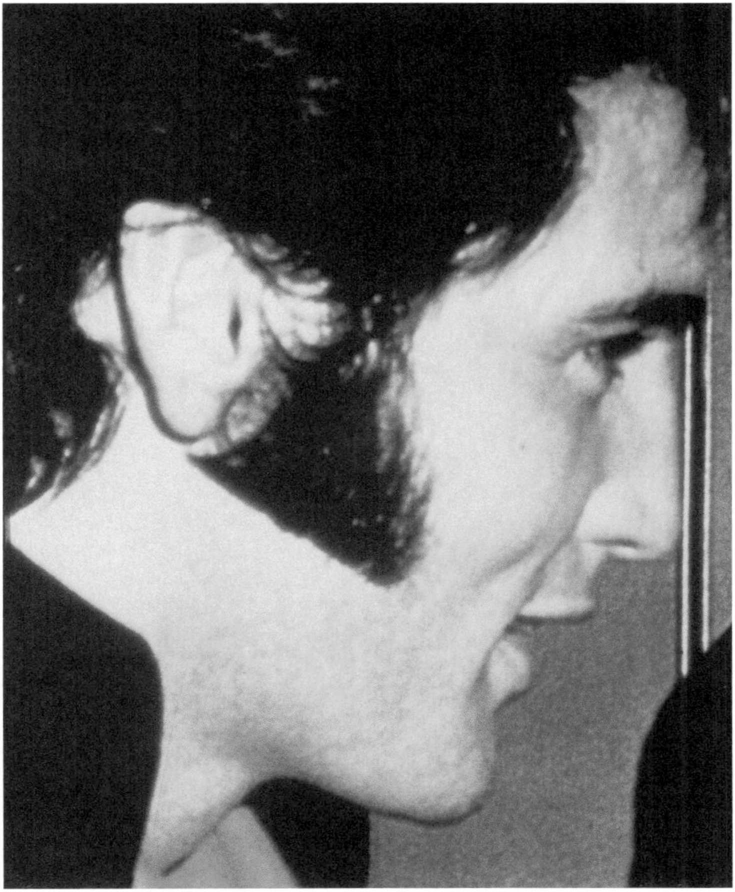

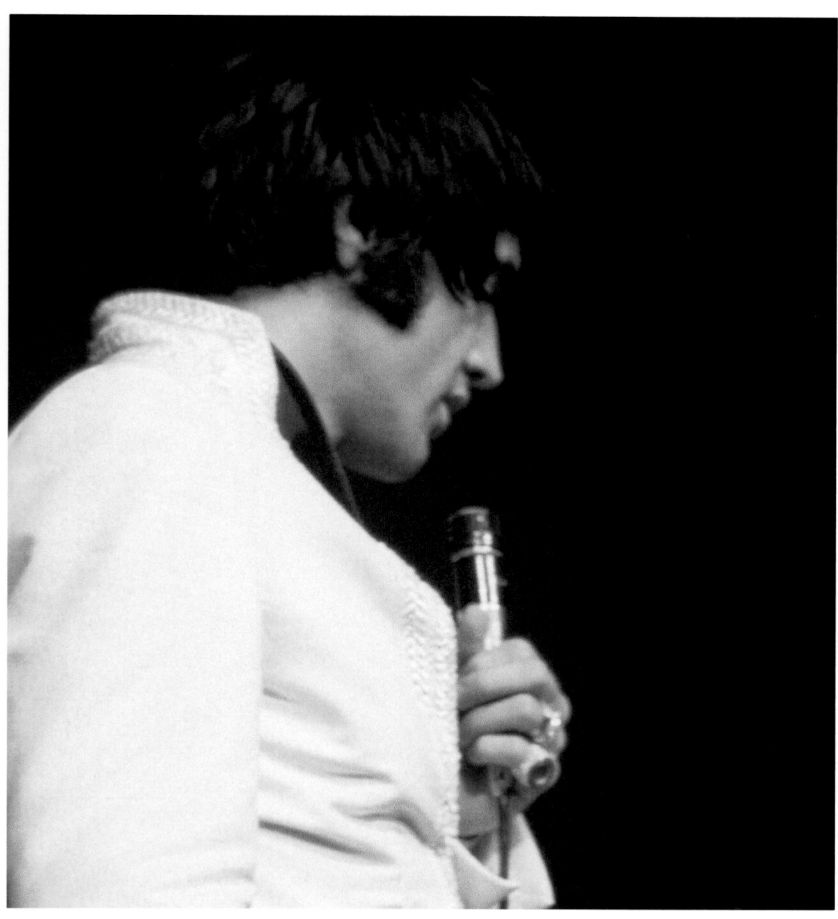

1969 LAS VEGAS The immediate impact of the TV special was clear from the offers of work that started flooding in. One was a proposal for Elvis to play the London Palladium, offering $28,000 for the week. The Colonel replied, "That's fine for me, now how much can you get for Elvis?" The offer that did bear fruit was four weeks of shows at the new International Hotel in Las Vegas, commencing July 31. He was to play two shows a night, for a reported $100,000 a week, and this was to represent the second phase of his comeback, this time in live concerts. The invite-only opening night saw Elvis perform in front of a star-studded crowd, plus a huge press contingent, which the Colonel had flown in on the hotel owner's private jet.

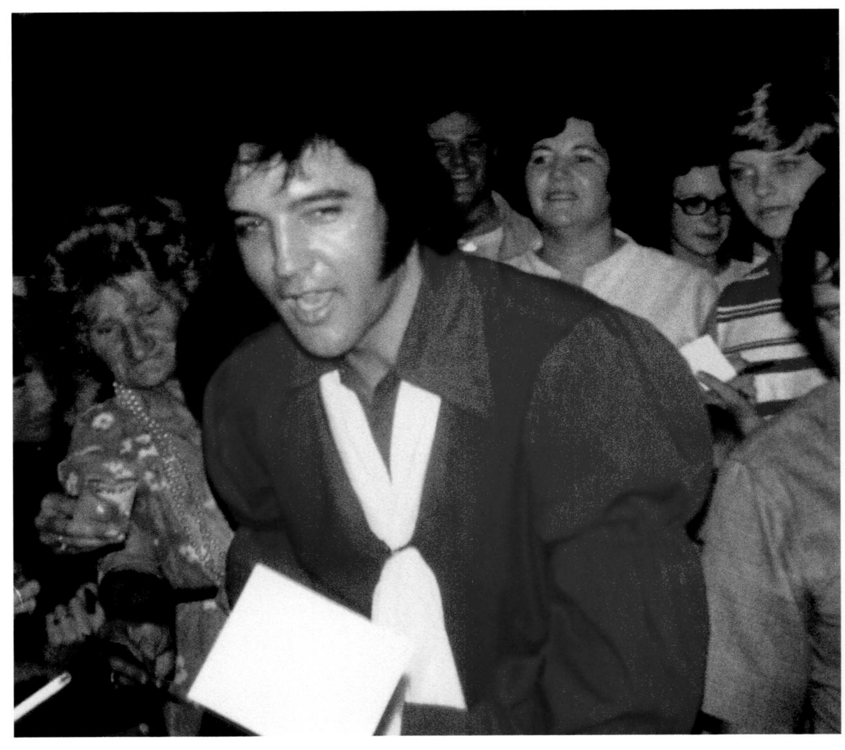

1969

1969 FANS, GRACELAND During the period leading up to his comeback appearances in Las Vegas, Elvis was increasingly in the habit of walking down to the gates at Graceland to sign autographs, talk, and even sing to the fans there.

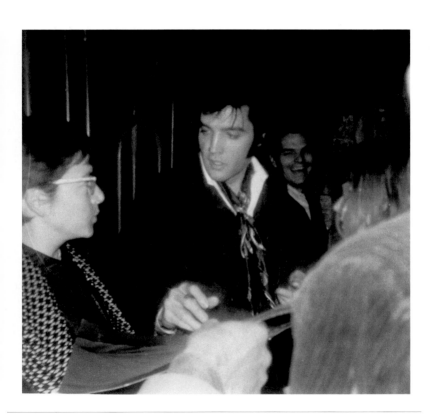

1969 **FANS, LOS ANGELES** Elvis meets with some fans who are gathered outside his West Coast home at 1174 Hillcrest Road, in the exclusive Trousdale section of Beverly Hills, Los Angeles. Elvis and Priscilla bought the three-bedroom, multi-level house in November 1967. The elegant home, which was just one of seven properties that Elvis rented or purchased in California over the years, was built in 1961 in the French Regency style, and included an Olympic-size swimming pool.

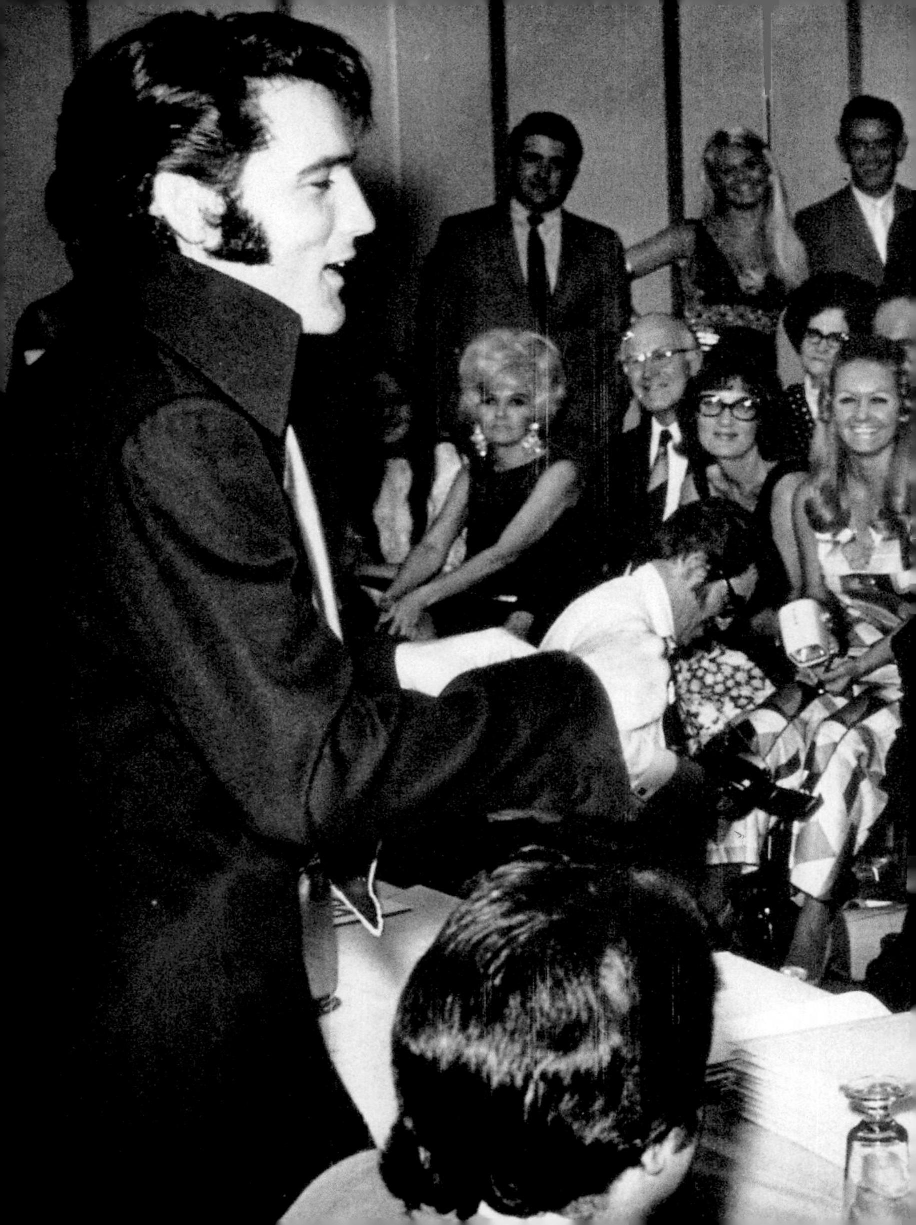

1969 PRESS CONFERENCE The morning after his opening night Elvis staged a press conference (*left*). The press reaction to his comeback was favorable. It augered well for future seasons in the Nevada city (*above*).

1969 THE FANS The reaction of the female members of the Las Vegas audience got wilder as the season progressed. They started throwing underwear at the stage, no doubt encouraged by Elvis who, leaning over to the front row, would kiss a fan here, touch a hand there, and after a few shows—noted by the ever-present press of course—his pants split for the first time. The crowds at the 1969 comeback season were redolent of the demonstrative fans he encountered during his touring concerts in the Fifties, screaming at his every gesture (*see also overleaf*), physically moved by his music. When he reached out to them, they stretched forward to touch him, hung on every lyric he sang. They moved with him, as one.

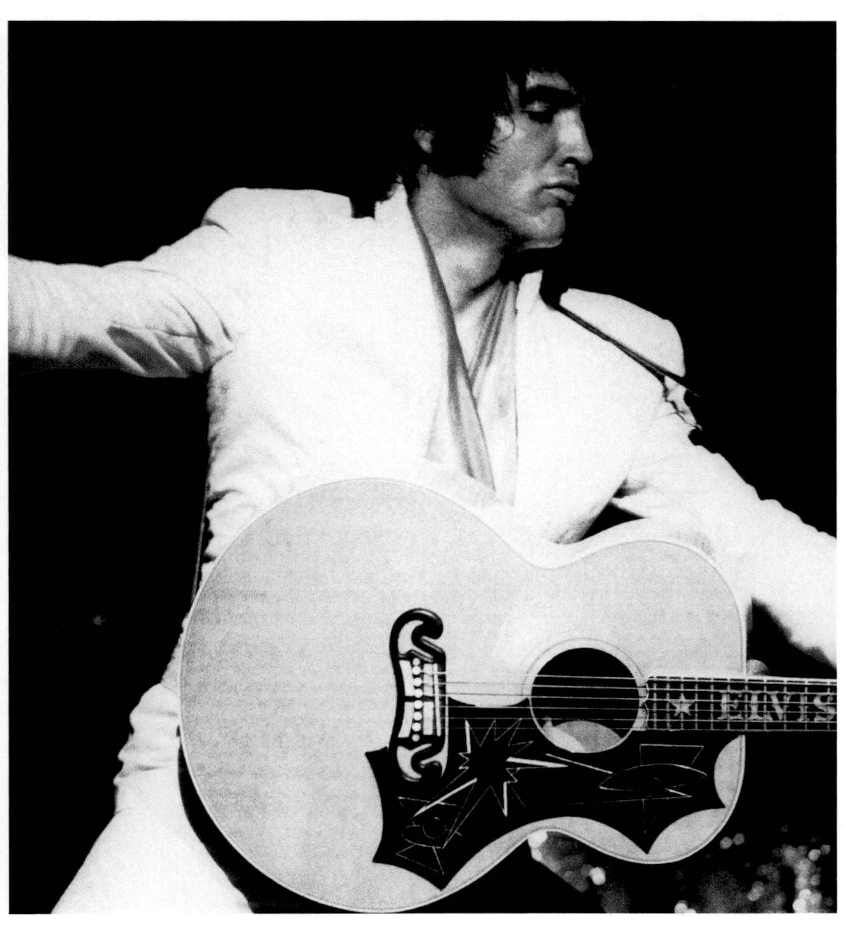

1969 **GUITAR MAN** For the International season Elvis was backed by the great James Burton on guitar, Jerry Scheff on bass guitar, Larry Muhoberac on piano, John Wilkinson on rhythm guitar, and Ronnie Tutt on drums.

1969

1969 THE MUSIC The core of the set for the opening Las Vegas shows (*see also previous pages*) consisted of: "Blue Suede Shoes," "I Got A Woman," "Love Me Tender," "Jailhouse Rock," "Don't Be Cruel," "Heartbreak Hotel," "All Shook Up," "Hound Dog," "Memories," "In The Ghetto," "Yesterday," "Hey Jude," "One Night," "Johnny B. Goode," and "Suspicious Minds." The selection relied on his own vast back catalog, and included songs made famous by Chuck Berry and the Beatles.

1969

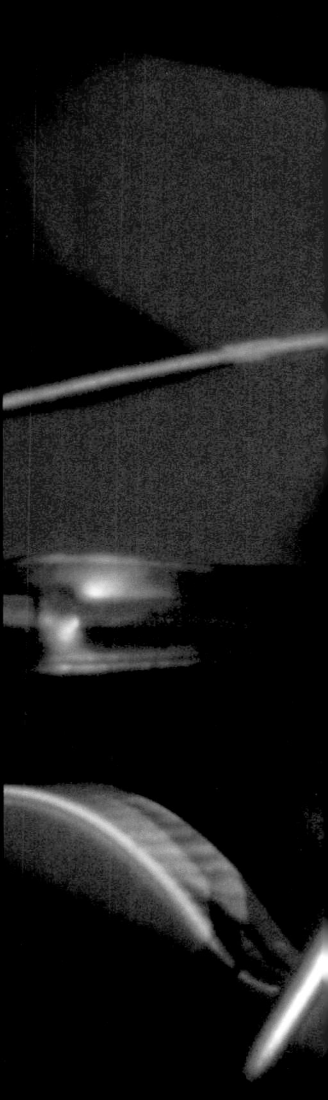

➔ **1969 RENAISSANCE** The comeback period of the late Sixties (*see also previous pages*) represented a true renaissance for Elvis, not just some nostalgia-driven retrospective but a true revival of his art in fresh terms. This was no live version of a "greatest hits" package, carbon-copied classics rolled out for the faithful fans—and that would have been easy, for there were certainly millions of them. This was an Elvis for a new decade, freed from what had become the artistic straitjacket of his movies. His ambitions to act were frustrated by plots usually constrained by the commercial demands of making "musical" films, while his musical horizons in the films were limited to these same often sterile scenarios. Hollywood had served its purpose, but it was time to move on. And with the TV special of 1968 and the Las Vegas season in 1969, Elvis had signaled in no uncertain terms that he had made that move.

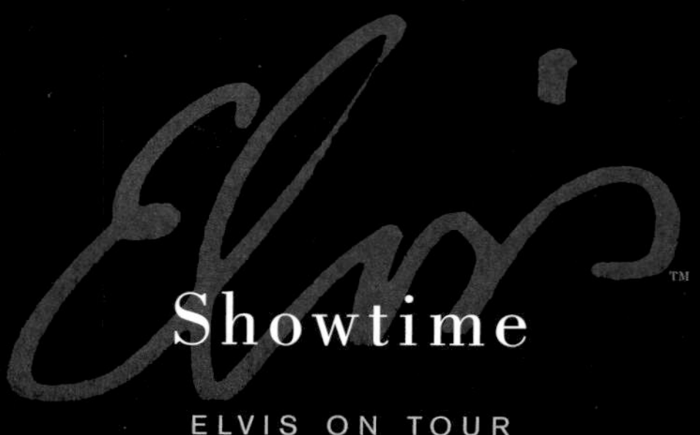

Showtime

ELVIS ON TOUR

[1970–1977]

1972 ON STAGE Following the "comeback" TV show and live dates at the close of the Sixties, the rest of Elvis' career was characterized by his spectacular stage act.

July 1970 *September 1970* *Spring 1972*

Once he had made his comeback, there was no going back for Elvis. The Seventies opened with him in the center of the action again as far as live appearances were concerned, with a new image rather than the slightly retro-Elvis that was a feature of the TV special. Honed to what quickly became a new Elvis look, the Elvis of the Seventies was indeed regarded by some as a parody of himself by the middle of the decade. But as the jumpsuits became more rhinestone-encrusted and the capes more flamboyant, it was his own self-created image that he was building on. It was not modified or copied from elsewhere: this was Elvis, and no-one else.

And, like his voice, no matter how the look was parodied, satirized, or imitated, it could never be duplicated. All the impersonators in the world can't come near to reproducing the way he moved, the way he used the clothes, the way he occupied the stage—and the way he was at one with the audience.

Elvis had become an icon once again, not in some "Fifties revivalist" mode, harking back to a past era he had indeed helped to define, but a true icon for the times. As with his stage shows, every aspect of Elvis' working life in the

Summer 1971 *Summer 1975* *August 1977*

Seventies was spectacular. While the touring became more grueling, and took its toll, media-driven events, including the "Aloha" satellite link-up and two major movie documentaries, took the stage show to fans around the world.

And as he became, once more, a pillar of the showbusiness establishment, so he received more and more accolades from the social establishment. An award as one of the Ten Outstanding Young Men of 1970 was followed at the end of that year by his unprecedented meeting at the White House with President Richard Nixon; in the light of subsequent history, it's not hard to guess which of them is more fondly remembered.

But by the middle of the decade, it had become apparent that things were not as they should have been. Elvis often looked physically tired on stage, his performances were frequently sloppy, and they increasingly lacked the surefire dynamic that had been their trademark.

When his death on August 16, 1977 was announced, the world was shocked, but many who had observed his career over the previous few months were not truly surprised. The King was dead. Long live the King.

1970

1970 MGM STUDIOS In July 1970, MGM started filming what would become a major movie documentary of Elvis as a live performer. This included rehearsals, life on the road, and concert performances, as well as his showcase at the International Hotel in Las Vegas. The director was Denis Sanders, who had won two Academy Awards, and whose other credits included three well-remembered television series: *The Defenders*, *Route 66*, and *The Naked City*.

←→ 1970 MGM STUDIOS The rehearsal session musicians were the core of Elvis' onstage band. They included Ronnie Tutt on drums, Charlie Hodge on guitar, Glen D. Hardin (from Buddy Holly's Crickets) on piano, Jerry Scheff on bass (*opposite*, behind Elvis), John Wilkinson on rhythm guitar, and James Burton on lead guitar. Burton (*top*, behind Elvis) cut his teeth on Ricky Nelson's seminal records in the Fifties, and went on after his work with Elvis to feature on tracks by such artists as Emmylou Harris, John Denver, and Elvis Costello.

1970 **MGM STUDIOS** Although doubtless under the close scrutiny of both Elvis' record company, RCA, and of course the Colonel, Denis Sanders managed to produce a candid portrait of Elvis making live music. The 97-minute movie, the first of two produced in the Seventies that followed Elvis' working life "on the road," was released in November 1970 with the title *Elvis: That's The Way It Is*. It was originally to be simply called *Elvis*, which was the working title throughout the film's production.

1970 **MGM STUDIOS** The rehearsal sequences for the documentary were filmed on the MGM sound stage at Culver City studios on July 15 and 29. The songs covered included early favorites, among them *"Baby Let's Play House"* and *"That's All Right,"* rock'n'roll standards such as *"Johnny B. Goode,"* country classics like *"I Can't Stop Loving You,"* the Beatles' hits *"Yesterday"* and *"Hey Jude,"* and Elvis' own classic hits, ranging from *"Love Me Tender"* to *"Suspicious Minds"*–over 50 songs in all.

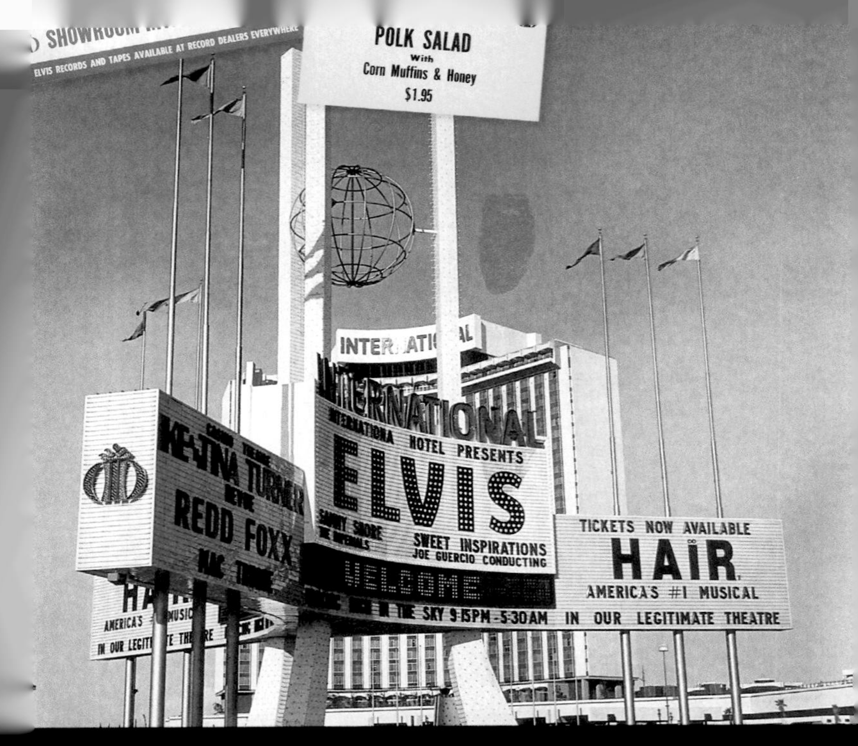

1970 LAS VEGAS At the end f February 1970, Elvis began a four-week eason at the International Hotel, Las Vegas, pening with an invitation-only date that arnered enthusiastic press reviews, many rawing attention to his new stage act.

1970 POLK SALAD A table card from the International Hotel Las Vegas, offering "polk salad," named after a song in Elvis' repertoire at the time, "Polk Salad Annie," which had been a 1969 hit for its composer, country singer Tony Joe White.

1970

⊖⊕ **1970 JUMPSUITS** This white suit featured in the Las Vegas shows, and was among the first of the jumpsuits that were to become Elvis' trademark in the Seventies. Designed by Bill Belew, they later became even more flamboyant.

1970

1970 SUMMER SHOW The image *above* was shot for *Elvis: That's The Way It Is*. The film was released in November. The images on the *facing page* and *following pages* were taken during Elvis' February 1970 engagement in Las Vegas.

ELVIS
INTERNATIONAL HOTEL
SOUVENIR MENU
1971
COMPLIMENTARY COPY

1970 **TOURING** Most of Elvis' jumpsuits (*here and overleaf*) were made out of 100% wool gabardine from Milan, Italy, chosen for its flexibility. The flared legs were typical Seventies; the collar was inspired by military styles from the Napoleonic period.

← **1970 WINTER** The choice of Las Vegas—regarded as a haven for supper club audiences—was initially seen as a curious one for Elvis' return to live performances. Elvis' fan base would have been more familiar with concert stadia.

↑ **1970 SUMMER** The summer dates at the International Hotel were presented by Colonel Parker as the "Elvis Presley Summer Festival" with thousands of specially printed menus, postcards, catalogs, and photo albums.

1970

⊖⊖ **1970 WINTER** Even the Colonel doubted whether the success in Las Vegas could be reflected nationwide. However, after the Houston shows he was confident enough to set up a six-day tour in September that took in Phoenix, St. Louis, Detroit, Miami, Tampa, and Mobile. During this tour, Elvis appeared before a total audience of over one million. The photos on this page and the following four pages are all from 1970 Las Vegas shows.

1972

➔ **1972 COLLARS** Inspired by the European military styles of the late 18th and early 19th centuries, the collars on Bill Belew's creations got bigger and bigger, as did the capes and the flares on the pants. These are parts of the Elvis Presley "stereotype" that has persisted–particularly with Elvis impersonators the world over–ever since.

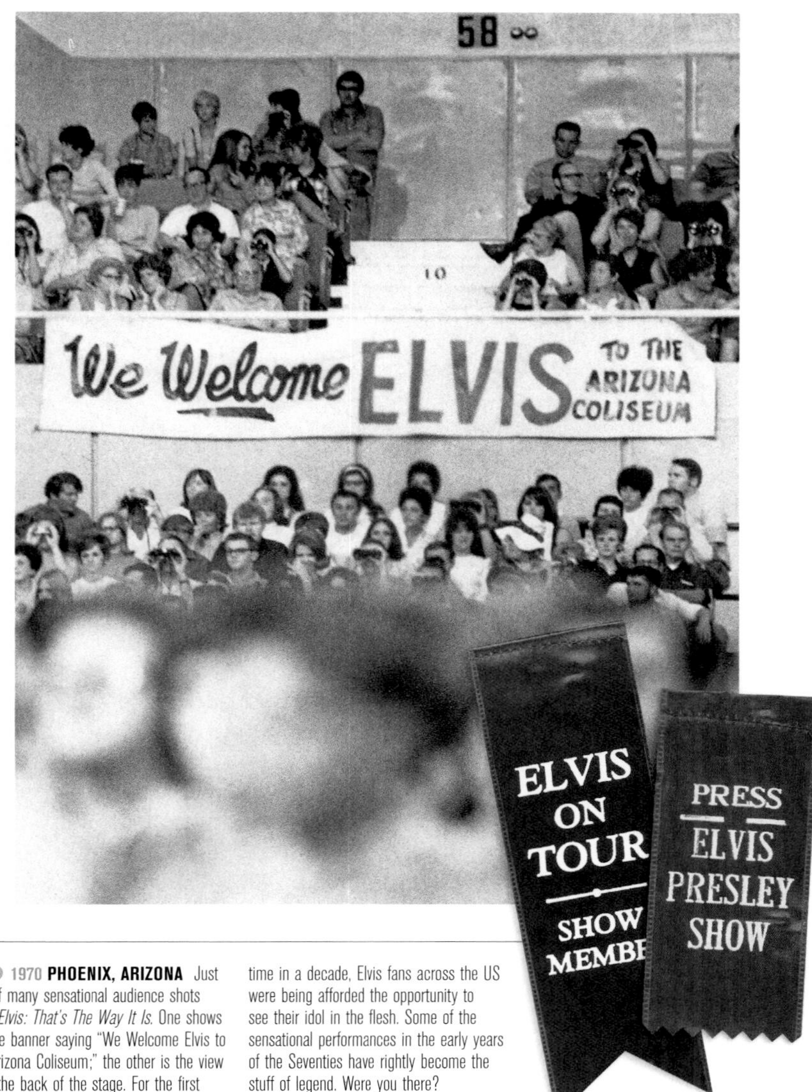

1970 **PHOENIX, ARIZONA** Just two of many sensational audience shots from *Elvis: That's The Way It Is.* One shows a huge banner saying "We Welcome Elvis to the Arizona Coliseum;" the other is the view from the back of the stage. For the first time in a decade, Elvis fans across the US were being afforded the opportunity to see their idol in the flesh. Some of the sensational performances in the early years of the Seventies have rightly become the stuff of legend. Were you there?

1970 **HOUSTON PRESS CONFERENCE** Elvis held a press conference after his final show at the Houston Astrodome on March 1, 1970. He was presented with a Stetson, a gold watch, and a gold deputy's badge from the local sheriffs' department, adding to his collection of honorary law-enforcement decorations. As Elvis admires his gifts (*left*)—wearing a military-style jacket probably influenced by the Beatles' "Sergeant Pepper" look of the late Sixties—the Colonel looks on.

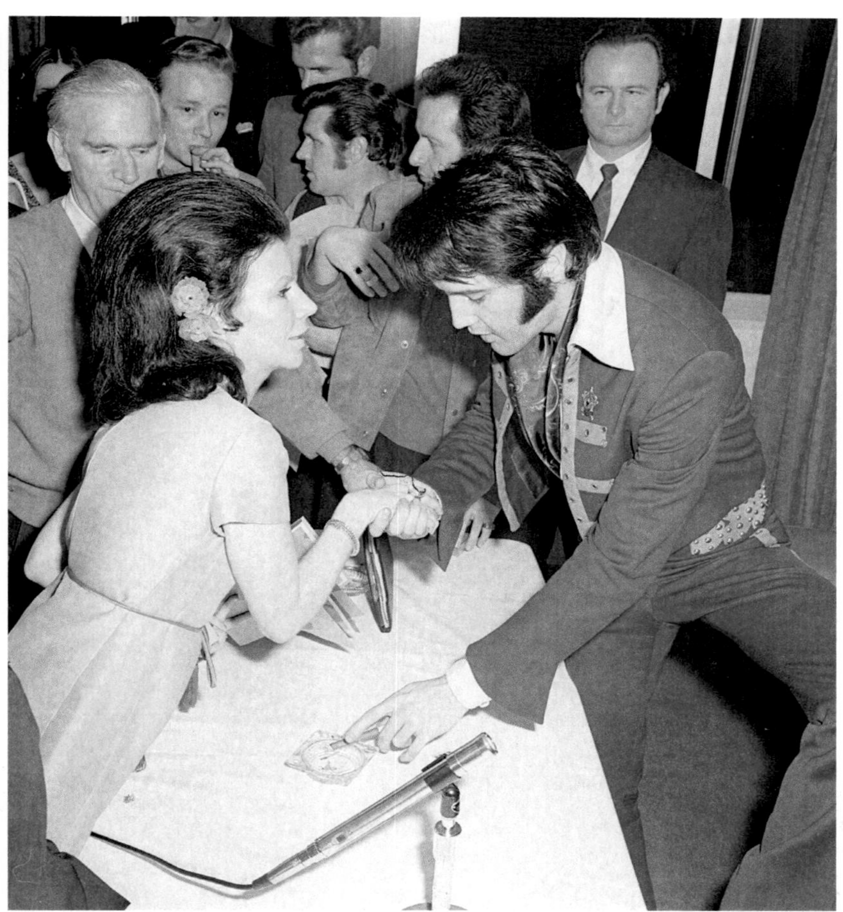

1974 HOUSTON ASTRODROME
Elvis returned to the Houston Astrodome on March 1 for two shows, which together set a world audience record for any indoor arena. He preceded the shows with a "lap of honor" around the auditorium in a jeep.

1970 HOUSTON ASTRODROME
At the press conference Elvis received gold records for five 1969 releases, including the single "In The Ghetto" and the albums, *From Elvis In Memphis* and *From Memphis to Vegas/From Vegas to Memphis.*

ELVIS
BIG
50
Records
ELVIS
SUMMER
FESTIVAL
ELVIS
50
FESTIVAL ELVIS
SUMMER FESTIVAL
ELVIS SUMMER
ELVIS
PERSON
NOW!
NOW!

1970 **SUMMER FESTIVAL** Captured on film in *Elvis: That's The Way It Is*, the Las Vegas Hilton Hotel lobby, pictured during what Colonel Tom Parker dubbed the "Elvis Summer Festival." The hotel lobby was filled with Elvis souvenirs. In the shot opposite, the Colonel is seen reviewing some of the 3,500 straw boaters he had provided for the hotel staff to wear. The Colonel organized the manufacture and sale of a variety of items, a logical extension of licensing merchandise.

1972 **SUMMER FESTIVAL** An army of stuffed hound dogs line the way to the souvenir stand in the Hilton lobby. The stuffed pooches were pure Colonel—one of Elvis' toughest rock'n'roll records became the inspiration for kiddies' playthings.

1973

↑ 1973 THAT'S THE WAY IT IS A shot from the film; the Colonel is watching over Elvis. His relationship with his charge was complex; he was business organizer, public relations man, father-figure, financial adviser, and–despite many suggestions to the contrary–a long-term friend.

→ 1973 ON THE ROAD Hotel room, limousine, dressing room, stage, and then back again: the story of Elvis' frenetic life on the road. Here Elvis leaves a hotel on his way to a concert date, as always becoming the center of attention.

1970 SAMMY DAVIS BACKSTAGE Elvis met with Sammy Davis Jr. backstage at the opening night of his summer season at the International Hotel. The event was recorded on film in *Elvis: That's The Way It Is*. Other celebrities who attended the opening included Juliet Prowse (who had starred with Elvis in *GI Blues*), Cuban bandleader Xavier Cugat, and the actor Cary Grant. Backstage encounters with celebrities were a constant feature of his appearances in Las Vegas.

1973 ELVIS AND ALI When Elvis was appearing at the Las Vegas Hilton in February 1973, he met up with Muhammad Ali—formerly Cassius Clay—simply the greatest boxer of his generation. Of course the meeting with Ali couldn't pass without a photo of the two kings sparring. Here, the King of the Ring is wearing a stud-encrusted robe presented to him by the King of Rock'n'roll. In this posed picture (*left*,) Elvis is wearing the pendant he was presented with in appreciation of his work through the Aloha project for the Kui Lee cancer fund.

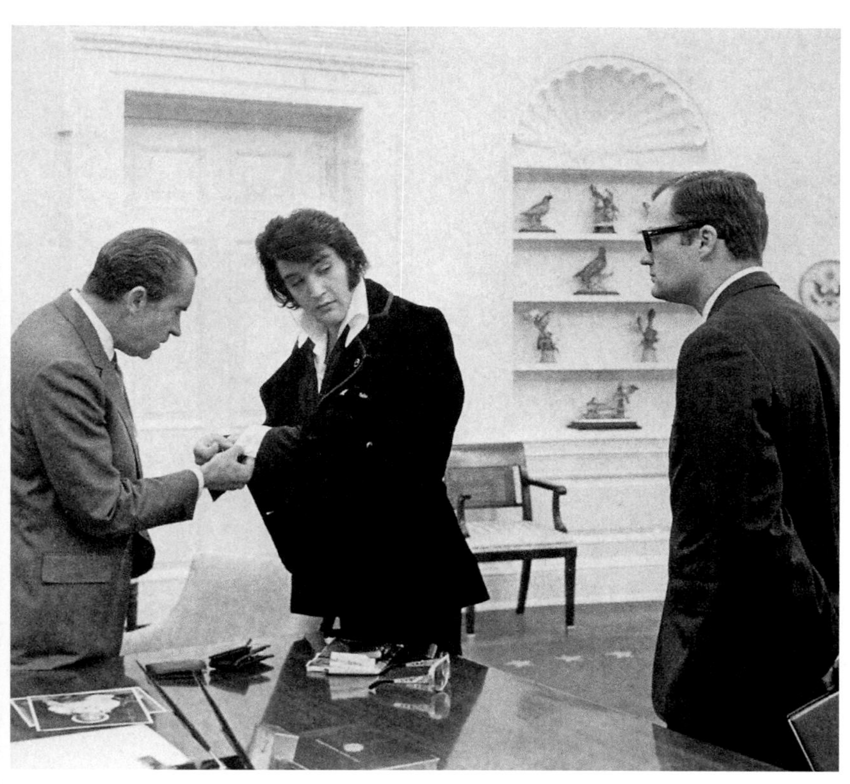

1970 THE WHITE HOUSE On December 21, 1970, after much personal lobbying of the President, Elvis met with Richard Nixon in the White House. After presenting the President with a World War II Colt .45 in a wooden case, he received the much sought-after badge as an honorary member of the Federal Narcotics Bureau, having written to the President voicing his concern about "the drug culture," and offering to use his status in the war against illicit narcotics.

1970

← 1971 **DENVER, COLORADO** An informal shot of Elvis taken in a motel room in Denver, Colorado. Life on the road, regardless of a star's status, is not all glamor. As well as the best hotels in town there were more modest motels.

↑ 1974 **THE TELEVISION ROOM** Elvis in the TV room at Graceland, where he had had television, hi-fi, and movie equipment since the Fifties. It was redecorated in 1974 by the designer Bill Eubanks. With its mirrored ceiling, it was pure Seventies.

1971

1971 THE "JAYCEE" AWARD In January, Elvis was selected by the Junior Chamber of Commerce as one of the nation's Ten Outstanding Men of the Year for 1970. Other recipients include Revd. Jesse Jackson and conductor Leonard Bernstein.

1970 BEST MAN Elvis was best man, and Priscilla matron of honor, at the Memphis wedding of Sonny West—who had been a friend since the late 50s and long-time member of Elvis' entourage—on December 28, 1970.

1971 ELLIS AUDITORIUM Elvis and Priscilla at a broadcast of the first Ali-Frazier fight, at Memphis' Ellis Auditorium on March 8. Elvis wore a "championship" belt awarded to him for record attendances at the International Hotel, Las Vegas.

1971 THE "JAYCEE" AWARD Elvis and Priscilla at the "Jaycee" prayer breakfast, January 16, where Elvis spotted Sam Phillips' former office manager Marion Keisker. It was she who had encouraged Elvis to make his first recording tests at the Sun studios.

1971 THE "JAYCEE" AWARD Elvis' speech ran: "When I was a child, ladies and gentlemen, I was a dreamer. I read comic books, and I was the hero of the comic book . . . every dream that I ever dreamed has come true a hundred times. I'd like to say that I learned very early in life that 'Without a song the day would never end / Without a song a man ain't got a friend / Without a song the road would never bend / Without a song.' So I keep singing a song. Good night. Thank you."

1970

1970 ALL THE KING'S MEN Shelby County Sheriff Roy Nixon awarded deputy badges to Elvis and his entire entourage. Here, displaying their badges after Sonny West's wedding in December, is the so-called "Memphis Mafia"–plus local law officers. *(Standing, left to right:)* Billy Smith, former Sheriff Bill Morris, Lamar Fike, Jerry Schilling, Sheriff Roy Nixon, Vernon Presley, Charlie Hodge, Sonny West, George Klein, and Marty Lacker. *(Front, left to right)* Dr. George Nichopoulos, Elvis, and Red West.

c1974 **ON THE ROAD** Another city, another hotel. Leaving with Elvis, on the way to another concert, are Jerry Schilling (to Elvis' right), Joe Esposito (behind Schilling), Red West (behind Elvis), and Dick Grob (to Elvis' left).

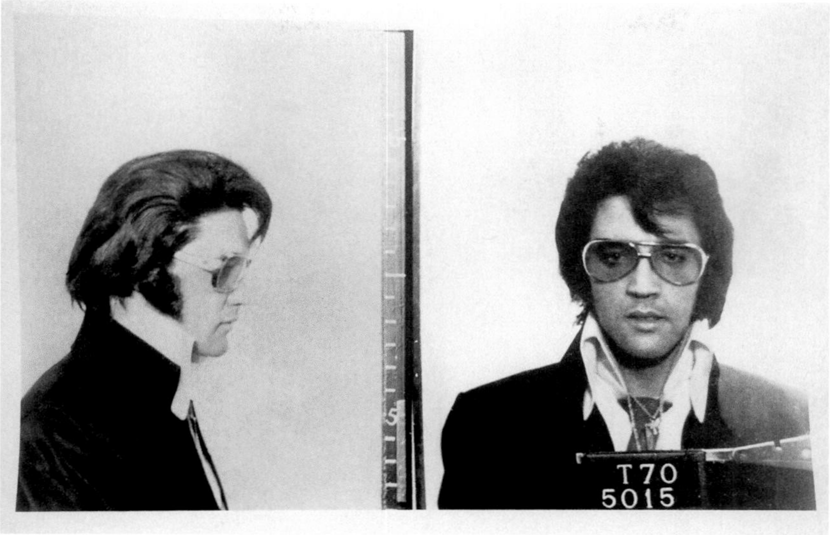

1975 CALIFORNIA Elvis astride one of his beloved Harleys outside the gates of his West Coast California home in Hillcrest Street, Bel Air. During and after his movie-making period, Elvis spent a lot more time on the West Coast.

1970 "MUG SHOTS" Elvis poses straight-faced in "mug shots" which were taken for use in an honorary police badge with which he was presented in Denver, Colorado, before playing the Coliseum there on November 17.

PHOENIX

1970 PHOENIX, ARIZONA
September 9: Elvis and the Colonel disembark from an aircraft at Phoenix, Arizona. Parts of the concert at the Phoenix Coliseum were filmed by MGM for the documentary *Elvis: That's The Way It Is.*

1972 BILLBOARDS, LAS VEGAS
On the route into Las Vegas from the Nevada desert, billboards announce current attractions. The Elvis concerts held there during the 1972 "Summer Festival" were always prominently advertised.

1970s THE RECORDS Throughout the Seventies, Elvis kept up his output of albums and singles. These included the single "Steamroller Blues," from his *Aloha From Hawaii* LP (1973), *Back in Memphis* (1970), *Elvis as Recorded at Madison Square Garden* (1972), *From Elvis Presley Boulevard, Memphis, Tennessee* (recorded in 1976 at Graceland), and the penultimate album released during his lifetime, *Moody Blue* (1977).

1976 ON STAGE For many of his touring dates between March and September that year, Elvis wore what became known as his "bicentennial" jumpsuit, designed by Bill Belew to mark the US bicentennial year. The patriotic tone of the red-white-and-blue outfit was emphasized by the number that was the highlight of many of the shows, a rendition of "America The Beautiful." During this period, the physical toll of touring was beginning to show in live performances.

1972 **CAPES** The famous capes (*also see over*) first appeared in the early Seventies. They got heavier and more unwieldy as they were encrusted with metal and rhinestone studs, and were phased out by 1975 as it became apparent that fans grabbing at them were threatening ito pull Elvis off stage. The capes shown opposite were captured on film during the spring of 1972 in the second MGM tour documentary, *Elvis On Tour*, the image above is from Honolulu in November.

c1974 **SCARVES** Another feature of live shows were the scarves, as seen in *Elvis On Tour*. In February 1973 the movie was honored with a Golden Globe Award, co-winner with the film *Wheels of Fire* as the best feature documentary of 1972.

RECORDS
DENMARK
MEXICO
NORWAY
FRANCE
ARGENTINA
PHILLIPPINES
KOREA

1972 **LAS VEGAS** Between Elvis' dinner and midnight shows at the Las Vegas Hilton on September 4, the Colonel organized a press conference at which Elvis and RCA Records president Rocco Laginestra (*above*) announced the *Aloha From Hawaii* broadcast planned for January 14. The familiar Hilton straw boaters were displayed, this time emblazoned with the names of the countries that the satellite link-up was going to reach. It would be seen by an estimated 1.4 billion viewers.

1973 ALOHA *"Elvis: Aloha From Hawaii Via Satellite"* was broadcast on January 14 at 12.30 AM Hawaiian time from the International Center Arena in Honolulu. It was seen live in Australia, Japan, South Korea, Thailand, South Vietnam, and the Philippines, and on a time-delay basis in 30 European countries. It was not shown in the US until April 4, when, with 57% of the nation's viewers tuned in, it was seen by more households than the live transmission of man's first walk on the Moon.

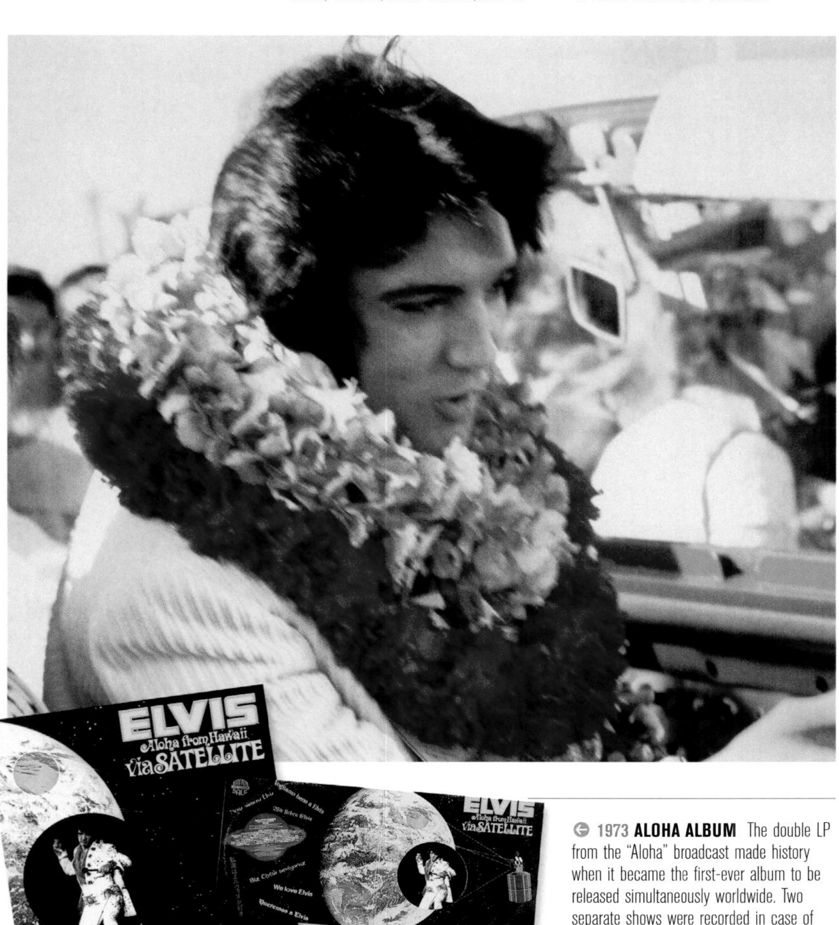

1973 ALOHA ALBUM The double LP from the "Aloha" broadcast made history when it became the first-ever album to be released simultaneously worldwide. Two separate shows were recorded in case of problems with the broadcast.

1973 **ALOHA JUMPSUIT** The regular jumpsuit designer Bill Belew was asked by Elvis to produce something that represented the US for the Hawaii show. He created the spectacular American eagle, outlined in studs on the front and back of the Aloha jumpsuit. At the finale of the broadcast show, Elvis flung both his belt and the jewel-laden "eagle" cape into the audience, providing one of the highlights of a sensational performance. The image above was shot straight from a TV screen.

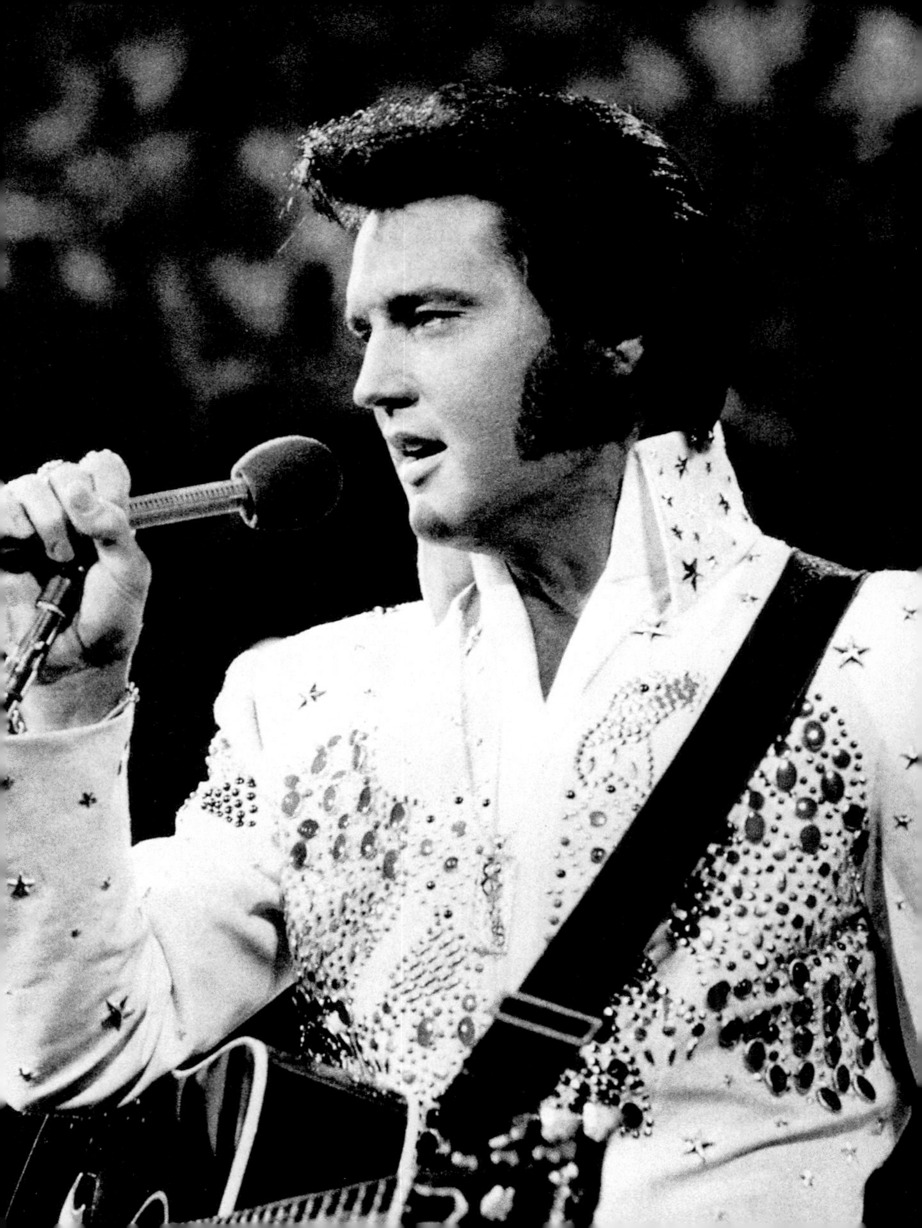

1973 **ALOHA** A back detail of the "eagle" suit. The show was a fund-raising event for the Kui Lee Cancer Fund (Kui Lee was a Hawiian composer who had died of cancer in his thirties), and Elvis announced audience donations of $75,000.

1975 **HUNTSVILLE, ALABAMA** At a June 1 concert during his April–July tour, Elvis—clearly starting to gain weight—is wearing his "blue phoenix" jumpsuit. All the Bill Belew outfits acquired specific names, dreamed up originally by the fans.

↑ 1976 **ON STAGE** On his bicentennial year tour, Elvis is wearing the "twin birds" jumpsuit. Given the demanding nature of his stage routines, it's not surprising the heavy rhinestone-studded suits gave way to lighter embroidered oufits in the mid-Seventies.

→ 1977 **"AZTEC" JUMPSUIT** The very last jumpsuit that Elvis wore on stage was the Mexican-inspired "sundial" suit, with its gold Aztec-style calendar design on the front and back, which he wore for the entire 13 days of his May–June tour.

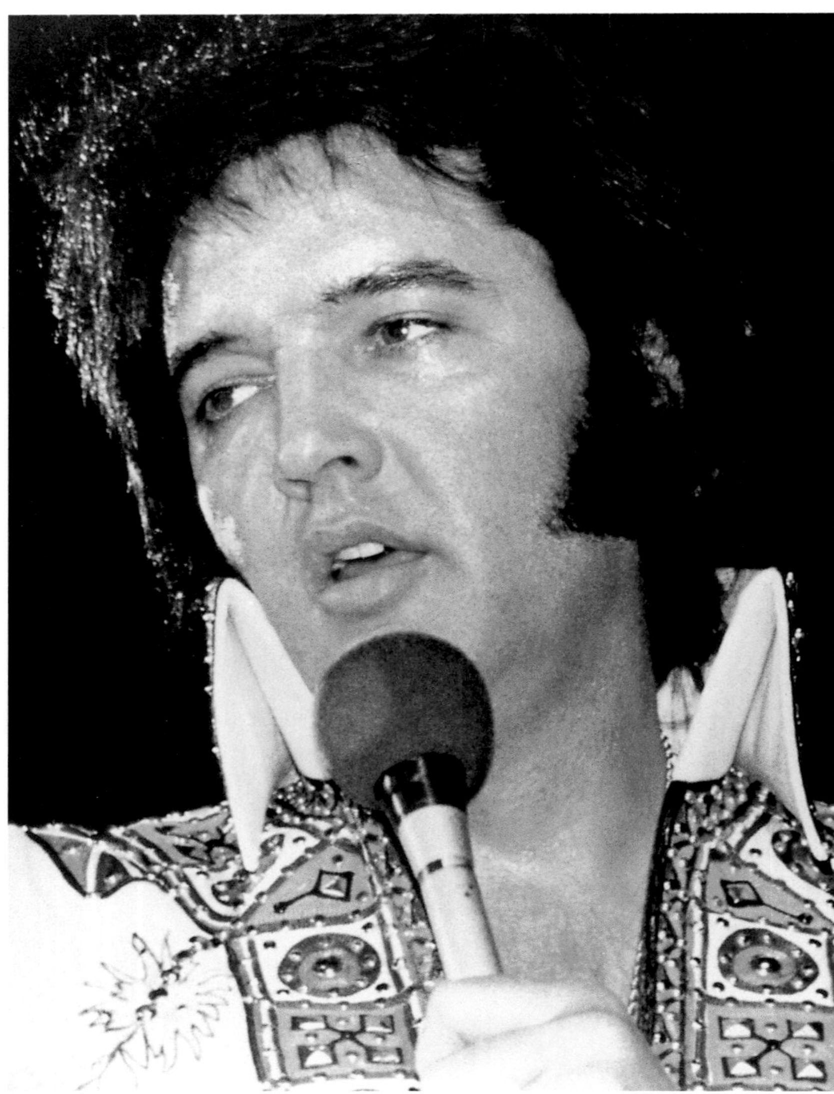

ELVIS
SUMMER FESTIVAL
INTERNATIONAL
A HILTON HOTEL
LAS VEGAS, NEVADA
RCA
RECORDS
ELVIS

1975 **"AMERICAN INDIAN" JUMPSUIT** The elaborate embroidery on this particular outfit incorporated elements of Native American design and culture, hence the name of the outfit most often used by Elvis afficianados to describe it.

1970 **WEBBED JUMPSUIT** This early example of the jumpsuit fashion, worn during the Fall concerts of 1970, predates outfits that featured a cape. Instead, it has a web of fabric from sleeve to torso with a long fringe hanging down.

1975 "BLACK PHOENIX" JUMPSUIT Elvis appeared in this jumpsuit–identical to the "blue phoenix" outfit in all but the colors–on the same midyear tour. It was a period when his health was beginning to cause concern.

1975 "GYPSY" JUMPSUIT For many of his performances during the tour dates in mid-1975–a period when he also seemed to be wearing more and more jewelry on stage–Elvis wore the so-called "gypsy" outfit.

1974

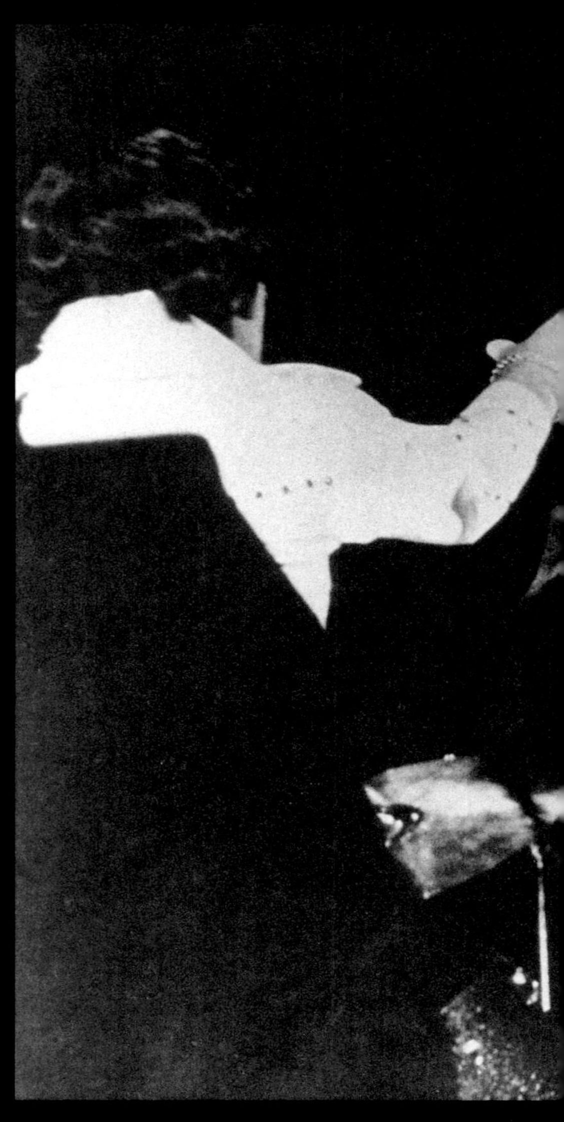

➔ 1974 ON TOUR Elvis in the Seventies, during the last few years of his life, is typified by this shot of him reaching out with the guitar on stage. His life was music, and in this period, despite the lows that often followed the highs, he expressed that in the most direct way possible, and the way he knew best–performing in front of live audiences. When he decided to go back on the road at the beginning of the decade, it was a way of reaching out once more for that contact with his fans that he had enjoyed 10 years before. This communication with his public could never be achieved via a movie camera or studio microphone. During the last years of his life that contact was made once again, and, perhaps fittingly, that is how Elvis Presley is best remembered.

1977

1977 THE FINAL WAVE
Thought to be the last ever picture of Elvis Presley alive, this candid shot was taken as he entered Graceland in a car on August 15, on his way from an evening dental appointment, and just hours before he was found dead the next day.

Epilogue

ELVIS LIVES:

THE LEGEND CONTINUES

← 1957 **PHOTO PORTRAIT**
This portrait is what used to be called a tinted photograph, a photo made to look like a painted portrait. For years it was thumbtacked to a wall in Vernon's office at Graceland, being framed and moved into the house itself when the tours began in 1982.

August 1977 *August 1977* *October 1977*

Once recorded on a scratchy acetate disc, "My Happiness" backed with "That's When Your Heartaches Begin"—made by Elvis at the Memphis Recording Service—now appear on a digital compact disc, elegantly designed with a postmodern knowingness of early-Fifties style. And true to the fan's insistence on authenticity, this is no "cleaned up" job—the detail is there, hisses and all. But what still astounds is the detail of the 18-year-old voice, the purity of sound that was once described as the "voice of an angel."

Strutting on stage at the Fort Homer Hesterly Armory in Tampa, Florida, in 1955, Elvis can be seen hitting that brand new Martin guitar, proclaiming his youth, reaching for the sky. That image burned in the imagination of millions, from the first 12-inch album cover through nearly 50 years of posters, postcards, theater programs, T-shirts, ballpoint pens, and pillowcases.

Down on Memphis' Beale Street, a young kid is casually leaning on a pink-and-white Cadillac outside of Lansky's clothing store, shirt collar turned up, with a draped jacket, cuffed pants and two-tone shoes in open imitation of the zoot-suit rhythm and blues singers who crackle across the airwaves from the

August 1992 July 1992 August 1998

car radio. Now 21st-century Beale has a whole nightspot dedicated to the kid, right where Lansky's used to be. Who'd have imagined it?

The lights dim, and as a hugely amplified rhythm section riffs an intro, a sudden spotlight reveals a virtual image looming huge over the stage. Diamanté glints off the white jumpsuit with the flowing cape and high collar, jet black hair and sideburns as familiar as family. It's the Mid-South Coliseum in Memphis on August 16, 1997, and, 20 years after his death, Elvis is "back."

Through video images, and accompanied live on stage by over 30 of his former band-mates and the Memphis Symphony Orchestra, the concert became the prototype for the touring production *Elvis—The Concert*. By being the first performer ever to headline a tour while no longer living, Elvis made history again. The 1998 tour included three shows at Radio City Music Hall in New York and Elvis' "return" to the Las Vegas Hilton. The 1999 European tour opened with a sellout at London's Wembley Arena and, in effect, marked Elvis' first-ever concerts outside of North America.

Elvis was back but, like all real icons, he never really went away.

FORD
55

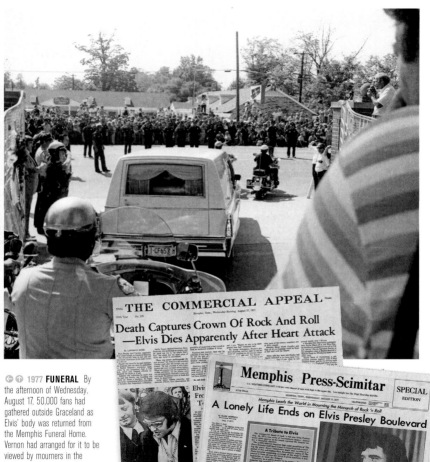

FINAL THE COMMERCIAL APPEAL FINAL

Memphis, Tenn., Wednesday Morning, August 17, 1977

138th Year No. 229

Death Captures Crown Of Rock And Roll —Elvis Dies Apparently After Heart Attack

Memphis Press-Scimitar

SPECIAL EDITION

97TH YEAR

MEMPHIS, TENN., WEDNESDAY, AUGUST 17, 1977

Memphis Leads the World in Mourning the Monarch of Rock 'n Roll

A Lonely Life Ends on Elvis Presley Boulevard

A Tribute to Elvis

Mourners In Waiting For Last Homecoming Of Revered Singer

1977 FUNERAL By the afternoon of Wednesday, August 17, 50,000 fans had gathered outside Graceland as Elvis' body was returned from the Memphis Funeral Home. Vernon had arranged for it to be viewed by mourners in the hallway of the mansion. The funeral was held the next day, when the body was carried in a white hearse to Forest Hill Cemetery. After a short ceremony Elvis was interred in a crypt a few hundred yards from his mother's grave.

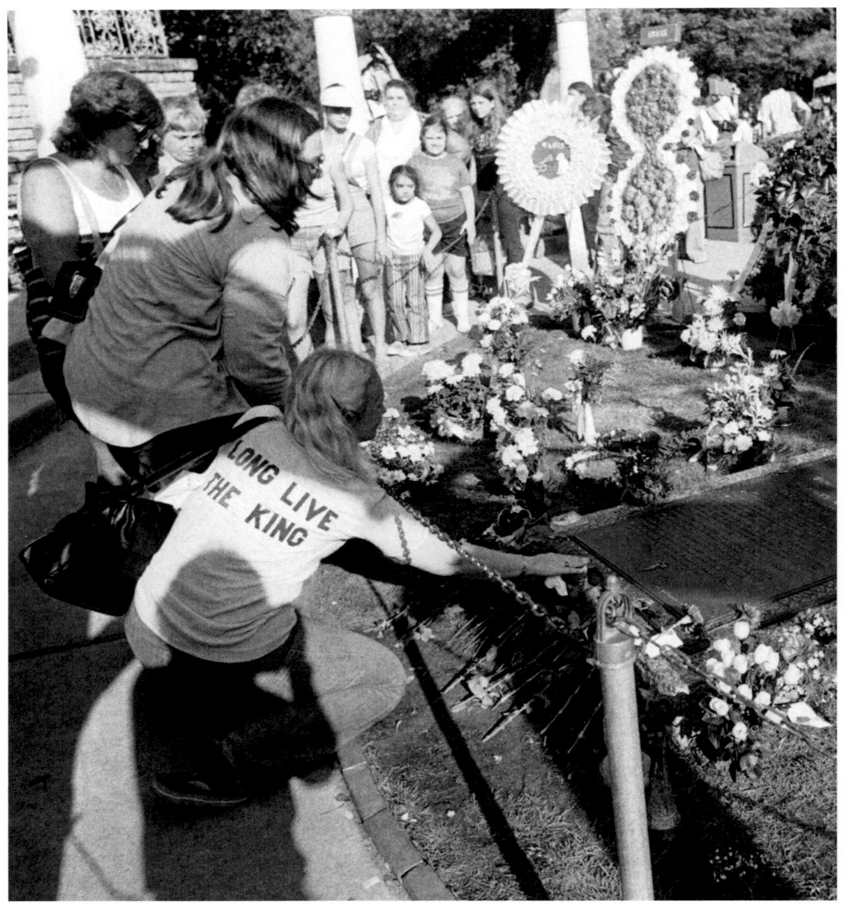

1977

1977 RESTING PLACE
On October 2, the bodies of both Elvis and his mother were moved to the Meditation Garden in the Graceland mansion grounds, their final resting place. Fans immediately treated it as a place of pilgrimage, as they still do today. After their deaths, Vernon and Grandmother Minnie were also buried in the garden. A plaque commemorates Elvis' twin brother Jesse Garon, who was stillborn and is actually buried in Tupelo, Mississippi.

CANDLELIGHT VIGIL Every year, during Elvis Week in mid-August, which commemorates the anniversary of Elvis' death, thousands of fans take part in the candlelight vigil that centers on the Meditation Garden at Graceland. The original Presley family monument was relocated from the family's plot at the Forest Hill Cemetery to the Meditation Garden. It brought to the garden a sacred element that made it even more a focus of pilgrimage for fans over the years.

1992 GRACELAND Elvis Presley's home and refuge for 20 years, Graceland attracts over 600,000 visitors annually. It is the most famous home in America after the White House, and in 1991 was placed on the National Register of Historic Places.

1992 MEDITATION The Meditation Garden was originally inspired by Elvis' interest in Eastern philosophies, and was built under his personal supervision. It was never intended as a place of burial, and was simply a place of quiet retreat.

SOME GOT TO
WE GO TO
GRACEL
FOR OUR
PILGRIMAG

1992

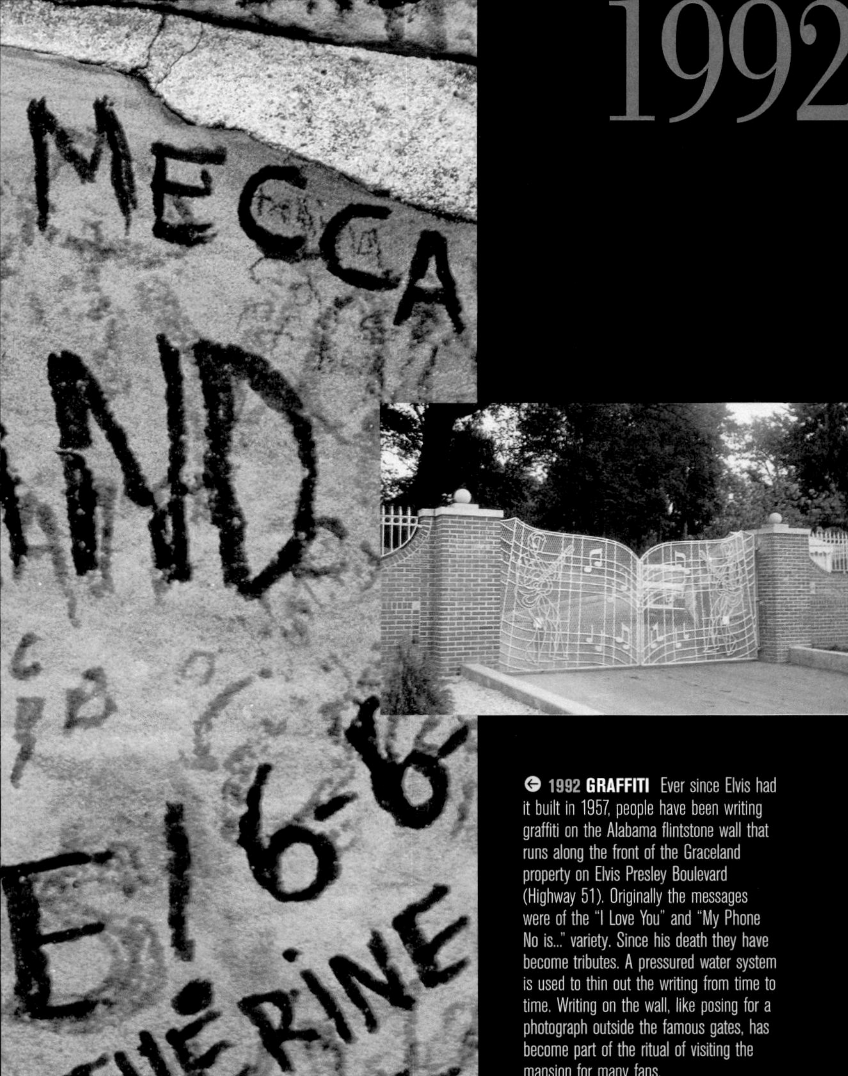

1992 GRAFFITI Ever since Elvis had it built in 1957, people have been writing graffiti on the Alabama flintstone wall that runs along the front of the Graceland property on Elvis Presley Boulevard (Highway 51). Originally the messages were of the "I Love You" and "My Phone No is..." variety. Since his death they have become tributes. A pressured water system is used to thin out the writing from time to time. Writing on the wall, like posing for a photograph outside the famous gates, has become part of the ritual of visiting the mansion for many fans.

THE KINGS
Heartbreak Hotel
RESTAURANT

1990s MERCHANDISE Representations of Elvis span all the iconic phases of his life, from the early rock'n'roll period of the Fifties to the jumpsuit "Las Vegas" image.

1992 HEARTBREAK HOTEL Across the highway from Graceland, in the visitors' reception area which includes the automobile museum and Elvis' private aircraft, stands the 128-room Elvis Presley's Heartbreak Hotel and Restaurant. The neon sign (*left*) now occupies a spot in the Graceland Visitor Center. Another popular attraction is Elvis Presley's Memphis restaurant and nightspot, a huge complex on the corner of Second Street and Beale, on the site of Lansky's clothing store where Elvis used to shop.

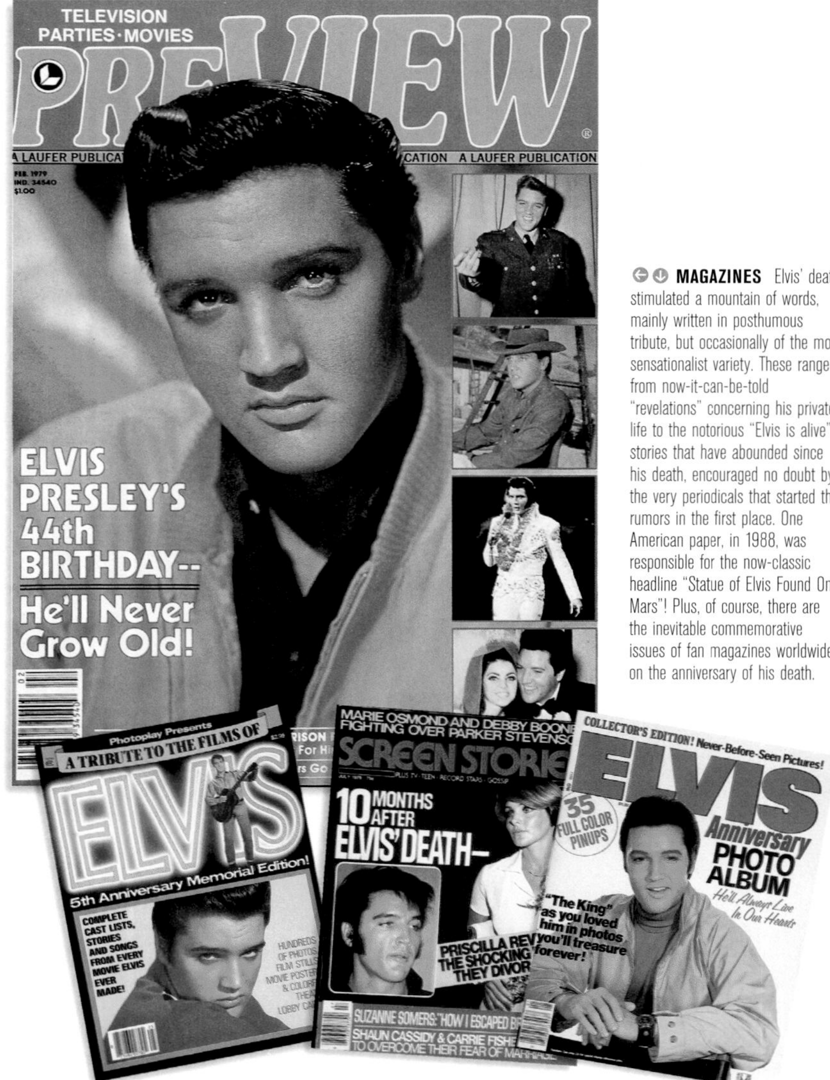

MAGAZINES Elvis' death stimulated a mountain of words, mainly written in posthumous tribute, but occasionally of the more sensationalist variety. These ranged from now-it-can-be-told "revelations" concerning his private life to the notorious "Elvis is alive" stories that have abounded since his death, encouraged no doubt by the very periodicals that started the rumors in the first place. One American paper, in 1988, was responsible for the now-classic headline "Statue of Elvis Found On Mars"! Plus, of course, there are the inevitable commemorative issues of fan magazines worldwide on the anniversary of his death.

1973/1992 **PROMOTION AND PACKAGING** RCA Records have produced a huge variety of material in the promotion and packaging of vinyl discs, tapes, and CDs. These two examples, which now constitute Elvis memorabilia, are the calendar-cards produced in 1973 (*left*); and the spectacular sheet of souvenir stamps featuring record sleeves from the 1950s, which was included in the *King of Rock'n'Roll: Complete 50s Masters* box set of CDs released in 1992.

1981

➲ **1981 THIS IS ELVIS** A row of posters advertising the showing of the drama-documentary film released in 1981 "This Is Elvis," in which authentic footage was spliced in with actors to form a collage picture of Elvis' life, done with the approval of the Elvis Presley Estate. The film starts just before Elvis' death with Johnny Harra acting as Elvis; then a series of flashbacks trace his career with the aid of news film, clips from TV shows and such, as well as more dramatized scenes from his personal life.

THIS IS ELVIS
THIS IS ELVIS
THIS IS ELVIS
THIS IS ELVIS
THIS IS ELVIS
THIS IS ELVIS
THIS IS ELVIS
THIS IS ELVIS
THIS IS ELVIS
THIS IS ELVIS

1993

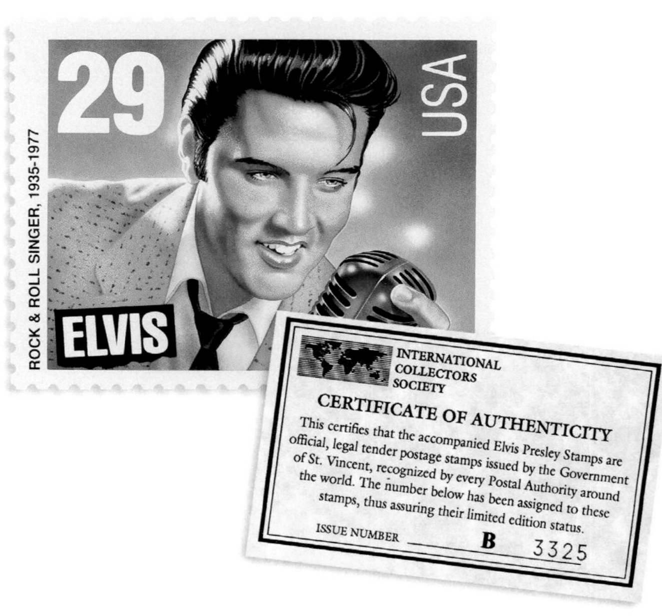

1993 ELVIS STAMPS In 1992, the US Postal Service announced that they were planning to use Elvis' image for a commemorative stamp. They organized a nationwide ballot to vote for one of two images: Elvis in the 1950s as a young rocker, or the still-svelte concert superstar in his 1973 "Aloha from Hawaii" special. Over 1.2 million votes were cast, and the image of the younger Elvis won. The stamp was released on January 8, 1993, and became the top-selling commemorative postage stamp of all time. Several countries outside the USA also have issued Elvis stamps over the years, such as those opposite from the Caribbean island of St. Vincent, confirming his continuing status as a truly universal icon.

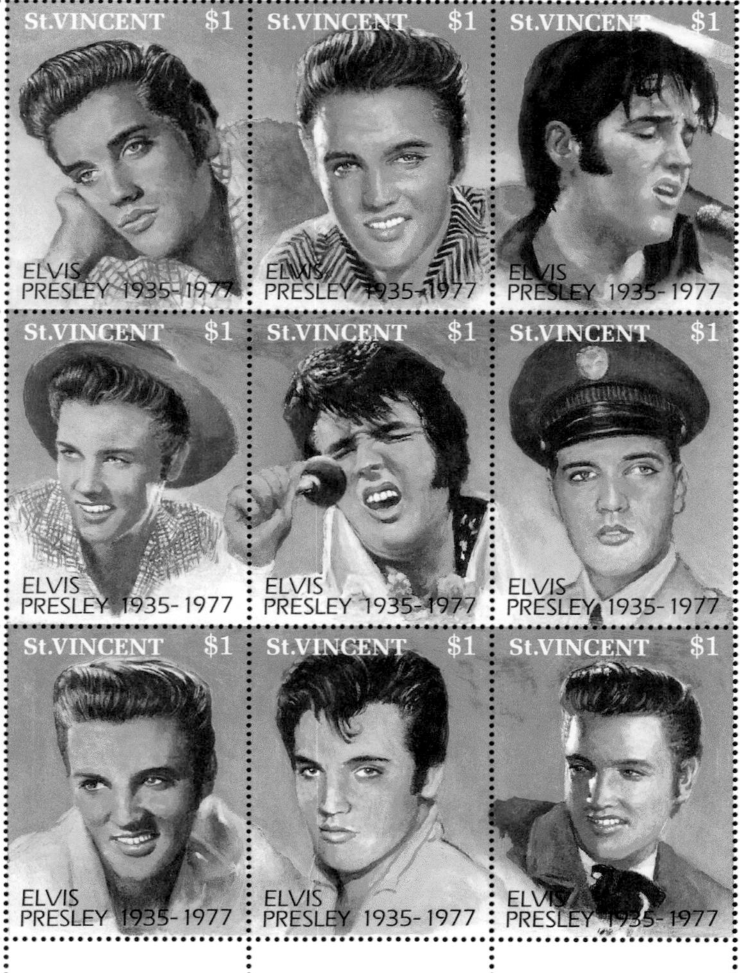
St.VINCENT $1
ELVIS PRESLEY 1935-1977
St.VINCENT $1
ELVIS PRESLEY 1935-1977
St.VINCENT $1
ELVIS PRESLEY 1935-1977
St.VINCENT $1
ELVIS PRESLEY 1935-1977
St.VINCENT $1
ELVIS PRESLEY 1935-1977
St.VINCENT $1
ELVIS PRESLEY 1935-1977
St.VINCENT $1
ELVIS PRESLEY 1935-1977
St.VINCENT $1
ELVIS PRESLEY 1935-1977
St.VINCENT $1
ELVIS PRESLEY 1935-1977

Appendices

← 1956 LOVE ME TENDER
A studio publicity shot used during the promotion of Elvis' first movie *Love Me Tender.* Although only a matter of months into his success as a major recording star, the picture established him as a multi-media entertainer on the concert stage, records, television, and the cinema screen–a pattern that would continue throughout his career.

Facts, figures, and statistics

RECORD SALES

It is estimated that Elvis Presley has sold over one billion record units worldwide, more than anyone in record industry history. In the US alone, Elvis has had 131 different albums and singles that have been certified gold, platinum, or multi-platinum by the Recording Industry Association of America (RIAA), with more certifications expected as research into his past record sales continues and as current sales go on. Research is also underway to document his record sales achievements in other countries. It is estimated that 40% of Elvis' total record sales have been outside the United States.

ELVIS' GOLD AND PLATINUM DISC AWARDS

The list below—as of August 1999, when the last presentation was made—is of Elvis albums, singles, and extended-plays the American sales of which had received gold, platinum, or multi-platinum designations from the Recording Industry Association of America (RIAA). Sales required are 500,000 copies for a gold single or album, 1 million copies for a platinum single or album. *(For double or multiple disc albums/CD packages, each disc's sales are counted, so a five-CD box selling 100,000 copies would count as 5x100,000 and go gold.)*

64 ALBUMS

Elvis Presley – GOLD
Elvis – GOLD
Loving You – GOLD
Elvis' Christmas Album (1957 Package) – PLATINUM (x3)
King Creole – GOLD
Elvis' Golden Records Vol. 1 – PLATINUM (x6)
50,000,000 Elvis Fans Can't Be Wrong (Elvis' Gold Records Vol. 2) – PLATINUM
Elvis Is Back – GOLD
G.I. Blues – PLATINUM
His Hand In Mine – PLATINUM
Something For Everybody – GOLD
Blue Hawaii – PLATINUM (x2)
Girls! Girls! Girls! – GOLD
Elvis' Golden Records Vol. 3 – PLATINUM
Roustabout – GOLD
Girl Happy – GOLD
How Great Thou Art – PLATINUM (x2)
Elvis, NBC TV Special – PLATINUM
Elvis' Gold Records, Vol. 4 – GOLD
Elvis Sings Flaming Star – GOLD
From Elvis In Memphis – GOLD
Elvis: From Memphis to Vegas, From Vegas to Memphis – GOLD
On Stage, February 1970 – PLATINUM
Worldwide 50 Gold Award Hits – PLATINUM (x2)
Elvis' Christmas Album (1970 Package) – PLATINUM (x6)
Elvis, That's The Way It Is – GOLD
Elvis In Person At The International Hotel – GOLD
Elvis Country – GOLD
Elvis: The Other Sides; 50 Gold Award Hits, Vol. 2 – GOLD
You'll Never Walk Alone – PLATINUM
Elvis Sings The Wonderful World Of Christmas – PLATINUM (x3)
Elvis Now – GOLD
He Touched Me – PLATINUM
Elvis As Recorded At Madison Square Garden – PLATINUM (x3)
Elvis Sings Burning Love And Hits From His Movies, Vol. 2 – PLATINUM
Separate Ways – GOLD
Aloha From Hawaii – PLATINUM (x3)
Elvis, A Legendary Performer, Vol. 1 – PLATINUM (x2)
Elvis Recorded Live On Stage In Memphis – GOLD
Pure Gold – PLATINUM (x2)
Elvis, A Legendary Performer, Vol. 2 — PLATINUM (x2)
From Elvis Presley Boulevard, Memphis, Tennessee – GOLD
Welcome To My World – PLATINUM
Moody Blue – PLATINUM (x2)
Elvis In Concert – PLATINUM
He Walks Beside Me – GOLD
Elvis, A Legendary Performer, Vol. 3 – GOLD
Memories Of Elvis – GOLD
Elvis Aaron Presley – PLATINUM
Memories Of Christmas – GOLD
The Number One Hits – PLATINUM (x2)
The Top Ten Hits – PLATINUM (x3)
Elvis, The King Of Rock 'n' Roll, The Complete 50's Masters – PLATINUM
Elvis, From Nashville To Memphis, The Essential 60's Masters I – GOLD
Elvis: His Greatest Hits (Reader's Digest Compilation) – GOLD
Blue Christmas – GOLD
Elvis' Golden Records, Vol. 5 – GOLD
Amazing Grace – GOLD
If Everyday Was Like Christmas – GOLD
Walk A Mile In My Shoes, The Essential 70's Masters – GOLD
50 Years – 50 Hits – PLATINUM
Worldwide Gold Award Hits, Vols. 1 & 2 (club version) – PLATINUM
The Elvis Presley Story – PLATINUM (x2)
Elvis Gospel Treasury – GOLD

51 SINGLES

Heartbreak Hotel/I Was the One – PLATINUM (x2)
Blue Suede Shoes/Tutti Frutti – GOLD
I Want You, I Need You, I Love You/My Baby Left Me – PLATINUM
Hound Dog/Don't Be Cruel

– PLATINUM (x4)
Love Me Tender/Any Way You Want Me – PLATINUM (x3)
Too Much/Playing For Keeps – PLATINUM
All Shook Up/That's When Your Heartaches Begin – PLATINUM (x2)
(Let Me Be Your) Teddy Bear/Loving You – PLATINUM (x2)
Jailhouse Rock/Treat Me Nice – PLATINUM (x2)
Don't/I Beg Of You – PLATINUM
Wear My Ring Around Your Neck/Doncha Think It's Time – PLATINUM
Hard Headed Woman/Don't Ask Me Why – PLATINUM
I Got Stung/One Night – PLATINUM
(Now and Then There's) A Fool Such as I/I Need Your Love Tonight – PLATINUM
A Big Hunk O' Love/My Wish Came True – GOLD
Stuck on You/Fame and Fortune – PLATINUM
It's Now Or Never/A Mess Of Blues – PLATINUM
Are You Lonesome Tonight/I Gotta Know – PLATINUM (x2)
Surrender/Lonely Man – PLATINUM
I Feel So Bad/Wild In The Country – GOLD
(Marie's The Name) His Latest Flame/Little Sister – GOLD
Can't Help Falling In Love/Rock-a Hula Baby – PLATINUM
Good Luck Charm/Anything That's Part Of You – PLATINUM
She's Not You/Just Tell Her Jim Said Hello – GOLD
Return To Sender/Where Do You Come From? – PLATINUM
One Broken Heart For Sale/They Remind Me Too Much Of You – GOLD
(You're The) Devil in Disguise/Please Don't Drag That String Around – GOLD
Bossa Nova Baby/Witchcraft – GOLD
Kissin' Cousins/It Hurts Me – GOLD
Viva Las Vegas/What'd I Say – GOLD
Ain't That Loving You, Baby/Ask Me – GOLD
Crying In The Chapel/I Believe In The Man In The Sky – PLATINUM
I'm Yours/Long Lonely Highway – GOLD
Puppet On A String/Wooden Heart – GOLD
Blue Christmas/Santa Claus Is Back In Town – PLATINUM
Tell Me Why/Blue River – GOLD
Frankie And Johnny/Please Don't Stop Loving Me – GOLD
If I Can Dream/Edge Of Reality – GOLD
In The Ghetto/Any Day Now – PLATINUM
Clean Up Your Own Back Yard/The Fair Is Moving On – GOLD
Suspicious Minds/You'll Think Of Me – PLATINUM
Don't Cry Daddy/Rubberneckin' – PLATINUM
Kentucky Rain/My Little Friend – GOLD
The Wonder Of You/Mama Liked The Roses – GOLD
I've Lost You/The Next Step Is Love – GOLD
You Don't Have To Say You Love Me/Patch It Up – GOLD
I Really Don't Want To Know/There Goes My Everything – GOLD
Burning Love/It's A Matter Of Time – PLATINUM
Separate Ways/Always On My Mind – GOLD
Way Down/Pledging My Love – PLATINUM
My Way/America – GOLD

16 EXTENDED-PLAY SINGLES

Elvis Presley (including Blue Suede Shoes) – GOLD
Heartbreak Hotel – GOLD
Elvis Presley (including Shake, Rattle & Roll) – GOLD
The Real Elvis – PLATINUM
Elvis, Vol. 1 – PLATINUM (x2)
Love Me Tender – PLATINUM
Elvis, Vol. 2 – GOLD
Peace In The Valley – PLATINUM
Loving You, Vol. 1 – GOLD
Loving You, Vol. 2 – PLATINUM
Jailhouse Rock – PLATINUM (x2)
Elvis Sings Christmas Songs – PLATINUM
King Creole, Vol. 1 – PLATINUM
King Creole, Vol. 2 – PLATINUM
Follow That Dream – PLATINUM
Kid Galahad – GOLD

RECORD CHART STATISTICS

Elvis has had no fewer than 149 songs to appear on *Billboard's* Hot 100 Pop Chart in America. Of these, 114 were in the top 40, 40 were in the top ten, and 18 went to #1. His #1 singles spent a total of 80 weeks at #1. He has also had over 90 charted albums with nine of them reaching #1. These figures are only for the pop charts, and only in America. He was also a leading artist in the American country, R&B, and gospel fields, and his chart success in other countries was substantial.

ELVIS' CHART ALBUMS

Every entry in the *Billboard* Top Twenty US Album chart during his lifetime.

Elvis Presley 1956 – 1
Elvis 1956 – 1
Loving You 1957 – 1
Elvis' Christmas Album 1957 – 1
Elvis' Golden Records 1958 – 3
King Creole 1958 – 2
For LP Fans Only 1959 – 19
Elvis Is Back! 1960 – 2
GI Blues 1960 – 1
His Hand In Mine 1961 – 13
Something For Everybody 1961 – 1
Blue Hawaii 1961 – 1
Pot Luck 1962 – 4
Girls! Girls! Girls! 1962 – 3
It Happened At The World's Fair 1963 – 4
Elvis' Golden Records, Vol. 3 1963 – 3
Fun In Acapulco 1963 – 3
Kissin' Cousins 1964 – 6
Roustabout 1964 – 1
Girl Happy 1965 – 8
Elvis For Everyone! 1965 – 10
Harum Scarum 1965 – 8
Frankie And Johnny 1966 – 20
Paradise, Hawaiian Style 1966 – 15
Spinout 1966 – 18
How Great Thou Art 1967 – 18
Elvis' TV Special 1968 – 8
From Elvis In Memphis 1969 – 13
From Memphis To Vegas, From Vegas To Memphis

(2-disc set) 1969 – 12
On Stage 1970 – 13
Elvis Country 1971 – 12
Elvis As Recorded At Madison Square Garden 1972 – 11
Elvis – Aloha From Hawaii, Via Satellite (2-disc set) 1973 – 1
Moody Blue 1977 – 3
Elvis In Concert (2-disc set) 1977 – 5

ELVIS' CHART SINGLES

Every entry in the *Billboard* Top Twenty US Singles chart during his lifetime. *(Where two songs are on one entry, it denotes both sides charted as part of the same single, whereas in some cases, such as "Hound Dog" and "Don't Be Cruel", both sides of a single sometimes charted independently.)*

Heartbreak Hotel 1956 – 1
I Was The One 1956 – 19
Blue Suede Shoes 1956 – 20
I Want You, I Need You, I Love You 1956 – 1
Don't Be Cruel 1956 – 1
Hound Dog 1956 – 1
Love Me Tender 1956 – 1
Anyway You Want Me 1956 – 20
When My Blue Moon Turns To Gold Again 1956 – 19
Love Me 1957 – 2
Too Much 1957 – 1
All Shook Up 1957 – 1
Teddy Bear 1957 – 1
Loving You 1957 – 20
Jailhouse Rock 1957 – 1
Treat Me Nice 1957 – 18
Don't 1957 – 1
I Beg Of You 1957 – 8
Wear My Ring Around Your Neck 1958 – 2
Doncha Think It's Time 1958 – 15
Hard Headed Woman 1958 – 1
One Night 1958 – 4
I Got Stung 1958 – 8
A Fool Such As I 1959 – 2
I Need Your Love Tonight 1959 – 4
A Big Hunk O' Love 1959 – 1
My Wish Came True 1959 – 12
Stuck On You 1960 – 1
Fame and Fortune 1960 – 17
It's Now or Never 1960 – 1
Are You Lonesome Tonight? 1960 – 1
I Gotta Know 1960 – 20
Surrender 1961 – 1
Flaming Star 1961 – 14
I Feel So Bad 1961 – 5
Little Sister 1961 – 5
His Latest Flame 1961 – 4
Can't Help Falling In Love 1961 – 2
Good Luck Charm 1962 – 1
Follow That Dream 1962 – 15
She's Not You 1962 – 5
Return To Sender 1962 – 2
One Broken Heart For Sale 1963 – 11
(You're The) Devil In Disguise 1963 – 3
Boss Nova Baby 1963 – 8
Kissin' Cousins 1964 – 12
Such A Night 1964 – 16
Ask Me 1964 – 12
Ain't That Lovin' You, Baby 1964 – 16
Crying In The Chapel 1965 – 3
(Such An) Easy Question 1965 – 11
I'm Yours 1965 – 11
Puppet On A String 1965 – 14
Love Letters 1966 – 19
If I Can Dream 1968 – 12
In The Ghetto 1969 – 3
Suspicious Minds 1969 – 1
Don't Cry, Daddy/ Rubberneckin' 1969 – 6
Kentucky Rain 1970 – 16
The Wonder Of You/ Mama Liked The Roses 1970 – 9
You Don't Have To Say You Love Me /Patch It Up 1970 – 11
Burning Love 1972 – 2
Separate Ways 1972 – 20
Steamroller Blues/Fool 1973 – 17
If You Talk In Your Sleep 1973 – 17
Promised Land 1974 – 14
My Boy 1975 – 20
Way Down 1977 – 18

GRAMMY AWARDS

Elvis received 14 Grammy nominations from the National Academy of Recording Arts and Sciences (NARAS). The three wins were all for gospel recordings, as follows:

How Great Thou Art 1967 (LP)
He Touched Me 1972 (LP)
How Great Thou Art (live Memphis recording) 1974

He also received the NARAS Lifetime Achievement Award (known then as the Bing Crosby Award) in 1971. Four of Elvis' recordings have been inducted into the NARAS Hall of Fame:

Hound Dog 1956 (inducted 1988)
Heartbreak Hotel 1956 (inducted 1995)
That's All Right 1954 (inducted 1998)
Suspicious Minds 1969 (inducted 1999)

ELVIS ON SCREEN

MOVIES

Title, year of release, director, studio, and length. *(Most movies are available on home video.)*

Love Me Tender 1956 (Robert D. Webb) 20th Century Fox (89 mins)
Loving You 1957 (Hal Kanter) Paramount (101 mins)
Jailhouse Rock 1957 (Richard Thorpe) Metro-Goldwyn-Mayer (96 mins)
King Creole 1958 (Michael Curtiz) Paramount (116 mins)
GI Blues 1960 (Norman Taurog) Paramount (104 mins)
Flaming Star 1960 (Don Siegel) 20th Century Fox (101 mins)
Wild In The Country 1961 (Philip Dunne) 20th Century Fox (114 mins)
Blue Hawaii 1961 (Norman Taurog) Paramount (101 mins)
Follow That Dream 1962 (Gordon Douglas) United Artists (110 mins)
Kid Galahad 1962 (Phil Karlson) United Artists (95 mins)
Girls! Girls! Girls! 1962 (Norman Taurog) Paramount (106 mins)
It Happened At The World's Fair 1963 (Norman Taurog) Metro-Goldwyn-Mayer (105 mins)
Fun In Acapulco 1963 (Richard Thorpe) Paramount (97 mins)
Kissin' Cousins 1964 (Gene Nelson) Metro-Goldwyn-Mayer (96 mins)
Viva Las Vegas 1964 (George Sidney) Metro-Goldwyn-Mayer (86 mins)
Roustabout 1964 (John Rich) Paramount (101 mins)
Girl Happy 1964 (Boris Sagal) Metro-Goldwyn-Mayer (96 mins)
Tickle Me 1965 (Norman Taurog) Allied Artists (90 mins)
Harum Scarum 1965 (Gene Nelson) Metro-Goldwyn-Mayer (95 mins)
Frankie And Johnny 1966 (Frederick de Cordova)

United Artists (87 mins)
Paradise, Hawaiian Style *1965* (Michael Moore) Paramount (91 mins)
Spinout *1966* (Norman Taurog) Metro-Goldwyn-Mayer (90 mins)
Easy Come, Easy Go *1967* (John Rich) Paramount (95 mins)
Double Trouble *1967* (Norman Taurog) Metro-Goldwyn-Mayer (90 mins)
Clambake *1967* (Arthur H. Nadel) United Artists (97 mins)
Stay Away Joe *1968* (Peter Tewksbury) Metro-Goldwyn-Mayer (102 mins)
Speedway *1968* (Norman Taurog) Metro-Goldwyn-Mayer (94 mins)
Live A Little, Love A Little *1968* (Norman Taurog) Metro-Goldwyn-Mayer (90 mins)
Charro! *1969* (Charles Marquis Warren) National General (98 mins)
The Trouble With Girls *1969* (Peter Tewksbury) Metro-Goldwyn Mayer (97 mins)
Change Of Habit *1969* (Wiliam Graham) Universal (93 mins)

DOCUMENTARY FILMS

Elvis, That's The Way It Is *1970* (Denis Sanders) Metro-Goldwyn-Mayer (97 mins)
Elvis On Tour 1972 (Pierre Adidge, Robert Abel) Metro-Goldwyn-Mayer (93 mins)

POSTHUMOUS BIOGRAPHICAL MOVIES

Elvis *1979* (John Carpenter) Dick Clark Motion Pictures 150 mins (TV movie)
This Is Elvis *1981* (Malcolm Leo, Andrew Solt) Warner Bros (101 mins)

TELEVISION SPECIALS

Elvis *1968* ***(AKA The '68 Comeback Special')***
Elvis: Aloha From Hawaii, Via Satellite *1973*
Elvis In Concert *1977*

TV GUEST APPEARANCES

Shows in their entirety have not been put out on home video, but extensive clips appear in various documentaries and specials.

January 28, 1956
Stage Show (The Dorsey Brothers)
February 4, 1956
Stage Show (The Dorsey Brothers)
February 11, 1956
Stage Show (The Dorsey Brothers)
February 18, 1956,
Stage Show (The Dorsey Brothers)
March 17, 1956
Stage Show (The Dorsey Brothers)
March 24, 1956
Stage Show (The Dorsey Brothers) *April 3, 1956*
The Milton Berle Show
June 5, 1956
The Milton Berle Show
July 1, 1956
The Steve Allen Show
September 9, 1956
Toast Of The Town (Ed Sullivan)
October 28, 1956
Toast Of The Town (Ed Sullivan)
January 6, 1957
Toast Of The Town (Ed Sullivan)
March 26, 1960
Frank Sinatra Timex Special ("Welcome Home, Elvis")

POSTHUMOUS TV AND VIDEO DOCUMENTARIES

Elvis '56 *1985*
A television documentary about the first year of Elvis' international fame. Lots of footage from the 1950s' TV appearances.

Elvis Presley's Graceland *1984*
A televised tour of Graceland hosted by Priscilla Beaulieu Presley. No longer available on home video.

Elvis, One Night With You *1985*
A TV special featuring unseen footage from the 1968 TV special.

Elvis, The Great Performances *1991*
(Original Version) A two-volume video collection of some of Elvis' greatest singing performances from movies, TV specials, and TV guest appearances.

Elvis, The Great Performances *1992*
(Televised Version).
A reedited version of the home video set, created for network television and hosted from Graceland by Priscilla Presley.

Elvis (TV Series) *1990*
A short-lived, but highly acclaimed network television series about Elvis' early career. Elvis is portrayed by Michael St. Gerard. Originally aired on ABC-TV in 30-minute episodes in 1990. In the years since, TNT has grouped the episodes together for several long-form broadcasts. No home video release.

Elvis, The Lost Performances *1992*
A home video release of unseen footage from the concert films *Elvis, That's The Way It Is* (1970) and *Elvis on Tour* (1972).

Elvis In Hollywood (The '50s) *1993*
Video documentary of Elvis' movie career in the 1950s. Footage from his first four films, including some previously unseen outtakes, and interviews with friends and colleagues associated with these films.

Elvis, His Life And Times *1987/1993*
A 1987 BBC TV documentary of Elvis' life, reedited in 1993 for a syndicated TV special hosted by Mac Davis and Lisa Hartman Black. A video without Davis and Black hosting was released in 1993.

America Comes To Graceland *1993*
A syndicated TV special about Elvis' life and legacy, hosted from Graceland by Mac Davis and Lisa Hartman Black. No home video release.

Elvis, Touch The Dream, A New Generation *1995*
A syndicated TV special about Elvis' life and today's new generation of Elvis fans. Hosted by Travis Tritt. No home video release.

Virtual Graceland *1995*
The critically acclaimed 2-disc CD-ROM tour of Graceland. Go on a programmed guided tour, or customizethe tour for yourself through the main choices of material to access. Includes home movie, newsreel and performance clips, interviews with people from Elvis' personal and professional life,

information about Elvis' life and career, and more. No home video version available. Primary production in 1993/94. Released in 1996.

Elvis Presley, The Alternate Aloha Concert *1996*
Taped in front of a live audience on January 12, 1973, this is the rehearsal show Elvis did for his January 14 satellite television special *Elvis: Aloha from Hawaii, Via Satellite*. Released on home video in 1996.

Elvis Presley's Graceland, Official Video *1997*
The official video tour of Graceland. Shot and released in 1997. Beautiful footage of the full tour of Graceland and its related attractions, plus photography, newsreel footage, and home movies. Highlights of Elvis' life and career and of his years at Graceland. Approximate running time: 50 minutes. *(This video was produced before Elvis' parents' bedroom was added to the tour in 1998. A revised edition sometime in the future will include this room.)*

Finding Graceland *1999*
First publicized with the working title "The Road to Graceland." A fictional film shot in 1997 with a few key scenes filmed on location at Graceland. It stars Harvey Keitel as a man of good deeds who thinks he is Elvis Presley and is making his way home to Graceland 20 years after his supposed death. Also stars Johnathon Schaech and Bridget Fonda. Premiered on Cinemax in May 1999 with home video and DVD release the following August.

The Century *1999*
ABC News'/Peter Jennings' 12-hour, six-part documentary of the events that shaped the 20th century. Original air dates: March 29, April 1, April 3, April 5, April 8, and April 10, 1999. The rise of Elvis Presley's career is the focus of half the installment that was presented on April 5. This documentary has also run on the History Channel and has been released in a home video set.

He Touched Me: The Gospel Music Of Elvis Presley *1999*
A two-part documentary produced by the Gaither Management Group in association with Elvis Presley Enterprises. It was aired as two 45-minute TV specials on TNN (one hour each with commercials). Part I first aired November 1999. Part II first aired January 2000. The home video set is an expanded version—two 90-minute tapes released in November 1999.

KEY DATES

1912 April 25
Gladys Love Smith is born.

1916 April 10
Vernon Elvis Presley is born.

1933 June 17
Gladys Smith and Vernon Presley are married.

1935 January 8
Elvis Aaron Presley is born.

1941 Fall
Elvis enters East Tupelo Consolidated School.

1945 August 18
Elvis sings "Old Shep" in a talent contest at the Mississippi–Alabama Fair and Dairy Show.

1946 January 8
His parents give him a guitar for his 11th birthday.

September
Elvis enters sixth grade at Milam Junior High, Tupelo.

1948 November
Elvis plays his guitar and sings "Leaf on a Tree" for his Milam Junior High class in Tupelo as a farewell.

November 6
The Presley family move to Memphis.

November 8
Elvis enrolls at Humes High School, Memphis.

1953 April 9
"Elvis Prestly" on the bill at the Humes High annual Minstrel Show.

June 3
High school diploma presented to Elvis at Ellis Auditorium, Memphis.

July
Elvis works at Parker Machinists Shop right after graduation.

Summer
He makes an acetate record at his own expense at the Memphis Recording Service (aka Sun).

Fall
Working at the Precision Tool Company, operating a hand drill and drill press.

1954 January
Elvis makes another demo acetate, attracting the attention of Sun boss Sam Phillips.

March 19
Elvis leaves Precision Tools.

April 20
Begins work at Crown Electric.

June 26
Sam Phillips' assistant Marion Kreisker rings Elvis to come in and try out a new song at the studios, though the result is not a success.

July 5
With guitarist Scotty Moore and bass player Bill Black, Elvis cuts "That's All Right" at Sun Studios.

July 8
Local DJ Dewey Phillips plays an acetate of the recording on his radio show.

July 12
Scotty Moore becomes manager and agent of the new group.

July 17
The trio of Elvis, Scotty, and Bill debut with two songs at the Bel Air Club, Memphis.

July 26
Contract signed with Sun Records.

August 28
His Sun single "Blue Moon of Kentucky" enters *Billboard* Country & Western chart for the Mid-South region.

October 2
Debut appearance on the Grand Ole Opry live/radio show.

October 16
Debut appearance on the Louisiana Hayride live/radio show.

November 6
One-year contract for 52 Saturday night Hayride appearances.

1955 January
Elvis signs a contract with Bob Neal, who becomes his manager.

Spring–Summer
Elvis, Scotty, and Bill continue touring on their own and in package shows, including shows with Hank Snow in which Colonel Tom Parker is involved.

August 15
Elvis signs a management contract with Hank Snow Attractions, owned equally by Snow and Parker. Bob Neal remains involved as

an advisor.
November 20
Elvis signs his first contract with RCA Records.
1956 January 10
First recording session for RCA, in Nashville. Songs include "Heartbreak Hotel."
January 27
"Heartbreak Hotel"/"I Was the One" is released by RCA and sells over 300,000 copies in its first three weeks on the market.
January 28
Appearance on *Stage Show*, starring Tommy and Jimmy Dorsey on CBS TV, his first network television appearance.
March 3
"Heartbreak Hotel" enters *Billboard* national chart.
March 13
RCA releases *Elvis Presley*, Elvis' first album.
April 1
Screen test for Paramount Studios in Hollywood.
April 3
Elvis appears on *The Milton Berle Show* on ABC TV.
April 6
Elvis signs a seven-year movie contract with Hal Wallis and Paramount Pictures.
April 23–May 9
Two-week engagement at the New Frontier Hotel in Las Vegas.
April 28
"Heartbreak Hotel" hits #1 in the US singles chart.
May 5
Elvis' first LP makes #1 in *Billboard* album chart.
July 1
Appearance on *The Steve Allen Show* on NBC.
August
Elvis begins shooting his first movie, *Love Me Tender*.
September 9
First of three appearances on *The Ed Sullivan Show*, the top television program of the era.
September 26
Triumphant "homecoming" at the Mississippi-Alabama Fair and Dairy Show in Tupelo, Mississippi.
October 28
Elvis makes his second of three appearances with Ed Sullivan.
November 16
Love Me Tender premieres at the Paramount Theater in New York City.
December 31
The front page of *The Wall Street Journal* reports that in the past few months Elvis merchandise has grossed $22 million in sales.
1957 January 6
Third and final appearance on Ed Sullivan's *Toast of the Town Show*, seen only from the waist up.
January 22
Elvis begins production of his second movie, *Loving You*.
March 25
Purchase of Graceland Mansion finalized, for himself, his parents, and his grandmother to live in.
April 2, 3
Elvis performs outside the United States for the first time, during which he plays the Canadian cities of Toronto and Ottawa.
May 6
Work begins on his third motion picture, *Jailhouse Rock* for MGM.
July 9
Loving You premieres and quickly reaches the top 10 at the box office.
August 31
Elvis performs in Vancouver, the last time he will perform in concert outside the United States.
September 27
Elvis returns once more to the town of his birth to perform, at a benefit for the proposed Elvis Presley Youth Recreation Center in Tupelo.
October 17
Jailhouse Rock premieres in Memphis.
November 10, 11
Elvis performs shows in Hawaii for the first time.
December 20
Elvis officially receives his draft notice for service in the US Army.
December 25
First Christmas at Graceland.
1958 January 20
Shooting begins on his fourth motion picture, *King Creole*.
March 15
Two shows in Memphis are to be his last stage performances until after his army release in 1960.
March 24
Elvis Presley is inducted into the US Army at the Memphis Draft Board and is assigned serial number 53310761.
March 25
Elvis gets his famous GI haircut at Fort Chaffee, Arkansas.
March 29
Private Presley arrives at Fort Hood, Texas for basic training and is stationed there for six months.
June 10
After basic training, while on his first leave, Elvis has a recording session, his last until 1960.
July
King Creole, Elvis' fourth motion picture, opens nationally. The reviews are the best he will ever have for his acting.
August 12
Elvis is granted emergency leave to visit his mother who has been hospitalized with acute hepatitis.
August 14
Gladys Presley dies in the early hours of August 14, at age 46.
August 15
Gladys Presley's funeral takes place at Memphis Funeral Home and Forest Hill Cemetery.
August 25
Elvis reports back to Fort Hood.
September 19
Elvis boards a troop train to New York, on his way to service in Germany. He boards the troop ship USS *Randall*.
October 1
Arrival in Germany, where he is stationed at Friedberg.
1959 January 8
Interview off-camera via trans-Atlantic telephone by Dick Clark on his *American Bandstand* show on ABC-TV.
June 13
Start of a two-week leave in which Elvis visits Munich, then goes clubbing in Paris, which includes a visit to the Lido.
September 13
Elvis meets Priscilla Ann Beaulieu, brought to his house in Germany by a mutual friend.
1960 January 20
Promotion to Sergeant.
March 1
Elvis leaves Germany, arriving in New Jersey the next day for a press conference.
March 5
Official discharge from active duty.
March 7
Arrival back in Memphis.
March 8
Press conference at Graceland in his father's office behind the mansion.

March 20
First post-army recording session.
March 21
Elvis receives a first degree black belt in karate, an interest he developed in the army.
March 26
Recording of a special "Welcome Home, Elvis" edition of Frank Sinatra's ABC-TV variety show.
April 21
Filming and recording begin for his first post-army movie, his fifth film, *GI Blues.*
May 8
ABC airs Frank Sinatra's "Welcome Home, Elvis" edition of his variety show, which attracts a 41.5% share of the national television audience.
July 3
Vernon Presley marries divorcee and mother of three sons, Davada (Dee) Stanley, an American whom he met in Germany.
August 1
Work begins on his sixth movie, *Flaming Star,* a drama with limited music.
November 6
Elvis begins recording and filming for his seventh film, *Wild in the Country.*
November 23
GI Blues opens nationally to warm reviews and big box office sales and is among the 15 top-grossing films of the year.
Late December
Flaming Star opens nationally to good reviews but, unlike *GI Blues*, this dramatic film with little singing does not set the box office on fire.
1961 February 25
"Elvis Presley Day" in Memphis includes a luncheon in his honor, and two shows at Ellis Auditorium to benefit around 38 charities in the Memphis area.
March 25
Elvis arrives in Hawaii for a concert at Pearl Harbor, a benefit to help fund the building of the USS *Arizona* Memorial.
March 27
Elvis remains in Hawaii to start location filming for his eighth motion picture, *Blue Hawaii.*
June 22
Wild in the Country opens nationally to mixed reviews.
July 2
Elvis starts recording and filming for his ninth motion picture, *Follow That Dream.*
October 23
Work commences on his 10th movie, *Kid Galahad,* which he will complete in January.
November 22
Blue Hawaii opens nationally to warm reviews and gets to #2 on the box office charts. It becomes the top-grossing film of Elvis' career thus far.
1962 March 26
Elvis begins filming and recording for his 11th motion picture, *Girls! Girls! Girls!*, working in Hollywood and location shooting in Hawaii.
May 23
Follow That Dream opens nationally and gets to #5 on the box office charts. It is warmly reviewed and does fairly well in sales.
August 28
Elvis reports for pre-production on his 12th motion picture, *It Happened At The World's Fair.* Shooting is in Hollywood and at the World's Fair in Seattle.
August 29
Kid Galahad opens nationally and does reasonably well financially with a brief stay in the top 10 on the box office chart.
November 21
Girls! Girls! Girls! opens nationally and rivals *Blue Hawaii* in box office success.
December 19
Priscilla Beaulieu arrives from West Germany to spend the Christmas holidays with him at Graceland.
1963 January 22
Soundtrack recording begins for Elvis' 13th film, *Fun In Acapulco.*
April 10
It Happened At The World's Fair opens nationally and does relatively well at the box office, though its plot is the most frivolous of any Elvis movie so far.
July 9
Elvis begins work on the music for his 14th motion picture, *Viva Las Vegas*, co-starring Ann-Margret.
October 7
Production begins for Elvis' 15th movie, *Kissin' Cousins.*
November 27
Fun in Acapulco opens nationally and quickly goes to #5 at the box office.
1964 February 13
Elvis presents the former presidential yacht *Potomac,* which he purchased for $55,000, as a gift to St. Jude Children's Research Hospital in Memphis.
March 5
Elvis reports for filming of his 16th motion picture, *Roustabout,* co-starring Hollywood legend Barbara Stanwyck.
March 6
Kissin' Cousins opens nationally.
June 10
Elvis begins recording the music for his next film, *Girl Happy.*
June 17
Viva Las Vegas opens nationally and goes to #8 at the box office. The picture is welcomed as one of the better Elvis movies of this period.
October 12
Elvis begins shooting his 18th motion picture, *Tickle Me.*
November 11
Roustabout opens, and hits #8 at the box office.
1965 March 15
Principal photography begins for *Harum Scarum,* Elvis' 19th motion picture.
April 7
Girl Happy is released nationally and does relatively good business.
May 24
Elvis starts filming for his 20th motion picture, to be released out of chronology as his 21st, *Frankie and Johnny.*
June 24
Elvis donates $50,000 to the Motion Picture Relief Fund, with Barbara Stanwyck and Frank Sinatra accepting for the organization.
July 7
Tickle Me opens nationwide.
August 2
Elvis commences work on the soundtrack music for his 21st motion picture, *Paradise, Hawaiian Style.*
August 27
The Beatles visit with Elvis for several hours at his home in California and have an informal jam session.
November 24
Harum Scarum opens nationally and hits #11 at the box office. The soundtrack album goes to #8.
1966 February 14
Elvis starts recording and filming for his 22nd movie, *Spinout.*
March 30
Frankie and Johnny opens

June 19
Elvis begins work on his 26th movie (to be the 27th released), *Speedway.*
July 12
On the movie set, Elvis announces the news of Priscilla's pregnancy.
September 9
Principal photography begins for Elvis' 27th movie (to be the 26th released), *Stay Away, Joe.*
November 22
Clambake is released nationally and goes to #15 at the box office.
1968 February 1
Priscilla gives birth to Lisa Marie Presley at 5.01 PM, at the Baptist Hospital in Memphis.
March 8
Stay Away, Joe opens to mixed reviews.
March 13
Filming begins for Elvis' 28th movie, *Live a Little, Love a Little.* A more adult kind of comedy/melodrama, a real departure from the typical Presley film.
June 12
Speedway is released nationally.
June 25
A press conference is held during rehearsals for his first television special.
June 27, 28, 29, and 30
Videotaping takes place for the TV special, usually known as *The '68 Special* or *The '68 Comeback,* the actual name being simply *Elvis.*
July 22
Principal photography starts for Elvis' 29th movie, *Charro!,* a dramatic western, again a very different kind of role. Elvis grows a beard for this.
October 23
Elvis starts work on the soundtrack for his 30th movie, *The Trouble With Girls (And How To Get Into It).*
October 23
Live A Little, Love A Little opens in the US, doing very well at the box office.
December 3
Elvis, the 1968 TV special, airs on NBC and is one of this biggest television hits of the year, receiving rave reviews from the public and the critics alike.
1969 January 13
Elvis begins recording sessions at American Studios in Memphis, the first time he has recorded in the city since he recorded for Sun in 1955.
March 5
Elvis returns to Hollywood to film his 31st, and final, acting role in a motion picture, in *Change of Habit.*
March 13
Charro! opens in theaters across the nation.
July 31
Elvis commences a four-week, 57-show engagement at the new International Hotel in Las Vegas, the largest showroom in the city.
September 3
The Trouble With Girls (And How To Get Into It) is released nationally.
November 10
Elvis' final fictional movie, *Change of Habit,* opens nationwide.
1970 January 26
Start of a month-long return engagement at the International Hotel. This time he breaks his own attendance records.
February 27
A press conference prior to shows at the Houston Astrodome on the same day, and the next, and March 1. The six shows attracted a record 207,494 people.
June 4
Start of five days of recording sessions in Nashville.
July 14
Back to Las Vegas for rehearsals for another month-long engagement at the International, MGM shooting the documentary *Elvis – That's The Way It Is.*
September 9–14
Elvis takes his show on a nine-city tour, with MGM filming portions of the first show for use in *Elvis – That's The Way It Is.*
November 10–17
Elvis does a successful eight-city concert tour.
November 11
Elvis, That's The Way It Is, his 32nd film, opens in theaters to good reviews and good box office.
December 21
Elvis meets with President Richard Nixon at the White House.
1971 January 16
Elvis is decorated as one of the Ten Outstanding Young Men of the Year by the United States Junior Chamber of Commerce (The Jaycees).
January 26
Another month-long engagement opens at the International Hotel in Las Vegas.
March 15
A recording session in Nashville is cancelled due to pain and inflammation in one eye. Elvis is diagnosed with secondary glaucoma.
May 15
Elvis has recording sessions in Nashville, some of the tracks being for his forthcoming album *Elvis Sings The Wonderful World Of Christmas.*
June 1
The two-room house Elvis was

born in opens to the public for tours, having been restored by the East Heights Garden Club in Tupelo.

June 29
Memphis City Council votes to rename a long stretch of Highway 51 South, part of which runs in front of Graceland, Elvis Presley Boulevard.

July 20
Elvis starts a two-week engagement at the Sahara Hotel in Lake Tahoe, Nevada.

August 9–September 6
Elvis plays the second annual "Elvis Summer Festival" at the International Hotel, which has been renamed the Las Vegas Hilton International Hotel.

August 28
Elvis is presented with the Bing Crosby Award from the National Academy of Recording Arts and Sciences (which also presents the Grammy awards).

November 5
Elvis commences a 12-city concert tour.

December 30
Elvis announces that he and Priscilla are to separate.

1972 January 26–February 23
Elvis plays another successful engagement at the Hilton in Las Vegas.

March 30
Filming begins in a Hollywood recording studio for another documentary, *Elvis on Tour,* which MGM will also film on and off stage during his 15-city concert tour.

June 9, 10, and 11
Elvis' first-ever concert shows in New York, at Madison Square Garden. John Lennon, George Harrison,and Bob Dylan are among the music stars attending.

June 18
Just nine days after it is recorded, RCA rush-releases a live album from one of the New York shows—*Elvis as Recorded at Madison Square Garden.*

July 26
Elvis and Priscilla's separation is formalized. A divorce is to come. Elvis has begun seeing Linda Thompson, his main female companion until late 1976.

August 4–September 4
Elvis plays a month-long engagement at the Hilton in Vegas.

September 5
Elvis holds a press conference in Vegas announcing plans for a TV concert to be broadcast via satellite around the world from Hawaii.

November 1
Elvis on Tour opens to good reviews and good box office, and later its producers receive the Golden Globe Award for Best Documentary of 1972.

November 8–18
A seven-city tour includes Honolulu, where Elvis announces that his upcoming satellite show will be a benefit for the Kui Lee Cancer Fund.

1973 January 14
Elvis makes television and entertainment history with his *Elvis: Aloha from Hawaii, Via Satellite* special, one of the all-time great moments of his career.

January 26–February 23
Elvis plays an engagement at the Las Vegas Hilton.

March 1
Elvis and the Colonel sell RCA the singer's royalty rights on Elvis' entire recording catalog up to that point in time.

April 4
The Aloha special is seen on American television for the first time, having been broadcast live to territories across the Pacific.

April 22
Elvis commences an eight-city concert tour.

May 4–16
An intended 17-day engagement at the Sahara Hotel in Lake Tahoe, Nevada, is cut short due to ill-health.

June 20–July 3
Another cross-country concert tour.

July 21
Elvis records a few songs at the Stax Recording Studio in Memphis—his first time back to record in Memphis since 1969.

August 6–September 3
Back to the Vegas Hilton for another engagement.

October 9
Elvis and Priscilla make a court appearance together and their divorce is granted. They will continue to be close friends.

October 15–November 1
Elvis is hospitalized in Memphis for recurring pneumonia and pleurisy, an enlarged colon, and hepatitis.

December 10
Elvis returns to the Stax Recording Studio in Memphis for a week of sessions.

1974 January 26–February 9
Another season of appearances at the Las Vegas Hilton.

March 1–20
Elvis tours with concert dates throughout the South.

March 3
Elvis returns to the Houston Astrodome and sets a one-day attendance record with his two shows.

March 16
Elvis plays Memphis, the first time since 1961, with four shows in two days. The LP *Elvis Recorded Live On Stage in Memphis* is recorded at one of the shows.

May 16–26
Another short season at the Sahara in Lake Tahoe.

June 15–July 2
Touring concerts dates.

August 19–September 2
Back to the Hilton in Vegas for an engagement.

September 27–October 14
Elvis is on tour again, including the Sahara Hotel, Lake Tahoe, October 11–14.

1975 January 29–February 14
Elvis is hospitalized with health and prescription problems again.

March
Elvis' live recording of "How Great Thou Art" from the *Live On Stage In Memphis* album wins the Grammy for Best Inspirational Performance.

March 18–April 1
Engagement at the Hilton.

April 24–July 24
Elvis tours in concert.

August 18–September 5
Elvis opens in Vegas but ends his engagement on the 20th and is hospitalized in Memphis until September 5.

November 27
The renovation of a Convair 880 jet Elvis bought earlier in the year is complete, and he takes his first flight in the *Lisa Marie.*

December 2–15
Elvis returns to the Hilton in Vegas to make up for the shows that were canceled during his previous engagement.

December 31
Elvis performs a special New Year's Eve concert in Pontiac, Michigan, and sets a single

performance attendance record of 62,500.

1976 February 2
During a week of recording in the den at Graceland, RCA bring in mobile equipment, for the album *From Elvis Presley Boulevard, Memphis, Tennessee.*

March 17–22
Elvis tours in concert.

April 21–27
Elvis tours in concert.

April 30–May 9
An engagement at the Sahara Hotel, Lake Tahoe in Nevada.

May 27–June 6
Elvis tours in concert.

June 25–July 5
Elvis tours in concert.

July 23–August 5
Elvis tours in concert.

August 27–September 8
Elvis tours in concert.

October 14–27
Elvis tours in concert.

October 29–30
Continuation of recording in the den at Graceland.

Early November
Elvis and Linda Thompson, his steady girlfriend since 1972, split up.

Late November
Elvis meets Ginger Alden who will be his steady girlfriend until his death.

November 24–30
Elvis tours in concert.

December 2–12
Elvis plays the Hilton in Vegas for what will turn out to be the last time.

December 27–31
Elvis tours in concert, ending with a special New Year's Eve concert in Pittsburgh, Pennsylvania.

1977 February 12–21
Elvis tours in concert.

March 23–30
Elvis tours in concert.

April 1–5
Elvis is hospitalized in Memphis and tour shows scheduled for March 31–April 3 are canceled.

April 2–May 31/June 1–2
Elvis tours in concert.

June 17–26
Elvis tours in concert. Shows on June 19, 20, and 21 are recorded for a live album and are videotaped for an upcoming television special.

June 26
A concert at Indianapolis, Indiana's Market Square Arena. This will turn out to be his very last concert performance.

June 27–August 15
Elvis relaxes in Memphis and prepares for the next leg of touring for 1977.

August 16
Shortly after midnight Elvis returns to Graceland from a late-night visit to the dentist. He retires to his master suite at Graceland around 7:00 AM. By late morning, Elvis Presley is dead of heart failure. It is announced by mid-afternoon. In a matter of hours the shock registers around the world.

SELECTED READING

Reel Elvis!
(Pauline Bartel) Elvis' movie information including cast lists, synopsis, and trivia.

Elvis Collectibles: Third Edition
(Rosalind Cranor) Pictorial and value estimates of Elvis memorabilia.

Did Elvis Sing In Your Hometown?
(Lee Cotton) All the available factscovering Elvis on tour in the1950s.

Did Elvis Sing In Your Hometown, Too?
(Lee Cotton) All the available factscovering Elvis on during the years 1968–1977.

Intimate & Rare
(Joe Esposito and Elena Oumano)
Longtime friend and staff memberJoe Esposito shares his memories of Elvis from their years together.

The King on the Road
(Robert Gordon)
A spectacular account of Elvis' live performances throughout his career.

The Elvis Treasures
(Robert Gordon) Biographicat textand removable facsimiles of documents and memorabilia from the Graceland Archives.

Elvis Presley's Graceland: The Official Guidebook
(Graceland) Photographic journey through the entire Graceland tour includes biographical and historical information.

When Elvis Died
(Neal and Janice Gregory)
Chronicles the reaction of the press and the world to Elvis' death. Revised edition in 1992 includes additional chapters on the Elvis phenomenon during the first 15 years following his death.

Last Train to Memphis
(Peter Guralnick) The first volume of the acclaimed biography of Elvis Presley.

Careless Love
(Peter Guralnick) The concluding volume of Guralnick's two-part biography.

Elvis: Day by Day
(Peter Guralnick and Ernst Jorgensen)
The definitive record of Elvis' career.

Memphis: Elvis Style
(Cindy Hazen and Mike Freeman)
A guide to all the places in Memphis that played a vital role in Elvis' life.

The Official Price Guide to Elvis Presley Records & Memorabilia: Second Edition
(House of Collectibles)
Descriptions of and value estimates of Elvis' records. Includes some memorabilia.

Elvis Presley–A Life In Music
(Ernst Jorgensen) Every recording session Elvis held between 1953 and 1977, including home and private sessions as well as live concert recordings.

Elvis: Word for Word
(Jerry Osborne) 43 years of collecting records and tapes of anything Elvis spoke into a microphone.

Elvis & Me
(Priscilla Beaulieu Presley)
Priscilla's own recollections of life with, and after, Elvis.

Index

Acknowledgments & Picture Credits

The author wishes to thank the staff at Elvis Presley Enterprises for their invaluable help in researching this book, particularly Pete Davidson, LaVonne Gaw, Kelly Hill, and Todd Morgan.

All images have been published with the permission of the official picture archive of Elvis Presley Enterprises, Inc., (including p55 From the Collection of John Heath; p266 © Alfred Wertheimer), with the exception of: p483 and p568 © Nancy Call; p574–575 © Corbis; p576–577 © Corbis; p582 © Corbis; p588 © Corbis; p590 stamp design © US Postal Service. Every effort has been made to trace copyright holders and obtain permission. The publishers apologise for any omissions and will make any necessary changes at subsequent printings.